MW01515627

Open Friendship in a Closed Society

Mission Mississippi and a Theology of Friendship

PETER SLADE

OXFORD
UNIVERSITY PRESS

2009

OXFORD
UNIVERSITY PRESS

Oxford University Press, Inc., publishes works that further
Oxford University's objective of excellence
in research, scholarship, and education.

Oxford   New York
Auckland   Cape Town   Dar es Salaam   Hong Kong   Karachi
Kuala Lumpur   Madrid   Melbourne   Mexico City   Nairobi
New Delhi   Shanghai   Taipei   Toronto

With offices in
Argentina   Austria   Brazil   Chile   Czech Republic   France   Greece
Guatemala   Hungary   Italy   Japan   Poland   Portugal   Singapore
South Korea   Switzerland   Thailand   Turkey   Ukraine   Vietnam

Copyright © 2009 Oxford University Press, Inc.

Published by Oxford University Press, Inc.
198 Madison Avenue, New York, New York 10016

www.oup.com

Oxford is a registered trademark of Oxford University Press

All rights reserved. No part of this publication may be reproduced,
stored in a retrieval system, or transmitted, in any form or by any means,
electronic, mechanical, photocopying, recording, or otherwise,
without the prior permission of Oxford University Press.

Library of Congress Cataloging-in-Publication Data

Slade, Peter, 1970–
Open friendship in a closed society : Mission Mississippi and a theology
of friendship / Peter Slade.
p. cm.
Includes bibliographical references and index.
ISBN 978-0-19-537262-5
1. Church work with minorities—Mississippi. 2. Race relations—Religious
aspects—Christianity. 3. Mississippi—Race relations. 4. Mission Mississippi
(Organization) I. Title.
BV4468.S53 2009
277.62'083089—dc22   2009002635

9 8 7 6 5 4 3 2 1

Printed in the United States of America
on acid-free paper

To Libby, Anna, and Jacob

Preface

Christian theologians call the Church the Body of Christ, but rarely do they go and look at this body to find what they might learn about Christ, the object of their study. Underlying this book is the conviction that they should. Congregations and faith communities develop their own *lived theologies* embodied in their practices and proclamations and theologians need to be in conversation with these lived theologies if academic theology is to stay true to its calling to serve the Church and if local churches' beliefs and practices are not to become intellectually impoverished. This book is a stumbling attempt to bring the lived theology of Christian reconciliation in Mississippi alongside recent theological work on reconciliation.

One immediate problem that such a conversation runs into is the great distance in vocabulary separating the lecture hall from the sanctuary. A key methodological concern shaping this book, therefore, is how to work with both the highly articulate and often obscure vocabulary of academic theology and the lived theology of the average churchgoer. The written word is the natural habitat of the academic theologian; in this medium, their words tend to carry more authority on the page thus making any equal exchange very difficult. The temptation is to remedy this imbalance by translating practices and stories of faith into the language of academic theology. To do this, however, is to lose the authentic voices of lived theology and to risk patronizing the subject. Accompanying this concern of equal exchange, is the conviction that, as far as is possible, this work must be accessible to the people who make up the subject of the study.

To address these concerns of equal exchange and accessibility, I present both academic and lived theologies using biographical narrative. Because I draw on transcriptions of interviews, participants in Mission Mississippi retain their own voice in this conversation. This use of narrative levels the playing field by demonstrating that the academic/lived theology dichotomy is in fact false. Just as for the regular person in the pew, theologians' religious beliefs and convictions spring, at least in part, from their reflection upon their own lived faith in their particular cultural context.

It is no coincidence that it was the findings of sociologists that precipitated my consideration of a theology of friendship in this book. As sociologist Robert Wuthnow recently observed, while theology and social science "are more often regarded as competing than as complimentary modes of inquiry," both disciplines agree on one point: "from whatever source theological inspiration originates, it manifests itself in the concrete realities of human life."[1] From a theological perspective, Christian communities and churches—such as those involved in Mission Mississippi—embody or incarnate their theology in a range of beliefs and practices. This means that an interdisciplinary attention to the social sciences is invaluable in the study of this theology.

This is a white Englishman's study of a Christian racial reconciliation movement in Mississippi. It is the work of an outsider welcomed into societies not his own—an academic researching the complex history of others' cultures. As such, there are some significant limitations to the project. The desire to study the lived theology of Mission Mississippi required not only reading the organization's documents and publications, but also hearing the personal narratives of its participants and observing its practices. In the course of field research conducted over a period of four years (2000–2004), I attended church services, rallies, conferences, prayer meetings, committee meetings, picnics, prayer breakfasts, and luncheons and interviewed over forty-five participants. Despite the generosity of all my interviewees and my best efforts, I found that the most candid conversations came from people who had most in common with me—white Episcopalians. Unsurprisingly, African Americans were guarded in their conversation about their experiences with, and feelings toward, whites. As an African American columnist with Jackson's *Clarion-Ledger* told me, "You'd be fascinated if I were to take a tape recorder...around black people to see what they think about white people and their fears and suspicions of white people—just how ingrained it is. You talk to eight black people and seven of them are going to think they can't trust you because you are a white guy."[2] It was beyond the scope (and means) of this project to engage an African American partner to conduct interviews. I have done my best to allow for this imbalance in my writing.

This work has its roots in friendships formed during three wonderful years I spent in Oxford, Mississippi, at the Center for the Study of Southern Culture. It was thanks to the encouragement of my teachers and colleagues there, Karen Glynn, Charles Reagan Wilson, Ted Ownby, David Wharton, Bill Ferris, and Tom Rankin, that I learned the importance and value of collecting oral histories. It was while in Oxford that I began to explore the complex history of race in the South and the ongoing legacy of the years of slavery and Jim Crow. I will always be grateful to Andy Beaird, Lloyd Holmes, Susan Glisson, Ethel Young Minor, Coulter Fussell, Lee Tyner, and all my Mississippi friends who were patient with a curious and opinionated Englishman. My understanding of race and religion in Mississippi would not be the same without the incredible experience of singing in the University of Mississippi Gospel Choir in churches and auditoriums across the region.

This book started its life as a doctoral dissertation and was almost about something entirely different, but misleading statements and obstruction of my research led me to Dolphus Weary's office in the summer of 2003. Weary's laughter when I told him my story of closed churches, suspicion, and threats was a liberating gift of grace to a desperate graduate student. I met the same understanding and support from Lee Paris, and so a proposal for a new dissertation rose from the crumpled ruins of my first project.

The generosity of Virginia Chase, Neddie Winters, Dolphus Weary, and everyone at Mission Mississippi made my field-research a joy and an adventure. This project would not have been possible without the willing participation of all the people who I interviewed. Although there are too many to mention here, each person was kind enough to share his or her stories of faith and race in the Closed Society. I have done my best to repay this gift with an honest and sensitive account of their stories.

Gregory Jones and Owen Brookes at the Smith Robertson Center in Jackson aided my research, as did Jennifer Ford in the Archives and Special Collections in the John D. Williams Library at the University of Mississippi and the staff in the Mississippi Department of Archives and History. I am also extremely grateful to Ed King for being so gracious as to answer all my questions and allowing me to include quotations from his unpublished history of the movement in Jackson. All the time that I spent in Mississippi was only possible with the generous hospitality of my friends Susan Glisson, Gibson Johnston Rayner, the Beairds, the Tyners, and the Barhams. I am particularly indebted to Lisa and Lee Paris for the use of their carriage house apartment that made my research in Jackson not only possible but also comfortable.

I would not have been in the predicament of having to write a dissertation were it not for Charles Marsh. He invited me to the University of Virginia, and both encouraged and facilitated my studies. While in Charlottesville, I studied under some inspiring teachers including Gene Rogers, Wallace Best, John Mason, Heather Warren, and Charles Mathewes. Graduate work was a strangely solitary exercise and I am grateful for those moments away from libraries and word processors when I could participate in a wider intellectual community. I owe my sanity to the support of friends in faith and work who include Jacqueline Bussie, Creston Davis, Jason Danner, Robert Erle Barham, and Scott Nesbitt. All of the people whom I met through Marsh's Project on Lived Theology kept me going through my PhD program, as did my colleagues at the Institute for Advanced Studies in Culture's Friday seminars, and the participants in the Colloquy on Race and the Reformed Tradition at Union Theological Seminary's Institute for Reformed Theology.

Writing *Open Friendship in a Closed Society* has been possible thanks to fellowships from the Louisville Institute for the Study of American Religion, and the Center on Religion and Democracy at the University of Virginia, which in addition to a writing fellowship also provided me with a subterranean bunker I could call my own for two years. Thanks is also due to Ashland University, which gave me a job and then a summer writing grant, and to my colleagues Kyle Fedler, David Aune, Don Rinehart, and Sue Dickson in the Religion Department.

I owe a debt of gratitude to my sisters and brothers in Christ in the congregations I have attended in the United States: St. Peter's Episcopal Church, Oxford, Mississippi; Trinity Episcopal Church, Charlottesville, Virginia; and First United Methodist Church, Ashland, Ohio. I am particularly grateful to Mount Olivet Church in Dyke, Virginia, for inviting me to be their preacher and helping me keep my theology grounded in the local church. In addition, the way to writing this book would have been significantly rockier without the love and support of my parents Sue and Charlie Slade and my in-laws Margaret and Don Moore.

The time spent writing this book has proven fruitful in other ways. I am dedicating this work with gratitude and love to Libby, my wife and best friend, who spent our first honeymoon driving between churches in Mississippi in the heat of August; to Anna, who was born in the middle of the first chapter; and to Jacob, who arrived in time to watch a dissertation turn into a book.

Contents

Open Friendship in
a Closed Society

I

Introduction

Today in Mississippi, a statewide ecumenical racial reconciliation initiative called Mission Mississippi brings Christians together across racial and denominational lines. Mission Mississippi strives to facilitate relationships between individuals and partnerships between churches. These new friendships, Mission Mississippi declares, are "changing Mississippi one relationship at a time."

Few Americans would contest the suggestion that Mississippi needs to change. Since the civil rights movement brought notoriety to the state, Mississippi has had a peculiar place in America's psyche: Mississippi became the exceptional other, the place in America that was not American. In 1962, when the historian James Silver first dubbed Mississippi the Closed Society, he was contrasting it with the rest of America, the Open Society. As opposition to integration spread outside the Deep South, historians and commentators quickly pointed out that perhaps Mississippi was not as distinct from the rest of America as Silver suggested.[1] In 1967, the historian Louis R. Harlan wrote, "The ghetto riots of the mid 1960s have weakened public belief in Mississippi's singularity as a rural cancer spot of bigotry isolated from an urbanizing, progressive America. It is now clear there is a bit of Mississippi in every metropolis, that the suburbs are still 'closed societies.' "[2] Still, Mississippi lingers in the popular consciousness as a byword for racism, bigotry, and poverty.

In 2003, as Mission Mississippi held a conference celebrating its tenth anniversary, the keynote speaker for the opening session was former governor of Mississippi William Winter. In the measured tones of an elder statesman, he addressed the African Americans and whites gathered: "I think God has placed us in this special location to carry out his mission of loving our neighbors."[3] Perhaps, Winter wondered, Mission Mississippi would have a unique part to play in changing not just the state but also the country.

What is one to make of these theological claims regarding the power of Christian friendship to bring reconciliation and change to—of all places—Mississippi?

The study by sociologists Michael O. Emerson and Christian Smith, *Divided by Faith: Evangelical Religion and the Problem of Race in America,* throws doubt on Mission Mississippi's "one relationship at a time" approach to transforming society. Despite white evangelicals' best intentions for racial reconciliation, Emerson and Smith argue that their individualistic perspective ignores the collective forces that perpetuate systemic injustice. Emerson and Smith go so far as to suggest that white evangelicals do more to perpetuate than reform the United States' racialized society.[4] Their findings, considered in the context of the work of Mission Mississippi, raise several important and interrelated questions with theological implications: Is Mission Mississippi wrong to build its hope for racial reconciliation and societal change on a theology of friendship? Does a close look at the fifteen-year history of the organization provide evidence to dispute Emerson and Smith's findings? If the sociologist's concerns prove founded, should churches abandon a theology of friendship in their search for racial reconciliation, or does Mission Mississippi's experience help in the development of a particular Christian understanding of friendship robust enough to address issues of systemic injustice and inequity in a racialized society? These are the questions that I try to answer in this book.

The chapters follow the logic of a theology of reconciliation. Starting with a theological worldview (chapter 2), the two sides meet desiring reconciliation (chapter 3). This meeting causes a theological reexamination and remembering of the past (chapter 4), which frees those seeking reconciliation to move forward exploring the possibilities of a reconciled future that will include restorative justice (chapter 5) and a true community of friends (chapter 6).

The book starts with the chapter "Open and Closed" to establish both the theological lens of open friendship and the object of scrutiny—Mississippi's closed society. Through the life and work of the German theologian Jürgen Moltmann, the chapter explores the powerful idea of Jesus' radical open friendship, which challenges the closed and exclusive systems of privilege and power found in closed societies and churches. Moltmann may seem an unlikely—not to mention white and male—choice of theologian for a study of racial reconciliation in Mississippi. He wrote his seminal works influenced by his experiences of life under the Nazis, as a prisoner of war in Britain, and as a churchman and professor in postwar Germany; but his description of closed churches and closed societies fits remarkably well with American historian James Silver's description of 1960s Mississippi as the Closed Society.[5] The second half of the chapter explores, through Silver's life and work, this closed society that shaped the lives of the people who would, thirty years after Silver's work, found Mission Mississippi.

With both a theology of open friendship in place and an understanding of Mississippi's history as the Closed Society, the third chapter lays out the short history of Mission Mississippi. Started in Jackson, Mississippi, in 1992, this extraordinary organization owes its existence to an alliance of white businessmen, African American ministers, and a pioneering community development and reconciliation ministry called Voice of Calvary. By the time Mission Mississippi celebrated its tenth anniversary, it had moved from holding large-scale events with big-name speakers to developing networks of church partnerships and personal relationships across the traditional divides of denomination and race. Mission Mississippi, through its call for Christians to form intentional relationships outside their social, denominational, and economic circles, has at its heart a theology of open friendship.

There is, however, just as Smith and Emerson describe, a reticence within Mission Mississippi to address any issues of systemic injustice. The fourth chapter demonstrates how this reticence is not simply the outworking of freewill individualism as Emerson and Smith suggest. Instead, it is in large part the result of the explicit application of the Southern Presbyterian doctrine of the spirituality of the church. This doctrine insists that the institution of the church must concern itself only with things spiritual and must not make pronouncements on political issues. The minister and members of First Presbyterian Church, Jackson, were very influential in the formation of Mission Mississippi; but less than a year after the first rally there was a backlash against the organization within this congregation. The roots of the protest against Mission Mississippi lie deep in the history of Southern Presbyterian resistance to abolitionism and this congregation's opposition to the civil rights movement.

Tracing the connections between the development of the doctrine of the spirituality of the church and white resistance to integration in the history of First Presbyterian Church, Jackson achieves three things: First, it adds historical and theological nuance and complexity to Emerson and Smith's account of why evangelical racial reconciliation initiatives fail to address systemic injustice. Second, it challenges a view propagated by historian David L. Chappell that white Southern churches "failed in any meaningful way to join the anti-civil

rights movement."[6] Revealed instead is a consistent and effective ecclesial strategy for maintaining the Southern white hegemony running unbroken from
the debates on slavery through to school desegregation. Third, it increases our
appreciation for the resistance faced by those who, within these historically
white closed churches, raise their voices for a gospel of open friendship.

The next two chapters consider ways that a theology of open friendship
rightly understood enriches a study of Mission Mississippi's strategy to seek
reconciliation across racial and denominational lines. In the fifth chapter, the
voice of the theologian Miroslav Volf joins the conversation. His influential
work on reconciliation, *Exclusion and Embrace*, emerging from his reflections
on the conflict in his native Croatia, shows the importance of open friendship
at the heart of the process of reconciliation.[7] His model of reconciliation as
embrace provides a template to consider the experience of Christians seeking
reconciliation through involvement in Mission Mississippi's programs. This
leads back to the question of how activities focused on individual relationship
building might lead to changing Mississippi.

The self-proclaimed central practice of Mission Mississippi's work is their
morning prayer meetings. Mission Mississippi considers these meetings essential to their work of reconciliation. The book ends by taking the claim of these
Mississippi Christians seriously, examining it in light of sociologists' findings
and a theological understanding of prayer and friendship. What emerges is
an understanding of Mission Mississippi's practice of interracial intercessory
prayer that prophetically challenges the idolatry of the Closed Society and its
closed churches.

In the prayer meetings, participants do not simply establish new relationships with individuals but build *networks* of relationships. Participation in
interracial networks, sociologists tell us, is the best hope for changing racialized perceptions of minority groups.[8] Gaining insight from the work of the
contemporary biblical scholars Stephen Fowl and Luke Timothy Johnson,
these networks are the community of the friends of God—the community of
forgiven sinners—engaging in the foundational practice of Christian friendship, listening graciously to each other's stories, and narrating them as part of
the drama of salvation. The emerging picture confirms Mission Mississippi's
emphasis on the importance of the prayer meetings, while at the same time
challenging its participants to explore further the importance of confession of
sin and forgiveness for intercessory prayer and reconciliation.

Taking a theological perspective on intercessory prayer from the work of
the German theologian and martyr Dietrich Bonhoeffer, this study of Mission
Mississippi's prayer breakfasts reveals how the logic of intercessory prayer

subverts the insistence that churches restrict their activities to the spiritual realm, leaving issues of justice and systemic inequality alone. In praying for the world, the fellowship of the friends of God identify with the other, extending to them the friendship of God at the same time as drawing them into the fellowship of the radical open friendship of Jesus.

2

Open and Closed

Jürgen Moltmann and Open Friendship

At the height of the civil rights movement, Martin Luther King Jr. warned churchgoers: "Desegregation will break down the legal barriers and bring men together physically, but something must touch the hearts and souls of men so that they will come together spiritually."[1] Five years later, on April 4, 1968, a bullet silenced this great voice, triggering riots in urban ghettos across the United States. That night Jürgen Moltmann, a German professor of theology on sabbatical at Duke University in North Carolina, watched images of burning cities on the television news. The assassination of King proved a pivotal point in the development of Moltmann's theology. In his subsequent work, he explores what it is that "must touch the hearts and souls" of people to bring them together spiritually—Moltmann challenges the Church to embrace the friendship of Jesus.

All theology develops in a particular context: it has a story. Some knowledge of that context is essential for the reader seeking to understand the work of the original author and then engaging with these ideas and insights in their own—different—context. The story of Moltmann's theology started years before Martin Luther King Jr.'s assassination and the rioting, looting, and arson in American cities; it began in the city of Hamburg in a far greater inferno.

Born in 1926, the second child of Herbert and Gerda Moltmann, Jürgen grew up in a "secular family of teachers in Hamburg."[2] His

father, a teacher of Latin, History, and German at the famous Lichtwark
School, learned in the trenches of the First World War, "to respect the hidden
God above us and the moral law within us."[3] As a result, Moltmann recalls,
"I wasn't very deeply socialized in a Christian sense but grew up with poets
and philosophers of German idealism."[4] His experience of Christianity was
as a dutiful member of a state church that made no extraordinary demands
on its members. "At home," he remembers, "Christianity was only a matter of
form...as something rather remote."[5] Jürgen and his three younger siblings
went to church only once a year on Christmas Eve. "And later [my father] confessed [we went] not to celebrate the birth of the redeemer, but to celebrate the
sacred family—father, mother and the first child."[6] Personal tragedy shaped
the family's religion: Herbert and Gerda Moltmann's first son, Hartwich, born
in 1924, contracted meningitis soon after birth. The resulting brain damage
meant their son lived in a home for handicapped children unable even to recognize his own parents.[7]

When the Nazis came to power in 1933, Jürgen was just seven years old.
The new government disbanded the Lichtwark School, known to be full of
social democrats. Herbert Moltmann moved to another school, but wishing to be free from Nazi Party control, he joined the Army reserve in 1936.[8]
Personal experience reinforced Herbert Moltmann's dislike of the Nazis. The
Moltmann family was friendly with the family of Fritz Valentin, a judge in
Hamburg and an outspoken Christian. In 1933, the Nazi's classified Valentin
as Jewish, and the Moltmanns watched Valentin lose his job and have to flee
for his life in 1938.[9] The Jews were not the only group in Germany that suffered under Hitler's social engineering. In 1941, the Moltmanns received news
that Hartwich, their disabled son, was dead—a victim of the Nazi's euthanasia
program.[10]

Along with his peers, Moltmann was a member of the Hitler Youth and
initially the nationalism harnessed by Nazi propaganda proved attractive.
"I remember the exalted and fascinating shiver which ran down my spine as
a boy when at school, on special Nazi occasions, we sang: 'Holy Fatherland, in
peril thy sons surround thee...' Then we were ready to die for Germany."[11] By
1943, with the war in its fourth year, any glamour nationalism had once held
for Moltmann was gone. He read the growing casualty lists in the newspaper
and felt himself surrounded by death.[12]

Under peaceful circumstances, Moltmann would have been making plans
for his summer vacation before his final year in high school. The demands of
the war effort, however, required all available hands. On February 16, 1943,
at the age of seventeen, he was conscripted into the *Luftwaffe* auxiliary to
defend his home city of Hamburg.[13] Moltmann worked with other boys his age

manning an anti-aircraft battery set on an artificial island raised on stilts in the middle of the Outer Alster, one of Hamburg's lakes.[14] Living in barracks in the central St. George district—not out in the leafy suburb of Volksdorf with his family—Moltmann made friends with others who had had their schooling interrupted by the demands of war. He particularly enjoyed the company of Gerhard Schopper with whom he shared a love of mathematics.[15] Night after night, Schopper and Moltmann kept watch as the air raid sirens warned of the bomber streams heading in their direction. Exposed on their small island, the two young men waited for the bombs to start falling. The alarms proved false; the aircraft passed over the city intent on other targets.[16] On the night of July 24, however, one schoolboy at his gun "heard the humming of engines, like a thousand bees."[17] This time the bombers were coming for Hamburg.

In secret orders issued in May 1943, Sir Arthur "Bomber" Harris, head of Royal Air Force (RAF) Bomber Command, stated his plans for the city of Hamburg. "The total destruction of this city," he wrote, "would achieve immeasurable results in reducing the industrial capacity of the enemy's war machine." He hoped to demonstrate his belief that area bombing could so reduce morale as to shorten, or even win, the war against Germany. This concerted effort to destroy an entire city by area bombing deserved a suitable title; Harris named the assault on Hamburg, "Operation Gomorrah."[18] Harris calculated that his planes could not destroy the city in one raid and so over the course of a week the RAF attacked the city three times at night with the United States Air Force bombing during the days. The British planes dropped a mixture of high explosive and incendiary bombs designed to rip the old town apart and set it ablaze. On their second raid, the aircrews were amazed to see not a patchwork of fires on the ground but a single raging inferno. The whole city appeared to be alight, "I saw not many fires, but one," recalled an RAF Flight Lieutenant. "Set in the darkness was a turbulent dome of bright red fire, lighted and ignited like the glowing heart of a vast brazier."[19]

Moltmann watched the apocalypse unfold from the relative safety of the lake. "We looked on as St. George's began to burn, and then the city hall, and finally Hamburg's churches, which flared up like torches."[20] The buildings set ablaze by the incendiaries grasped for more oxygen to feed their flames. Sucking in air already heated by other fires, they created a blast furnace of tornadic winds and walls of flame that whipped through the burning streets. Temperatures at the center of the blaze reached 800° Centigrade.[21] The fire trapped many citizens of Hamburg huddling in the basement shelters of their apartment buildings. The nightmarish images experienced by those who escaped the shelters and tried to outrun the fire come straight from Hieronymus Bosch's vision of hell. "There were people on the roadway, some already dead, some still lying alive but stuck in the asphalt," remembers Käte Hoffmeister, then nineteen years old. "Their feet had got stuck and then they had put out their hands to try to get out again. They were on their hands and knees screaming."[22] Moltmann saw others sucked back into the burning buildings they hoped to escape.[23]

It was either that night, or the night of the third and final RAF raid, that Moltmann's gun platform received a direct hit. The explosion wounded Moltmann with shrapnel in the head and shoulder, but Gerhard Schopper— standing right next to Moltmann—was blown to pieces.[24] Forty-four years later, Moltmann looked back on those terrible experiences and saw the beginning of his theological journey.[25] "In the night, for the first time I cried out to God. 'My God, where are you?' was my question. 'Why am I alive and not dead like the others?' "[26]

By the time the raids ended, Moltmann found "the whole city covered with ash."[27] Slave laborers filled mass graves with the forty-five thousand dead and Operation Gomorrah added a new word to the lexicon of war: *Feuersturm*, or Firestorm.[28]

The following year, recovered from his wounds, Moltmann took his place in the infantry. The terrifying experience of the air raids and the senseless death of school friends had shaken him, but despite his religious crisis during the destruction of Hamburg, Moltmann was far from embracing religion. Rather than a Bible, for which he had no use, he carried pocket editions of Goethe and Nietzsche printed on India paper in his knapsack.[29] With only the briefest of training, Moltmann joined his division in Holland. In September 1944, after a long night march, his company dug in by the Albert Canal at Asten.[30] That evening the young conscripts faced an assault—part of the allies' Operation Market Garden planned to establish a bridgehead over the Rhine. The fighting was fierce and allied tanks overran Moltmann's position killing half the men in his company.[31] Again, Moltmann found himself alive while those around him died.

Moltmann surrendered to British soldiers in Belgium on February 14, 1945. They sent him with thousands of other defeated and dispirited soldiers to Camp 2226 in Zedelgem near Ostend. The camp was crowded and conditions were miserable. With the war still raging, Nazis among the prisoners brutally punished their fellow prisoners who expressed doubts regarding Hitler or Germany's inevitable victory.[32] From Belgium, Moltmann's captors moved him to a labor camp in Kilmarnock, Scotland, where conditions improved.

The end of the war in May 1945 brought new trials for the prisoners. With his fellow prisoners of war, Moltmann experienced what today would be termed post-traumatic stress disorder. With the collapse and destruction of their homeland, the prisoners had no idea of the fate of their loved ones. "Cold despair laid an iron ring round the heart and took away the air we needed to breathe."[33] Haunted by his own experiences of violence and destruction, Moltmann struggled to deal with Germany's defeat while shut up as a prisoner. At night, memories of the firestorm and the horrors of infantry warfare haunted Moltmann's dreams.[34] He describes his generation as "burnt children" who were "shattered and broken."[35]

In September 1945, the guards at the camp in Scotland posted horrifying photographs from the liberated death camps of Auschwitz and Belsen. Moltmann had watched as many fellow prisoners in the camp in Belgium collapsed inwardly, gave up hope, and even died.[36] Now, facing the truth of the Nazi's Final Solution, he found that his own inner world fell to pieces, too. He could not face "the horrors of the Second World War, the collapse of an empire...the guilt and shame of one's own nation" and "stand up to it all inwardly."[37]

The daily battle was not only with despair but also, as a result of the harsh rationing, with hunger. British army chaplains working in the camps tried to minister to the prisoners. When one gave Moltmann a New Testament & Psalms, the young prisoner found it an odd gesture; "I would rather," he opines, "have had something to eat."[38] Nevertheless, as he read the cries of lament in the Psalms, his "experience of misery and forsakenness and daily humiliation gradually built up into an experience of God."[39] Turning from the Psalms to the Gospel of Mark, Jürgen Moltmann had a decisive encounter. In the gospel account of the crucifixion, he read Christ's cry of dereliction from the cross, "My God, My God, why have you forsaken me?" Moltmann heard echoes of his own cry in the Firestorm. He recalls, "When I came to Jesus' dying cry, I knew, 'There is your divine brother and redeemer, who understands you in your godforsakenness.'"[40] Describing this experience, Moltmann concludes: "I think I never made a decision for Jesus, but I am certain that he found me when I was lost and accepted me."[41]

Moltmann attributes his own survival to this encounter with God, but this was no retreat into a private spiritual world; it was quite the opposite. Those who gave up hope withdrew in despair from the realities afflicting them, while, paradoxically, his newfound hope made Moltmann increasingly aware of his suffering and imprisonment. Moltmann had found God's presence "most of all behind the barbed wire" with the broken-hearted; yet, the hope that this discovery engendered made his continued captivity harder to bear. In what would guide his life's work, Moltmann started to understand the connections and contradictions of suffering and hope—crucifixion and resurrection.[42]

A year after the end of the war Moltmann remained a prisoner. In July 1946, he had the opportunity to go to Norton Camp outside Mansfield in Nottinghamshire, England. Norton was a camp for the reeducation of German prisoners run by the Young Mens Christian Association (YMCA); here Moltmann finished his high school education. Before his experiences as a prisoner, Moltmann had wanted to pursue physics and mathematics at university; now, he had developed a taste for theology. At Norton, prisoners with the help of the YMCA and the British Army had established a Protestant theological school. The YMCA assembled a library and printed its own editions of theological works. The students and lecturers were prisoners of war, but the camp invited prominent theologians and churchmen to visit. These guests included the influential Swedish theologian Anders Nygren and the Confessing Church leader Martin Niemöller.[43] Moltmann, who had had no previous exposure to Christian theology found everything "fabulously new."[44] "It was marvelous, a richly blessed time. We were given what we did not deserve, and received of the fullness of Christ 'grace upon grace.'"[45]

Released in April 1948, Moltmann returned to Hamburg and the family home now full of refugees from East Prussia. Moltmann applied to the University in Göttingen to study theology, much to the dismay of his father who feared that his son would become a priest. Göttingen had a reputation as "a mecca of a Reformation theology which was critical of the church and society," which suited the young Moltmann's theological and political inclinations.[46]

To understand Moltmann's theology, one needs to understand the crisis that gripped the German church in the years after the war. Thirteen years of Hitler's Third Reich had left the Protestant churches in Germany in crisis. These churches, with their particularly close association with the state, had presented little resistance to the Nazification of Germany. Following their rise to power, the Nazis imposed their monolithic totalitarian logic of "One party, one Fuhrer, one people" on the churches. There must now be "one church."[47] A new Reich church (Reichskirche) replaced the existing Federation of Churches (Kirchenbund), and the state installed the Nazi stooge, Ludwig Müller, as the first Reich bishop (Reichsbischof).[48]

In 1933, a few churchmen formed the Pastors Emergency League to resist the takeover of the protestant churches by the pro-Nazi German Christians. Particularly disturbing to the League were the Aryan Laws, passed in 1933, which excluded ministers with Jewish heritage from the church.[49] Swiss theologian Karl Barth, then teaching in Germany, gave the opposition a firm theological footing when he helped draft a radically simple confession of faith at the League's synod in Barmen in 1934. At the heart of this Barmen Confession was this affirmation: "Jesus Christ, as he is attested to us in Holy Scripture, is the one Word of God whom we have to hear, and whom we have to trust and obey in life and in death." The delegates at Barmen made their challenge to the Nazis explicit as the confession continues: "We reject the false doctrine that the Church could and should recognize as a source of its proclamation, beyond and besides this one Word of God, yet other events, powers, historic figures and truths as God's revelation."[50] Those who stood by the Barmen Confession formed the Confessing Church, a church with no recognition from the state. As the Nazi state's power grew and times became more desperate, many of its leaders were imprisoned and some were executed.

With the war's end, the church in a defeated Germany had to come to terms with its complicity in the Nazi's crimes against the Jews and decide what form it could take in a country divided between occupying forces. Bishop Theophil Wurm called church leaders to attend a conference held in the Hessian town of Treysa. Eighty-eight delegates—half of whom had been imprisoned or placed under house arrest by the Nazis—met between August 27 and September 1, 1945. Karl Barth and Martin Niemöller, as part of a twelve-man delegation of the Confessing Church, tried to call the German church to a time of spiritual conversion and cleansing.[51] They wanted the Protestant Church in Germany to adopt the Confessing Church model, completely free from the state. They failed to convince the gathered church leaders who were concerned for the German church's survival under occupation. Otto Dibelius, the bishop of Berlin, believed that the Confessing Church would be incapable of running the "whole ecclesiastical organism"; furthermore, the Russians would not tolerate a church critical of the state.[52] The church in Germany would continue as the single German Evangelical Church (*Evangelische Kirche Deutschland* (EKD)) with its organization of regionally autonomous churches (*Landeskirchen*).

Out of prison camp and studying theology at Göttingen in West Germany, Moltmann found the church's desire to maintain the old structures disturbing. The church had had the opportunity to learn from its terrible mistakes. Why, Moltmann wondered, did the leaders of the EKD not heed the lessons from the Confessing Church and move forward with this "church from below"?[53] Instead, they returned to "the misalliances of 'throne and altar,' 'faith and the bourgeoisie,' [and] 'religion and capitalism.' "[54] The post-war Protestant church seemed to want to continue on its traditional way as if the Nazi era was simply an unfortunate interruption to the *status quo*. "Even the much admired leaders of the 'Confessing church,' " Moltmann realized with horror, "took possession of the traditional offices...and poured their new wine into old bottles."[55]

While at Göttingen, Moltmann allied himself with the Council of Brethren and the Society for Protestant Theology, who represented the continuing voice of the Confessing Church in the EKD.[56] These followers of Karl Barth and

"Barmen orthodoxy" believed Christianity in Germany, with its bureaucratic relationship with the state, had lost its center. The center of the Church, they maintained, could be nothing other than Christ. The political implications of Barmen had not ended with the defeat of the Nazis; Moltmann and his colleagues believed in a free church "supported only by committed Christians and making no attempt to placate nominal Christians—a church prepared to take clear stands on social and political issues."[57]

At Göttingen Moltmann found time for less academic pursuits. He met and fell in love with a fellow theological student, Elisabeth Wendel. They married in 1952 when Moltmann completed his doctorate. The newlyweds hoped to move to the German Democratic Republic (DDR), where Jürgen would pastor a congregation and Elisabeth could teach theology. The challenge facing the church under communism attracted Jürgen, and Elisabeth's family lived in the East. Jürgen found a job as a hospital chaplain in Berlin while they waited for the necessary work permits from the Russians. After a year in Berlin, they met with disappointment; because of his three years as a prisoner in England, the communists considered Jürgen Moltmann "politically unreliable."[58]

During this stay in Berlin, the Moltmanns joined with other like-minded Christians sharing their hopes and concerns for the German church calling themselves the "group on the way."[59] There they became friends with Eberhard Bethge and his wife Renate. Only the previous year Bethge had published Dietrich Bonhoeffer's *Letters and Papers from Prison*.[60] The book, including Bonhoeffer's reflections smuggled from his cell in Tegel Prison, gave strength and direction to the sidelined postwar Confessing Church. Their reliance on the reformed theology of Karl Barth, that had inspired and guided them through the Nazi years, did not seem to address the new problems of the Cold War. In tantalizing theological fragments scattered through his correspondence, Bonhoeffer had wrestled with the future of Christianity in a postwar "religionless" Germany. Such a church, Bonhoeffer anticipated, would have to regard itself not "from a religious point of view as specially favoured, but rather belonging wholly to the world."[61] Moltmann and the group around Bethge discovered in these writings a new direction that moved them beyond the strictly confessional theology of Karl Barth.[62]

Historian Victoria Barnett believes the direction Moltmann and his contemporaries found was suggested by Dietrich Bonhoeffer in his idea that "the morality of certain political decisions became a *status confessionis*, a view point so fundamentally derived from Christian teaching that acceptance of it is implicit in the Christian confessions."[63] The legacy of the Confessing church in the postwar years, she argues, is a political activism as Christian witness. Moltmann certainly fits this model. In the years after Berlin, he threw himself into protesting the Federal Republic of Germany (FDR)'s rearmament, nuclear weapons, and the church's collusion with the military in providing chaplains.

Prevented from pastoring in the DDR, Moltmann looked for a position in the West. After a couple of temporary appointments, Moltmann took the job as community pastor in Wasserhorst, a suburb of Bremen. There, he says he "experienced the meaning of Christian community."[64] His time as a pastor ended in 1958 when the seminary at Wuppertal appointed him as professor of theology.

In 1960, on a family holiday in Switzerland, Moltmann read Ernst Bloch's *The Principle of Hope.* Elisabeth noticed that "despite the radiant spring sun and the mountains glittering with snow, Jürgen immersed himself in [the book]...saw nothing and heard nothing."[65] As his family enjoyed the scenery, Moltmann was enthralled. "All that is not *hope* is wooden, dead, hampering, as ponderous and awkward"; Moltmann read, "There there is no freedom, but only imprisonment."[66] Here he found talk of hope matching his own experience as prisoner of war. Bloch, a Jewish Marxist philosopher, saw in his Marxist atheism a ground for hope based in "social utopias for the 'weary and heavy laden' and his utopias of justice for the 'humiliated and the injured.' "[67] But why, Moltmann wondered, "has Christian theology paid no attention to the subject of hope?"[68] Prompted by Bloch's work, Moltmann placed hope at the center of his theological work. Christian hope, Moltmann realized, far exceeded Bloch's secular hopes. Christians, Moltmann proclaimed, have "the eschatological horizon of the resurrection of the dead."[69]

This eschatological hope is not just an appendix to the Christian faith. This hope does not lead to Christians resting quietly, awaiting the return of Christ or their own death. Drawing on his own experience of renewed hope while in captivity and the political activism of the Confessing Church, Moltmann showed the impact for believers in the here and now of a hope in the resurrection of the dead. "The resurrection of Christ is not merely consolation in suffering," he explained. "It is also the sign of God's protest against suffering. That is why whenever faith develops into hope it does not make people serene and placid; it makes them restless."[70]

Moltmann published his book, *Theology of Hope,* in Germany in 1964 and started work on a follow-up volume entitled *Ethics of Hope.*[71] In 1967, he accepted an invitation to spend a year as a visiting scholar at Duke University in the United States. Moltmann was in the United States for the publication of the English translation of *Theology of Hope.* It perturbed him that "Americans received it as a statement supporting American optimism." Moltmann felt far from optimistic about America's role in the world. "During the Vietnam war," he explains, "I could not support American optimism."[72]

At the beginning of April 1968, Duke Divinity School hosted a symposium to consider "the task of theology today."[73] Moltmann was the main speaker, delivering a lecture on his Theology of Hope. What occurred during this gathering changed the direction of Moltmann's theology. He recalls the night of April 4, 1968, as theologians from across the United States gathered in Page Hall: "I was just discussing with Van Harvey the English concept of history and the German concept of *geschichte*—When *geschichte* happened!"[74] "Harvey Cox burst into the room crying 'Martin King has been shot.'"[75] The conference broke up and the participants returned home. Watching the news reports of Martin Luther King Jr.'s assassination and the ensuing rioting in cities across America, Moltmann felt he should no longer be writing about hope. "On that night the idea came to me not to go on with the theology of hope but [to] write about the crucifixion and the assassination of the prophets."[76]

Returning to Europe, the situation that greeted him confirmed Moltmann in his new theological direction. In July 1968, the World Council of Churches met in the Swedish city of Uppsala. Responding to the revolutionary climate, the Council chose as its theme, "behold I make all things new." Elisabeth and Jürgen Moltmann took part in a parallel student conference in Turku. Elisabeth remembers that, in the charged atmosphere, "revolutionary theories and actions were discussed instead of Christian topics."[77] Any hopes generated at this conference turned to disillusionment when the next month Soviet tanks rolled into the streets of Prague stomping on the "human face" of Czech socialism.

Shelving the *Ethics of Hope,* Moltmann decided to "speak no more about hope, but only about the cross."[78] He started work on a book that he would entitle *The Crucified God.* Recalling his own cry of dereliction as bombs fell and his experience of despair as a prisoner of war, Moltmann wrote, "Jesus died crying out to God, 'My God, why hast thou forsaken me?'" In his new work, he realizes this cry is the critical moment for Christian theology. "Either Jesus who was abandoned by God is the end of all theology," Moltmann asserts, "or he is the beginning of a specifically Christian, and therefore critical and liberating, theology and life."[79]

Typically, theologies ask what the crucifixion of the Son of God means for humans. In writing his theology, Moltmann reversed this traditional question by asking, "*What does the cross of Jesus mean for God himself?*"[80] Here, Moltmann develops his connection and tension between suffering and hope, because "Golgotha becomes the revelation of the suffering of the passionate God for us."[81] This notion of "the suffering of God in Christ, rejected and killed in the absence of God," Moltmann argues, is completely alien and abhorrent to any human notion of religion.[82]

Published in 1972, *The Crucified God* found a wide audience with the proponents of liberation theology in the Americas and South Africa.[83] These theologians understood and embraced Moltmann's assertion that a theology of the cross is a "dangerous and liberating reality" that becomes "aware...of its own strangeness and homelessness in its own Christian world."[84] The powerful Eurocentric colonial churches marginalized theologians who were developing "dangerous and liberating" contextual theologies.[85] These theologians understood what it meant to feel strange and homeless within the Church. They discovered in Moltmann's writing a way to reclaim the Christian faith as central to their struggle for liberation.

Moltmann had focused on Easter Sunday in *Theology of Hope* and Good Friday in *The Crucified God;* his next work revisited Pentecost. In *The Church in the Power of the Spirit,* published in 1975, Moltmann hoped to "help the church find its bearings" in an age of "uncertainty."[86] With his experience of the worldwide church from Korea to Manila and Kenya to El Salvador, he explored " 'the sending of the Spirit,' its messianic history and the charismatic power of its church."[87] Continuing in the Confessing Church tradition, he argued against "national and established churches" that, following a pastoral model, "looks after the people." Instead, he wished to see "missionary churches" or "fellowship churches." These free-church congregations should be "the people's own communal church among the people."[88] In a brief section of the book, Moltmann calls on the church to know Christ as *friend,* and in a seemingly innocuous descriptor, Moltmann challenges the church to be the community of "Open Friendship."[89]

A Theology of Friendship

To understand the meaning and significance of open friendship in Moltmann's theology, we must retrace our steps back to the prison camp in Belgium. While a prisoner of war, Moltmann watched his comrades as they "collapsed inwardly, how they gave up hope, sickening from the lack of it, some of them dying."[90] Reflecting on this experience of hopelessness, he realized that the hopeless person, unable to deal with the difficult reality of their future, engages in an anesthetizing withdrawal from reality. "The withdrawn and introverted person—*homo incurvatus in se*[91]—has no future and desires no alteration," writes Moltmann. "He is twisted in on himself, in love with himself and imprisoned by himself. He can only desire the prolongation of his present in the future."[92] This person is *closed* to the world, to others and to new possibilities.

We can best understand this closedness of despair by considering the opposite: the openness of hope. In a heavily symbolic description of his own

FIGURE 2.1. Jürgen Moltmann, University of Virginia, 2005. (Courtesy of
R. Stan Runnels)

spiritual awakening as a prisoner of war, Moltmann recalls the Norton camp
with the chapel at its center and his nightly walks inside the barbed wire perim-
eter. The chapel represents the young Moltmann's newfound spiritual hope
"without which it is impossible to live at all." This hope, "provided the strength
to get up again after every inward or outward defeat; on the other hand it made
the soul rub itself raw on the barbed wire, making it impossible to settle down
in captivity or come to terms with it."[93] In this metaphor of Christian hope,
the prisoner gaining his strength from the mystery of God pushes up against
the barbed wire of his existence. He does not withdraw from the barbed wire
because beyond the fence he has a hope in the future; he has his eyes fixed
in Christian hope on "the eschatological horizon of the resurrection of the
dead."[94] Thus, a person formerly closed, withdrawn, and protected from disappointment and hurt, is now open "for experience of the future in the hope of
what is to come. But," warns Moltmann, "this also makes him vulnerable and
capable of being hurt."[95]

Moltmann moves from his observations of "the withdrawn and introverted person" to "the closed and introverted society." The closed society, for
Moltmann, is the hopeless individual writ large. With a fundamental lack of
hope, the closed society "wants to corroborate itself, to perpetuate itself and
to write its possession of the present into the future." An open society, in contrast, is "open for the experience of the future in the hope of what is to come."

There is a desperate need for such an open society, Moltmann believes, "For what closes itself within itself is condemned to death and has a deadly effect on other life."[96]

Moltmann describes the state of an open society as "perilous openness" because in opening "society's institutions and society itself for others," it "also makes it vulnerable and alterable."[97] The infusion of hope into a closed society breaks the fear of the future, of the other, and of change. It is the responsibility of the Christian Church, Moltmann states, to bring the good news of this hope to society, "in the missionary proclamation of the gospel, that no corner of this world should remain without God's promise of new creation through the power of the resurrection."[98] The problem, of course, is that the Christian Church, far from being a model of this openness, is often as closed and deathly as the society in which it is located.

Moltmann issues the challenge of openness to the Church in bold theological terms deeply rooted in his understanding of Jesus and his crucifixion. The Church must open itself not simply to the possibilities of the future but also open itself to those who are different, particularly those who suffer. Why? Because "this is what God has done in the cross of Jesus Christ."[99] In his book *The Crucified God,* Moltmann employs the dialectical principle—that truth is only revealed in its opposite—to understand the cross. Moltmann explains that "God is only revealed as 'God' in his opposite: godlessness and abandonment by God," and this is what he finds at the heart of the story of the crucifixion. Moltmann explains the ramifications of this dialectical principle for Christian th eology in a beautifully simple and profound passage:

> In concrete terms, God is revealed in the cross of Christ who was abandoned by God. His grace is revealed in sinners. His righteousness is revealed in the unrighteous and in those without rights, and his gracious election in the damned...the deity of God is revealed in the paradox of the cross. This makes it easier to understand what Jesus did: it was not the devout, but the sinners, and not the righteous but the unrighteous who recognized him, because in them he revealed the divine righteousness of grace, and the kingdom. He revealed his identity amongst those who had lost their identity, amongst the lepers, sick, rejected and despised, and was recognized as the Son of Man amongst those who had been deprived of their humanity.[100]

The implication of this revelation of God in the godforsaken dictates the way that the Church should approach its "missionary proclamation of the gospel." "If a being is revealed only in its opposite," Moltmann reasons, "then the church which is the church of the crucified Christ cannot consist of an assembly of like persons who mutually affirm each other, but must be constituted of unlike persons."[101] In Moltmann's continued exploration of this challenge to the Church, he discovers in the gospel accounts a description of the very openness he sees as the result of hope in the crucified and risen Christ: it is the friendship of Jesus. "Friend," argues Moltmann, should become one of the church's titles for Jesus alongside "prophet," "priest" and "king" and the Church should again become the friends of Jesus as well as the communion of saints.[102]

Jesus is called friend on two occasions in the gospels. In two of the synoptic accounts, Jesus compares his reception to that of John the Baptist. Whereas John had been criticized for his strict asceticism, now "the Son of man has come eating and drinking; and you say, 'Look, a glutton and a drunkard, a friend of tax collectors and sinners!'" (Luke 7:34).[103] Moltmann sees in this friendship the radical openness to the other that a closed society is bound to condemn. This extension of friendship toward those deemed antisocial gains its energy, according to Moltmann, from Jesus' eschatological vision of the messianic feast of the kingdom.

In the second instance, found in the gospel of John, Jesus proclaims to his disciples that they are now no longer his "servants...but...friends" (John 15:15). This is no easy designation. Jesus indicates the import and cost of such a statement by linking friendship with the greatest possible human love for, as Jesus explains, "No one has greater love than this, to lay down one's life for one's friends" (15:13). "When he cites friendship," Moltmann reflects, "as the motive for Jesus' sacrificing his life, John means a love that sees, that is faithful unto death. He means a knowing sacrifice for the sake of friends' lives. Through Jesus' death in friendship the disciples become friends forever, and they remain in his friendship if they follow his commandments and become friends to others."[104] The disciples must now participate in the prefiguring of the messianic banquet—they, too, must be known as friends of tax collectors and sinners if they are to be friends of Jesus. The motivation for the friends of Jesus to extend friendship to the godforsaken and the sinner is not a masochistic practice of self-denial, a trade-off for some delayed cosmic reward. No, the motive comes from the overflowing joy of God—"that my joy may be in you" (15:11). Moltmann calls this hopeful, joyful, risky friendship of Jesus and his friends *Open Friendship.*

Moltmann means something very specific by friendship when he claims, "the concept of friendship is the *best* way of expressing the liberating relationship with God, and the fellowship of men and women in the spirit of freedom."[105] One enters into friendship, unlike other relationships—one's family for instance—by free choice. As Moltmann says, "friendship...springs from freedom, exists in mutual freedom and preserves that freedom."[106] "Rightly understood," Moltmann explains, "the friend is the person who 'loves in freedom.' "[107]

Open friendship lies at the very heart of Moltmann's theological model, not just of the Church but also of God. The Trinity is a fellowship in which Father, Son, and Spirit are distinct persons through their relationship with one another. One person is not subordinate to another; instead, there is only mutual love in freedom. This mutual love in freedom is open, not just to the persons of the trinity but also to creation.[108] As a result, when Jesus calls his disciples friends, he is extending the open friendship of the Trinity to godforsaken humanity. Thus, Moltmann shows how the title of friend is the best title "to describe the inner relationship between the divine and the human fellowship."[109]

Moltmann does not just describe individuals and societies as closed: friendships can be closed as well. Closed friendship, Moltmann recognizes, is what most people consider real friendship. Since Aristotle, friendship has most often been characterized as "Like seeks after like."[110] One finds true friendship with another who is like you and is your peer. The friendship of Jesus, however, is radically opposed to this privatization of friendship to the "inner circle of one's equals."[111] The Church above all must realize this because as Moltmann points out: "The closed circle of friendship among peers is broken in principle by Christ, not only in relation to the despised humanity of "bad society," but in relation to God. Had he abided by the peer principle, he would of necessity have had to stay in heaven."[112] Unlike the closed friendship of peer relations, for Jesus' disciples, friendship must mean the complete disregard of hierarchy and social station. They are not to "lord it over" one another Jesus tells them; rather, "whoever would be great among you must be your servant" (Mark 10:42–43). When Jesus no longer calls them servants but extends his friendship to the disciples, then "open friendship becomes the bond in their fellowship with one another, and it is their vocation in a society still dominated by masters and servants, fathers and children, teachers and pupils, superiors and subordinates."[113]

Moltmann's own experience in the EKD and the World Council of Churches showed him that churches are rarely prepared to enter and stay in the world of open friendship. "People grow tired of maintaining the open situation of dialogue and co-operation with others, in which the boundaries are always fluid," he observes.[114] Churches usually revert to a closed church position by insisting on "an orthodoxy which feels threatened and is more rigid than ever. It occurs wherever, in the face of the immorality of the present age, the gospel of creative love for the abandoned is replaced by the law of what is supposed to be Christian morality."[115] The solution is not, as so many of the student radicals at Turku in 1968 believed, in letting go of the particular claims of Christianity. Moltmann found this "decay [of the gospel] through uncritical assimilation" as disturbing as churches' "withdrawal into the ghetto without self-criticism."[116] Those who think the choice presented to the church is between evangelism and social action, Moltmann argues, could not be more wrong. The church practicing the open friendship of Jesus will be a missionary church bringing the hope of the crucified and risen Jesus to the world.[117]

Where the open friendship of Jesus becomes the practice and witness of a church, then that church will be at odds with a closed society. Such a church does not bring a word of comfort or escape to a cowering, reactionary society frightened of change. "The Christian Church has not to serve mankind in order that this world may remain what it is, or may be preserved in the state in which it is." Instead, expounds Moltmann, the church serves society "in order that it may transform itself and become what it is promised to be."[118] This church must avoid co-option by a secular ideological or social agenda because the world does not share the same hope. "[The church's] mission is not carried out within the horizon of expectation provided by the social roles which society concedes to the Church," warns Moltmann, "but it takes place within its own peculiar horizon of the eschatological expectation of the coming of the kingdom of God."[119] In other words, the Church should be worried when it finds itself fitting comfortably into the larger society. Rather, the Church should always find itself rubbed raw against the restrictive barbed wire of society because it sees the coming kingdom on the other side of the fence.

James Wesley Silver and the Closed Society

In 1964, thirteen years before Jürgen Moltmann had written of closed societies, readers of the popular magazine *Life* knew that the Closed Society existed in America and that its name was Mississippi. That summer a photo-essay featuring a history professor from the University of Mississippi could be found on coffee tables and in waiting rooms across the country. History professors rarely share the pages of popular magazines with celebrities and politicians but extraordinary times and extraordinary timing threw Professor James Wesley Silver into the national spotlight.

On Sunday June 21, 1964, in events recreated over two decades later in the movie *Mississippi Burning*, three civil rights activists—Andrew Goodman, James Chaney, and Michael Schwerner—disappeared in Philadelphia, Mississippi.

The following day, Harcourt, Brace & World published Silver's book, *Mississippi: The Closed Society*. The book, as the *Life* magazine article explained, was "an explosive attack on the powers that run the university and the state."[120] In its first year, *Mississippi: The Closed Society* sold thirty thousand hardback editions and the *New York Times* and *Time* listed it as a best seller.[121] Silver presented an attractive hero for the national media. The handsome fifty-seven-year-old professor's blunt manner and wry humor supplied newspaper reporters with memorable quotes: when a *New York Times* journalist asked the "6-foot 1-inch educator with the sharp tongue and piercing blue eyes" why he remained in Mississippi, he replied, "Hell, I like it there."[122]

While the murders in Philadelphia, Mississippi, and the voter registra-tion drives of 1964 fueled the sales of the book, it was the events surround-ing James Meredith's integration of the University of Mississippi in 1962 that had precipitated its writing. The violence, threats and lies that surrounded the "Meredith event" shocked Silver into action. The historian's diagnosis he presented in *Mississippi: The Closed Society* was not a sudden revelation to its author, it came instead from years of teaching and struggling for academic freedom at Ole Miss. Silver believed that his "entire life had unquestionably been a preparation" for this book.[123]

Born in Rochester, New York, in 1907, the son of a grocer, when Silver was twelve, the family moved to the small town of Southern Pines in North Carolina. The Silvers were a Methodist family and sent the young James Wesley to Sunday school.[124] With the move South and his father's agnostic drift away from the Methodist Church, Silver found his way to the regionally dominant Southern Baptist denomination. From high school he went to the University of North Carolina at Chapel Hill, majoring in history. At Chapel Hill he found his "Baptist fundamentalism underwent severe attack from class lectures and dormitory bull sessions."[125] Baptist piety did not mark Silver's undergraduate existence; instead, he displayed an irascible spirit with a disregard for authority and a love for high-stakes poker. Halfway through his senior year, the univer-sity threw him out for gambling. Despite his expulsion, he had accumulated enough academic credits to graduate and used his unsought free time to travel before enrolling as a graduate student in history at Vanderbilt. Silver wrote his doctoral dissertation on the Confederate General Edmund Pendleton Gaines, receiving his doctorate in 1935.[126] He left Nashville with a young bride, Margaret "Dutch" McLean Thompson, for a teaching post in Kansas. Then, only a year later, Jim and Dutch Silver moved to Oxford, Mississippi, where he took a position in the history department at Ole Miss.

Life on the leafy campus of the University of Mississippi suited Silver. He found many opportunities to play poker and go fishing, and he and Dutch threw themselves into the social life of the University. Their circle included the author William Faulkner, whom Silver considered an "awesome figure."[127] Silver supplemented his low salary by coaching the men's tennis team and traveling with the football squad making slow motion movies during the games.

Silver came to Mississippi a liberal and a supporter of the labor movement; he described his beliefs as a tendency to support the underdog.[128] Soon after arriving in Mississippi, disturbed by the views he encountered at the heart of the Jim Crow South, he started considering the question of "Negro inferiority," reading any sociological, historical or anthropological works he could find. He engaged in some mild mannered activism by attending biracial meetings at Oxford's Methodist Church in 1939.[129] However, it was Silver's views on labor, not race, which first brought him to the attention of the state authorities. Only three years after his appointment, following a lecture at the Clarksdale courthouse on the 1938 Wages and Hours Act, the University's Board of Trustees received a complaint that Silver was a "Red." The board, well disposed to Silver thanks to his ties with the Ole Miss football program, dismissed the charges out of hand. Silver would not get off the hook so easily in the future.[130]

During his twenty-eight years at the University of Mississippi, Silver exerted his greatest influence through his students who graduated to fill the courtrooms, boardrooms, and corridors of power in his adopted state. One of these students, William Winter, went on to become the governor of the state. Winter considers Silver his mentor who set his life's course, reflecting, "he helped me to understand the changes that had to take place in Mississippi."[131]

Winter came to Oxford as a freshman in the fall of 1940. He had grown up in Grenada, Mississippi, where his great-great grandfather had settled in 1837 having secured the first land deed from the governor after the Treaty of Dancing Rabbit Creek. He came from a line of gentleman farmers with impeccable Mississippi credentials; his father had been elected to the state senate in 1920.[132] As the young William Winter found his feet on campus, Silver organized a student-run lecture series on current affairs called the Omicron Delta Kappa (ODK) Mortar Board Forums to provide "the best chance for a student from one of the smaller towns of Mississippi to become acquainted with world-famous statesmen."[133] Silver kept an eye out for promising young students from these "smaller towns," and Winter caught his attention. As a history major, Winter came under Silver's influence in the classroom and in extended personal conversations.[134] The Second World War disrupted both Winter's education and Silver's lecturing. In 1943, Winter went into the army serving as an infantry officer in the United States; Silver volunteered with the Red Cross and served in the Pacific.[135]

Winter's wartime experience as a white officer in an African American regiment showed him the Jim Crow South for the first time through the eyes of his black fellow officers. He returned to Oxford and law school, "convinced that when [he] got back to civilian life things would never be the same."[136] Pleased to find Silver still at the school, Winter resumed his relationship with his mentor spending hours discussing how change would come to the region. "Jim Silver was a man way ahead of his time," Winter remembers, "he was one of the most perceptive, incisive observers of the Southern scene of anybody I ever knew. And one of the most courageous...[He was] one of the true prophets of the thirties and forties and fifties in Mississippi."[137]

Winter became the chairman of the ODK and worked closely with Silver in inviting the speakers to Oxford. Sixty years later, Winter still proudly keeps the fliers for these meetings in his desk drawer. Printed on faded color paper, one announces: "the public is cordially invited" to "Hear Alexander Karensky...The man whom Lenin succeeded as ruler of Russia," give a talk on "Russia and the International Situation." Another flier advertises Hodding Carter II, the Pulitzer Prize–winning editor of the Delta-Democrat Times, speak on "The Liberal Spirit and the South."[138] This invitation to Carter in 1946 started raising the suggestion at the state level that Silver was brainwashing his students. "Pressure was put on the chancellor by a certain conservative legislator to cancel the invitation to Hodding Carter," recalls Winter. "We went to see the chancellor and urged him not to cancel the invitation, and he did not...In introducing Hodding Carter that night to the assembly, I thanked the chancellor for letting academic freedom prevail."[139]

This conflict between Silver and the state of Mississippi over academic freedom characterized the rest of his time as an employee of the state. In 1950, state legislator Hamer McKenzie from Benton leveled accusations against particular university faculty including Silver of "molding the minds of Mississippi students" with their liberalism. Hamer introduced a "subversive activities bill" to the House of Representatives.[140] Particularly troubling to Hamer were the political views of the speakers Silver brought to the university for ODK Mortar Board Forums. William Winter, then a state legislator, vigorously defended Silver.[141]

The intransigent and outspoken Silver might have continued as a minor annoyance to the white Mississippi establishment were it not for the Supreme Court of the United States concluding that separate was not in fact equal. The Brown v. Board of Education of Topeka ruling in May 1954 sensitized segregationists in Mississippi to any threat to their segregated way of life enshrined in Jim Crow laws. Those voices calling for Silver's removal, once easily dismissed, now gained the weight of popular support. The window of tolerance for dissent from the segregationist orthodoxy was closing and the reaction to outspoken heretics grew increasingly severe. Silver's observation of the events that followed *Brown vs. Board* in Mississippi formed the nucleus of his understanding of The Closed Society.

In the summer of 1954, as the South held its breath waiting to see what would happen following the Supreme Court's ruling against segregated schools, Reverend Will D. Campbell came to Ole Miss. Campbell, a Baptist preacher from Amite county, Mississippi, had gone to war then to Yale Divinity school and now he was taking the job of Director of Religious Life at the university.[142] Returning to his home state to settle near family, he looked forward to joining "a university community where, I assumed, there would be freedom to speak on issues as I pleased."[143] He aimed to use his freedom of speech to subvert white supremacy in the state. He moved into his office in the Y building and Malcolm Guess, his predecessor and now a dean, showed him the ropes. That summer, Guess received a visit from Tom Brady. Brady, a former student of Guess's and now a judge, was on his way to deliver a speech to the Sons of the American Revolution in Greenwood. Campbell noted Guess's somber aspect after Brady's departure. Asking why Guess was downcast, the retired dean responded, "You'll know soon enough. That's a speech that will be heard for a long, long time."[144] Historians credit Brady's speech, entitled *Black Monday,* with providing the impetus for the foundation of the Citizens' Councils of Mississippi and the South and their resistance to federal calls for desegregation.[145] The *Monday* of the title is the day of the Brown decision, and *black,* using Brady's words is the "embodying [of] grief, destruction and death."[146]

The Citizens' Councils organized quickly and in huge numbers. They rapidly expanded from their base in the heart of the Mississippi Delta. As early as September 1954, there were seventeen counties with Citizens' Council organizations.[147] Hodding Carter III, the son of the liberal newspaper man Winter had secured for the ODK forum, in a piece written for the *New York Times* in 1961, tried to impress on the non-Mississippi reader just how powerful, pervasive and respectable the Citizens' Councils were. "Membership in the Citizens' Council," he explained, "has come to be akin to membership in the Rotary or Lions Club." There was "one central purpose" to all this organizing, and that "was to retain control of resistance to desegregation in the hands of 'better people.'" By the time Carter was writing, this "uptown Klan" had constructed "a political machine whose power is publicly unchallenged by any major state official."[148]

Campbell watched the formation of the Councils with concern, but did not consider it cause for major alarm, certainly not enough to deflect him from his mission to subvert the system of white supremacy. It did not take long for the university's administration to realize that, in Campbell's words, "this little Yaley may be up to something."[149] Silver observed the new arrival, but kept a discrete distance from the new Director of Religious Life. He suspected Campbell's "uncomplicated Christian logic" was likely to unsettle the *entente* he had worked out with the administration over a decade.[150] Campbell remembered, "[Silver] didn't have anything to do with me the first year I was there because he was afraid I would ask him to come and do something with one of my religious programs." For his part, Campbell did not consider this much of a loss. He had heard of Silver, "But I never considered him a radical. I had been [so] radicalized myself that in a way I considered Silver a conservative." He was, however, "a good historian and he was bright and he knew what time of day it was."[151]

Silver was right to be concerned. Only nine months after *Brown*, under pressure from the Citizens' Councils, the Board of Trustees of the university decided that the chancellor should investigate and approve all outside speakers.[152] This decision directly threatened academic freedom at the university and all that Silver had fought so hard to create with his forums. The students of the ODK petitioned the board to rescind this new decision, but to no avail.[153] They stood little chance of success. The political tide in Mississippi was now set against any free speech that might harbor dissent from the segregationist line.

The Citizen's Councils exerted social and economic pressure on those who supported integration and the state's legislature had officially opposed the Supreme Court's decision to interfere in the state's education system declaring that Mississippi had a right "to interpose for arresting the progress of evil."[154] In March 1956, House Speaker Walter Sillers, with the support of the Citizen's Councils, introduced House Bill No. 880 to create the Mississippi State Sovereignty Commission.[155] The bill defined the commission's task:

> It shall be the duty of the commission to do and perform any and all acts and things deemed necessary and proper to protect the sovereignty of the State of Mississippi, and her sister states, from encroachment thereon by the Federal Government...and to resist the usurpation of the rights and powers reserved to this state and our sister states by the Federal Government or any branch, department or agency thereof.[156]

William Winter was one of twenty-three house members who opposed the bill when they realized the Citizens' Councils were sponsoring it.[157] The opponents were, however, unable to stop the bill, which proved a triumph for the Citizens' Councils and a testament to their power.

The Commission set about securing Mississippi's "sovereignty" through a campaign of national and domestic propaganda. It arranged speaking tours of the United States promoting the state's right to perpetuate segregation. It also brought "experts" to Mississippi to speak on the evils of communism and the dangers of integration. The commission had a less public and more sinister dimension. In an attempt to silence any dissenting voices, it employed investigators who cultivated informants in the black and white communities and amassed files of information on thousands of Mississippi citizens. Campbell and Silver were two men at the University of Mississippi who attracted particular scrutiny.

Will Campbell proved a constant irritant to the university through his often mischievous acts of subversion. One of his duties was to organize students to say a prayer before the sacred Ole Miss football games. Offering Campbell such a platform proved too delicious an opportunity to miss. Ascending to the box overlooking the stadium, Campbell handed a prayer he had written to the student president of the YMCA. As the white Mississippi football faithful bowed their heads, they found themselves listening to a prayer for God in his justice to come to the aid of the oppressed. "It wasn't intended to be any kind of knock out punch," recalled Campbell with a chuckle, "but the people knew what the prayer was praying for." To avoid any repeat performances, Ole Miss stopped praying at their football games.[158]

Campbell hoped to challenge the ideological stranglehold that the segregationists had over the university. "If racial justice could not be discussed in the classroom," reasoned the chaplain, "then it would be proclaimed from the podium of the Religious Forum."[159] The forum he had in mind was Religious Emphasis Week to take place in February 1956. For one week each year, the students' Committee of One Hundred invited outside speakers to address the student body in Fulton Chapel. Campbell guided the committee to choose his recommendations for speakers. "If I had had to name one bit of subversion," Campbell boasted, "and I have been involved in a host of subversive activities in terms of the culture, that would be the only one I would name that turned out exactly as I planned from beginning to end...it was a direct challenge of the status quo."[160]

The success of Campbell's plans owed a great deal to luck as well as his judgment: following his invitation and acceptance to participate in Religious Emphasis Week, Rev. Alvin Kershaw, an Episcopal priest from Ohio, gained national publicity when he appeared on the TV quiz show *The $64,000 Question*. The university's administration—initially pleased that Campbell had attracted a celebrity—was horrified when Kershaw quit the game at $32,000 and donated some of his winnings to the NAACP's Legal Defense

Fund. The *Clarion-Ledger* ran the story alongside Campbell's announcement of the speakers.[161] John D. Williams, the university's chancellor, faced questions from the Board of Trustees as to how Kershaw had been invited. The Monday night before the start of Religious Emphasis Week, Will Campbell was sitting in James Silver's house on faculty row sipping bourbon. A knock on the door brought a summons for the director of religious life to report to the chancellor immediately. Williams told the recalcitrant Campbell that he needed him to "uninvite" Kershaw. Campbell refused the chancellor's request, leaving Williams to do his own dirty work. When the other invited speakers heard that the chancellor had removed Kershaw from the program, they all in turn withdrew.[162] Williams tried to invite local clergy to fill the empty schedule, but they, too, refused. Campbell drove his subversion home. Every day of Religious Emphasis Week, he went to the Fulton Chapel auditorium, and with an empty chair floodlit on the stage, he sat in silence. He was not alone as "each morning several hundred students, faculty, and townspeople joined [him] in the silent hour."[163]

Under the scrutiny of the Sovereignty Commission and with the political power of the Citizens' Councils, it only took a few months from Religious Emphasis Week for Campbell to find the situation at Ole Miss untenable. The official line was that he resigned because, "he found the University 'climate' incompatible."[164] The reality was that he had started to fear for his safety. In addition to inviting supporters of the NAACP to campus, Campbell had broken the taboos of white Mississippi when he had invited Carl Rowan—a black reporter from the *Minneapolis Tribune*—to stay in his house. This had not been a secretive transgression: he had invited Silver's history class to meet with the reporter after their class.[165] The last straw had been the discovery that Campbell had played ping-pong with a local African American minister in the Y building. This resulted in physical threats as well as ping-pong balls, painted half white and half black, dumped on the preacher's lawn under cover of darkness and, more seriously, human excrement placed in a bowl of punch at a YMCA function. When the National Council of Churches invited Campbell to set up its Southern Office of the Department of Racial and Cultural Relations in Nashville, he announced to the university that he would be leaving.[166]

The day that the university announced the Director of Religious Life's departure, Silver spent the afternoon on the Campbells' porch unsuccessfully trying to persuade him to stay. As Silver stood up to leave, Campbell asked him, "Jim, explain something to me. I've been here two and a half years. The first year and a half I was here you would walk all the way across the Grove to keep from speaking to me, afraid I was gonna invite you to meet with one of my programs. Now you're begging me to stay. What's going on?"[167]

"I don't give a damn about your religious program," Campbell remembered Silver replying. "Before you came I was number one on the state legislature's list to get rid of. You came in here and you bumped me to number two. Now you leave and I go back up to number one for them to run off; so I want you to stay."[168] The reactionary assault on freedom of speech at the university that Campbell helped stir up, and that Silver feared, was not long in coming.

In the fall of 1958, State Representative Wilburn Hooker and former representative Edwin White made allegations of integrationist, socialistic and communistic teachings at Ole Miss to the University's Board of Trustees. Both men were attorneys from Lexington, Mississippi, prominent members of the Citizens' Council, and alumni of the university; Hooker was a member of the Sovereignty Commission.[169] Silver referred to them sarcastically as "super patriots."[170] On November 18, they presented their accusations in a thirty-six page document.[171] White and Hooker, to create maximum pressure on the university, released their allegations to the press in "installments" over the summer of 1959.[172] "They didn't have subversive teachings up there when my grandfather, my father or I went to the University," explained Hooker to the readers of the *Clarion-Ledger*, "and I don't want my children to be exposed to such when they go to Ole Miss."[173] Defending their actions against the allegation that they were hurting the university, Hooker explained, "we don't want to kill the University, we just want to get rid of the liberal element." This would not have an adverse effect because, as he continued, "you don't kill the church when you oust a few backsliders."[174]

Hooker and White's documents included the names of Campbell and Silver. Reading the charges helps one appreciate the level of hysteria surrounding the fear of communism and integration. "Will Campbell in June 1956 was seen playing ping pong in the Y building with a nice looking well-dressed negro man." If that were not bad enough, "After this ping pong game Campbell got into his car with the negro and drove leisurely around campus."[175] They had to work hard to produce a case against Silver, claiming that a Master's thesis written by John Ben Nelson, a student in the history department, "defames the internal government of the people of Mississippi during the period of the Civil War. This thesis could well be the fruit of Dr. Silver's lectures."[176] Dr. Silver, they noted ominously, "went to Vanderbilt University which is well known for its integration sentiments."[177] The charges named fourteen other faculty and staff as well as broader accusations against the YMCA, the graduate school, the Psychology department, and the library.

The university administration answered all the charges to the satisfaction of the Board of Trustees, but the court of white public opinion fueled by the Citizens' Council and Sovereignty Commission's publicity machines continued to consider Silver a communist sympathizer. In a Sovereignty Commission sponsored speaking tour of the state, the "self styled communist hunter," Myers G. Lowman, accused Silver of being a "red." As Mississippi moved towards the showdown with Federal forces, Silver became increasingly outspoken. His response to Lowman came in an address to the Mississippi Historical Society in 1961. "I have been called a communist before by some pretty good local demagogues," Silver noted wryly, "but hiring someone from Ohio and then charging me taxes for him to come down here and accuse me is worse."[178]

As the pressure built against Silver, James Meredith's seemingly suicidal decision to be the first African American student to attend Ole Miss pushed the history professor to, in his own words, "take a public stand regardless of the personal consequences."[179] Meredith, an African American student wishing to transfer from Jackson State University, believed he had been born with a "Divine Responsibility." God, he said, had given him the mission of "directing civilization toward a destiny of humaneness." Applying to the state's premier all white school served his "immediate objective [which] was to break the system of 'White Supremacy.'"[180] Meredith's divine mission coincided with the interests of Medgar Evers, the secretary for the state's chapter of the NAACP. Evers helped Meredith secure the assistance of the NAACP defense fund for the legal battle ahead.[181] The state of Mississippi, under the arch-segregationist governor Ross Barnett, tried repeatedly to stop the federal rulings that said they must register Meredith. Negotiations between the Kennedy administration and Barnett ended on Sunday September 30, 1962, when 123 deputy federal marshals, 316 U.S. border patrolmen, and 97 federal prison guards escorted Meredith onto the Ole Miss campus.[182] With Meredith safely, and secretly, installed in his room in a hall of residence, the marshals took up positions around the white-columned Lyceum, the building housing the registrar's office.

Silver watched that Sunday afternoon as students gathered in front of the Lyceum in the area called the Circle. As their numbers swelled, Silver noted the way a mob forms and slowly moves toward violence. The students taunted the federal marshals and ruffed up a reporter. The word spread through the crowd that the marshals would try to register Meredith that night. At eight o'clock, they pressed in on the line of marshals who responded with a volley of tear gas. As marshals drove around the Circle to reinforce their beleaguered colleagues, they came under a barrage of bricks. "This really scared me," wrote Silver in a letter to his daughter, "for I knew then that this was a first class riot."[183] Evans Harrington, an English professor, recognized students from his poetry class raiding a building site for missiles, "They had a bunch of bricks and also broken concrete and whatever else wasn't too big to carry."[184]

As the night continued, agitators answering the call to defend Mississippi against federal aggression joined the students. With them came hunting rifles and gasoline for Molotov cocktails. Refraining from shooting back, the marshals stood their ground. With tear gas running low, the marshals managed to hold out until two o'clock in the morning when units of the Mississippi National Guard, federalized by the Kennedy administration, rode to the rescue in their jeeps.[185]

By the morning, with the National Guard reinforced by regular troops, Meredith walked past burned out cars to register at the bullet scarred Lyceum. The university resembled an army camp; Silver estimated that there were about ten thousand troops in Oxford in the days following the riot.[186] The cost of integration was a sad one: a French journalist and a local bystander had been killed during the riot. The rioters had shot 28 marshals and injured a further 160; undoubtedly, the marshals' incredible restraint in refusing to shoot back at the mob avoided a much greater tragedy.[187]

Mississippi's governor and state media, with a wanton disregard for the truth, cast the marshals as the villains claiming, "students...were gassed without just provocation" and were then "run down like rabbits by armed marshals."[188] Silver considered this distortion of the truth irresponsible and likely to incite further violence. Only three days after the riot, he released a resolution, signed by sixty-five faculty and staff stating, "We have evidence that the blame for the riot on the United States marshals is not only unfair and reprehensible, but is almost completely false."[189]

The deliberate attempt to distort the history of a significant historical event that Silver himself had witnessed pushed the professor to take action. "Until some moment in the Meredith affair," reflected Silver, "I had been running through life scared."[190] With nearly thirty years in the academy, Silver claimed he spent his life "desiring above all to be accepted in my work and play by my contemporaries."[191] Silver believed his fear of ostracism and loss of employment, "held me prisoner for most of my life."[192] Now, with the smell of tear gas lingering in the classrooms, Silver arrived, "as if by the wave of a magical wand at the point where there was no doubt as to my course."[193] The course he chose was publicly to counter the historical distortions of Mississippi's state propaganda machine and reveal the oppressive forces that maintained white supremacy. He hoped "to set the record straight and have some impact on Mississippi thinking."[194]

The platform for his message was to be his presidential address to the Southern Historical Association in Asheville, North Carolina, on November 7,

1963.[195] The title of the speech was "Mississippi: The Closed Society." With the benefit of hindsight, he could see his life leading up to this moment; "I have believed for a long time," he reflected, "that when he has made himself ready, the good teacher will have something to say beyond his classroom."[196] After spending nearly a year preparing the speech, Silver went to considerable effort to make sure that the widest possible audience heard what he had to say; he had contacted the press and before giving the speech, he had gone over his text with Claude Sitton of the *New York Times* highlighting the salient points of his argument. The next morning the front page of the *Times* carried the headline: "Mississippi Professor Declares That His State Is 'Totalitarian.'"[197] The Associated Press ran the story and papers across the country carried Silver's denunciation of Mississippi as a closed society.[198]

At the height of the Cold War, to label Mississippi "the Closed Society" was a particularly powerful and shocking statement. The United States believed itself to be an open society standing against the threat of international communism and totalitarian closed societies led by the Soviet Union and the People's Republic of China. Silver argued that since the Civil War, Mississippi's whites "on the defensive against inexorable change...had developed a closed society with an orthodoxy accepted by nearly everybody in the state."[199] This closed society defended the state's rigid racial caste system. "The all-pervading doctrine, then and now," Silver wrote, "has been white supremacy...[where] a never-ceasing propagation of the 'true faith' must go on relentlessly, with a constantly reiterated demand for loyalty to the united front, requiring that nonconformists and dissenters from the code be silenced, or, in a crisis, driven from the community."[200]

Silver's description of the Closed Society as "defensive against inexorable change" bears a striking resemblance to Jürgen Moltmann's *societas incurvatus in se*—the closed and introverted society. Moltmann's closed society, frightened by changes happening around it, lacks hope in the future. Such a hopeless society shies away from openness to the ambiguities and possibilities of an unknown future; instead, it "wants to corroborate itself, to perpetuate itself and to write its possession of the present into the future."[201]

There is another striking parallel between Silver's critique of Mississippi and Moltmann's theology. For Moltmann, the closed church that "is fearful and defensive...struggling to maintain itself and reaching out for security and guarantees...usually occurs in the form of an orthodoxy which feels threatened and is more rigid than ever."[202] Silver's description of Mississippi characterizes the threatened and rigid ideology of the Closed Society using the religious language of "orthodoxy," "doctrine" and "faith." His employment of these terms is not mere metaphor; rather, it points to both the religious

FIGURE 2.2. James W. Silver, University of Mississippi, picture taken sometime between 1961 and 1962. (Dain Collection, Southern Media Archive, University of Mississippi Special Collections)

nature of the intense and non-negotiable belief in white supremacy and to the religious sanctioning of the belief from the white pulpits. Silver summarized the main tenets of this threatened and rigid "segregation creed" of the closed society as: "1) the biological inferiority of the Negro, 2) the sanction of the Bible and Christianity, 3) the aptitude of the Negro for menial labor only, 4) racial separation as an absolute requirement for social stability, and 5) the necessity of the Negro earning his way to a higher and more responsible citizenship."[203]

The Mississippi State Sovereignty Commission, tasked with preserving orthodoxy and monitoring heretics, received a five-page closely typed report of Silver's Ashville speech from an informant identifying himself only as "a graduate of Emory University."[204] Erle Johnson Jr., the director of the Sovereignty Commission, wrote in a widely circulated letter, "I believe the best interest of the state, the University and all other state supported schools would be served by a request through proper channels that Dr. Silver be relieved of his duties."[205] His call for action resulted in the swift formation of a sub-committee of the College Board "to investigate Dr. Silver's situation and determine what grounds, if any, may justify his dismissal from the University staff."[206] While the sub-committee did its work, Johnston kept a close eye on the troublesome professor. The Sovereignty Commission's files show that agents monitored meetings at Silver's house and tried to identify the visitors by tracing the registered owners of the parked cars.[207]

The Board's sub-committee investigated the charge of "contumacious conduct" against Silver, a charge he took a perverse pleasure in repeating in front of numerous audiences. They summoned him to appear before them in the spring of 1964. Silver remembers the chairman stating, "Professor Silver, we have decided to drop the charges against you if you will agree to stop speaking about Mississippi outside the state."[208] Silver, of course, had no intention of doing any such thing. Realizing that his position at the University of Mississippi was fast becoming untenable, he was considering an invitation to teach at Notre Dame.[209] Shortly after *Mississippi: The Closed Society* reached the bookstores, he accepted the position, and the Silvers moved to Indiana.

When Silver left Mississippi in 1964, he had little hope that he would see a significant change in the Closed Society. "[It] is only in the distant future where the new society will be established," he had written. The possibility of such an open society might, he guessed, be no more than an eschatological hope, "a matter of faith, as something beyond a temporal Jordan."[210] As students and activists joined with local black community organizers for the voter registration drives of Freedom Summer, Silver believed the chances of white Mississippians supporting the civil rights movement were "minimal indeed."[211] Silver believed he did see African Americans successfully starting to challenge white supremacy through boycotts and sit-ins, but he remained pessimistic that change could come without great conflict and violence. After twenty-eight years of censorship Silver reasoned, "The strongest preservation of the closed society is the closed mind." Surveying the political scene he concluded, "As yet there is little evidence that the closed society will ever possess the moral resources to reform itself, or the capacity for self-examination, or even the tolerance of self-examination."[212] White Mississippians, who Silver describes as "a proud religious people," would not respond to "being told with increasing shrillness by outsiders that what three generations had accepted as historical truth was so much mythology. Furthermore," Silver continued, "separation of the races and absolute control of every facet of society by the whites—universally assumed to be not only constitutional but the work of God—were not to be challenged from within as evil and immoral."[213]

Silver, who said of himself "I was once a good Methodist" and claimed he was an atheist, had a low opinion of the role the church had played in Mississippi and held out little hope that change would come from that direction.[214]

"Mississippians torture the Scriptures into sacred sanction for inequality and inhumanity," he wrote, and that despite the "courageous stands" made by individual ministers, "the church as a whole has placed its banner with the status quo."[215] Some of these courageous ministers were very familiar to Silver. On September 16, 1962—just before the riots at Ole Miss—eight of Oxford's ministers read a joint statement in their churches urging their congregants to "act in a manner consistent with the Christian teaching concerning the value and dignity of man."[216] Duncan Gray, an Episcopal priest and one of the eight, remonstrated with the crowd on the night of the riot calling them to refrain from violence and go home.[217]

Will Campbell, another courageous minister, now working for the National Council of Churches and living a healthy distance from Mississippi on a farm in Mt. Juliet, Tennessee, placed more hope than Silver in the white churches of the South. In a short book, *Race and the Renewal of the Church,* published in 1961, Campbell had already addressed the problems posed to the church by the Closed Society. In *Race and the Renewal of the Church,* Campbell addressed the socially liberal churchmen and women engaging in the struggle for civil rights. Just as Moltmann warned the church against "uncritical assimilation" with society's social programs,[218] Campbell cried out against a church that pinned its moral pronouncements on the coattails of the Supreme Court. Liberal churches, bemoaned Campbell, far from taking the initiative and speaking a prophetic word against racism, were "imitat[ing] the action of the state" and "confirm[ing] such action with a pious benediction."[219] If the Supreme Court had not ruled favorably in 1954 on race, then perhaps it would have forced churches to speak from the Christian gospel. In that case, Campbell suggests, "We would have been required to say, Thus saith the Lord! Not, Thus saith the law!"[220]

Despite Campbell's protestations that he was "just a preacher," not a theologian, his work was profoundly theological. Campbell's ecclesiology combined a healthy Niebuhrian suspicion that all human institutions are self-serving with a Barthian insistence on the sovereignty of God. Greatly influenced by the Barmen declaration and the theology of the Confessing Church, he argued that segregation and racism are merely symptoms. "The sin," he declared, "is that the whole issue of race is an effort to deny the sovereignty of God, to negate the absolute supremacy of God."[221]

Although liberal scholars and ministers dismissed the conservative white Southern churches—as Silver did—as being racist and supportive of segregation, Campbell believed that hope for the region lay with them. Although they were playing little to no role in bringing about change to the closed society, Campbell believed that conservative Southern congregations had an important role in "cleaning up the mess" left in the wake of change. Campbell's argument, written in 1961 before the March on Washington and the Civil Rights Act, is prescient. It is also unexpected from a man, employed by the liberal National Council of Churches, who saw and shared Silver's closed society. Campbell wrote:

> As significant as the prophetic edge of the church is, and as much as most of us regret the present dearth of prophets in the land, it may well be that heroic deeds will come, not by the appearance of more and greater prophets, but as God uses the conserving edge which is, from our point of view, the weakness of the church. Making the conscious decision to play the conserving role and put our house in order is far from what the church might fairly have been expected to do. And if even this much is done it is not something of which we can boast, for it will have been that which God has done through us and often despite ourselves. And if it is done, the Kingdom will not have come, only the starting point will have been reached—that which was established at Pentecost concerning race will have been realized.[222]

The chapters that follow study a movement from within the "conserving edge" of the church that emerged in Mississippi thirty years after Campbell made this prediction. Inspiring the founders of this movement in Mississippi to put their racial "house in order," was a vision for unity across the whole of Christ's Church. Transformation in the racial landscape of the state would come, they believed, through the power of new relationships, made possible by the reconciling work of Christ. They intentionally forged relationships across the existing restrictive boundaries of the state's closed churches: the boundaries of race and denomination. Calling themselves Mission Mississippi, the participants placed their hope in changing the Closed Society on something that looked remarkably like Moltmann's Open Friendship of Jesus Christ.

3

Mission Mississippi

From Rallies to Meaningful Relationships

In Jackson, Mississippi, on January 15, 1993, the officers of a new organization called Mission Mississippi filed articles of incorporation stating it was "to be operated to promote Christian unity and racial reconciliation."[1] The following day the state's main newspaper, *The Clarion-Ledger*, broke the news with the headline, "Mission Mississippi takes religious tack toward racial harmony."[2] In a carefully worded statement, Mission Mississippi's chairman Lee Paris told the reporter, "Our vision is a mission outreach to unify the body of Christ from every walk of life by continuing to break down the walls that divide us by race and denominational backgrounds."[3] The article contained details of the "mission outreach" that would "culminate with a gathering Oct. 28–30 at Mississippi Veterans Memorial Stadium."[4] With its roots firmly planted in the conservative churches of Mississippi, Mission Mississippi was part of a wider movement for racial reconciliation in the American evangelical church in the 1990s. Often focusing on large-scale stadium and arena rallies, the movement had its highest public profile in the evangelical men's movement Promise Keepers.[5]

The stadium event in 1993 was not, as the *Clarion-Ledger* reported, the "culmination" of Mission Mississippi. Thirteen years later in 2006, with an annual budgeted income of nearly $700,000, Mission Mississippi had 133 actively participating churches spread across the state with chapters in six cities.[6] Proclaiming its strategy and vision from every letterhead, tee shirt, and bumper sticker, Mission Mississippi hopes it is "changing Mississippi one relationship at a time." The emphasis on individual relationships has survived while the large-scale rallies have gone by the wayside. At the time of writing, the largest event Mission Mississippi holds is the Annual Governor's Prayer Luncheon. Instead of mass meetings, one finds Mission Mississippi about its stated task of "providing specific opportunities for Christians to fellowship on neutral ground for the purpose of developing relationships."[7] In cities across the state, these "specific opportunities" include regular prayer breakfasts and luncheons, restaurant discounts for two couples to eat together, and churches partnering in activities ranging from picnics to preaching. At all of these public events, African Americans and whites sit down together, eat together, talk together, and pray together: actions unthinkable in the Mississippi of the 1960s that James Silver described.

Mission Mississippi owes its particular character and sustained presence to a confluence of three streams within Jackson's churches: African American ministers, white Christian businessmen, and Voice of Calvary Ministries. To engage in a gross generalization, preachers in historically black churches are singularly powerful individuals within their own congregations and wield great influence within their own communities. This does not tend to be the case in white protestant congregations where power lies with the church officers who hire and fire their ministers.[8] Filling these positions of deacons and elders in the white churches in Jackson are men who have attained standing within white society—the businessmen and professionals. These men, of course, rank among the largest financial contributors to their churches.

The third stream contributing to Mission Mississippi, Voice of Calvary (VOC), has been operating in West Jackson since 1974. Its founder, John Perkins, is a black preacher who mixes evangelical theology with a radical grassroots social activism; he is one of the main catalysts behind the contemporary revival in evangelical's involvement in so-called faith-based urban regeneration.[9] Many of Mission Mississippi's founders, both black and white, trace their interest in racial reconciliation to the influence of John Perkins and VOC's thirty-two-year ministry in Mississippi. In Mission Mississippi, the most powerful people in the city's black and white churches came under the influence of the ministry at the heart of a national faith-based community development movement. How these three groups came together is a story of unlikely friendships.

Victor Smith, John Perkins, and the Christian Businessmen's
Committee of Jackson

The Christian Businessmen's Committee of Jackson (CBMC), meeting once a month over breakfast or lunch, was not the sort of organization one would expect to produce a racial reconciliation movement. The meetings were opportunities for these suited white Rotarians at prayer to invite their work colleagues to listen to an evangelistic presentation of the gospel. The founder and first chairman of the Jackson chapter was Victor Smith, a businessman who had made a small fortune in oil extraction and in real estate development.

Victor Smith was born in 1930, the only son of a cottonseed oil mill manager in the small town of Hazlehurst, thirty-five miles south of Jackson in Copiah County. He grew up learning the social mores of life in a small segregated cotton town in Jim Crow Mississippi: Smith confesses, "We grew up very prejudiced people."[10] He went to the University of Mississippi, but in 1951, he dropped out of school and volunteered for the Army. While in the serving as an infantry officer, he married a woman from back home, the daughter of Aleck Primos, a Jackson restaurateur. On his discharge from the Army, Smith returned to Mississippi to work for his father-in-law as a manager in one of the Primos restaurants in Jackson. Although the sign on the street read, "Welcome—come as you are," following the conventions of Jim Crow Mississippi, the restaurant only served whites.[11]

Life as a restaurant manager did not suit the ambitions of the twenty-three-year-old Smith; then, in 1954, everything changed. "A guy came by one day and said, I am in the oil business and we can get rich," Smith recalls, "And I said that appeals to me... I invested a little money in an oil well. Sure enough the well hit."[12] Through an accident of birth, marriage, a stroke of luck, and hard work, Smith became a wealthy member of Jackson's white society, wholeheartedly subscribing to its doctrine of white supremacy.

As the 1960s progressed, the civil rights movement brought increasing turmoil into the neatly ordered world of the Closed Society and Smith's own family became targets of civil rights activists. His father-in-law Aleck Primos was one of the directors of Jackson's Citizens Council involved in secret meetings with the state's Sovereignty Commission to try to thwart attempts at integrating Jackson's public spaces.[13] When the student sit-in movement challenged whites-only seating at Primos' restaurants in 1963, Smith's wife (as part-owner of the business) became a named defendant in a long-running court case brought by the NAACP.[14] Smith's upbringing and loyalty to his family placed him at odds with his church. Despite a Presbyterian upbringing, he took his young family to St. Andrews Episcopal Cathedral in downtown Jackson. The cathedral was one of the bastions of Jackson society, but its leadership supported the integration of public schools and opposed the Citizens' Councils' call for massive resistance.[15] What Smith heard from the pulpit one Sunday morning angered him. "The man said you've got to start inviting blacks in your home," Smith remembers. "Well, I just basically said, I am not going to do that. I'm not going to stay here at this church!" He moved his family across town to First Presbyterian Church where he would not have to listen to such liberal pronouncements.

One evening in 1971, Smith experienced a religious conversion that led to a radical change in his views on race. Participating in First Presbyterian Church's Evangelism Explosion outreach program, Smith and another man were going door-to-door with tracts and a message of salvation. "I was going out as a trainee," Smith recalls, "[but it was] me and the church member [who] got saved that night...I was like Paul—I was knocked off the donkey!"[16] The energy that Smith poured into his business, he now turned on his newfound faith. He opened a Christian bookshop and publishing business from a desire "to know what it was to be a successful Christian."[17]

While volunteering as the treasurer for Billy Graham's 1975 crusade to Jackson, Smith met John Perkins. Perkins saw the Crusade as a marvelous opportunity to build contacts in the white community and here was a wealthy white Christian with a new and voracious appetite to hear the implications of the gospel of Jesus Christ for his life.[18] Perkins asked Smith if he knew any poor people, and when Smith sheepishly admitted he did not, Perkins invited Smith to travel with him to the poor black sections of Mendenhall and New Hebron. This was the first of many trips Smith took with Perkins who, during the ride down to Mendenhall, preached his gospel principles of Christian community building—reconciliation, relocation, and redistribution. "He was the one," Smith acknowledges, "who really led me into reconciliation."[19]

Smith's conversations with Perkins prepared him for the series of events that led to the start of Mission Mississippi. In 1991, CBMC invited Patrick Morley, a successful property developer from Florida recently turned author and evangelist, to speak in Jackson.[20] Morley impressed Lee Paris, the chairman of CBMC, another young property developer and protégé of Smith. Paris invited him back to speak at the 1992 CBMC sponsored Mayor's Annual Leadership Prayer Breakfast.[21] After these engagements, Morley still felt that he had unfinished business in Jackson. He called Paris proposing that CBMC sponsor a citywide crusade conducted by his organization, Patrick Morley Ministries. Paris was not sure that CBMC was in the business of organizing a "Billy Graham type thing," but agreed to bring it before the board.[22] The board, meeting in Lee Paris' office, raised a simple objection: how could a white evangelist hold a successful citywide crusade in a majority African American city?[23] Morley met this objection with a second proposal. He asked Lee Paris, "What if my friend Tom Skinner and I did this together?"[24]

Paris and Smith knew of the African American evangelist Tom Skinner. Since his Harlem Evangelistic Association held a series of meetings at Harlem's Apollo theatre in 1962, Skinner had spoken at crusades, revivals, and missions all over the country. With his tale of conversion from the violent street gangs of New York, Skinner mixed the traditional evangelists' message of repentance and personal salvation with an appeal for reconciliation between races.[25] Smith and Paris decided Morley and Skinner's proposal was worth exploring, but lacking a consensus from CBMC's board, the two men mailed out three hundred letters to ministers and businessmen on plain paper inviting them to come to Primos in November to hear the two evangelists pitch their vision for an interracial Metro-Jackson Outreach Mission.[26]

Smith and Paris's contacts with the white business community were incomparable; however, their connections with black churches in Jackson were negligible. James Baird, the minister at First Presbyterian Church where Lee Paris was an active member, with James Washington, the minister of St Peter Missionary Baptist Church, had formed a group consisting of black and white ministers who had been quietly gathering every month for conversation and prayer. This group, meeting since the mid-1980s, encouraged their members to attend the interest meeting with Pat Morley and Tom Skinner. Of the 130 curious guests who showed up at Primos, a core group of between thirty and forty ministers came from Washington and Baird's monthly meetings.[27]

This monthly ministers' meeting is very significant in the story of Mission Mississippi. The group's approach to racial reconciliation grounded in personal friendships formed through the practice of regular conversation and prayer predates the emphasis on large-scale events that dominated the early years of Mission Mississippi. Today, when Mission Mississippi recounts its own story, it chooses to locate its origins, not in the Christian Businessmen's Committee of Jackson or Pat Morley's suggestion to hold a citywide crusade but in the prayer meetings started by this group of ministers.[28]

James Washington, James Baird, and the Monthly Ministers' Meeting

The monthly ministers' meeting began in the mid-1980s when James Washington, the minister of St. Peter Missionary Baptist Church, deliberately sought to establish a relationship with First Presbyterian Church's James Baird. The two men sat next to each other at a meeting of Jackson ministers concerned over the city's rising crime and then shared an elevator on their way out. Washington remembers that he had a sense God was prompting him to talk with this white man. "The Holy Spirit kind of convicted me. He said, 'You know that's a shame both of you men are ministers of the gospel and yet you seem to be so far apart.' "[29] Meeting first on neutral ground at a Chinese restaurant, the two men simply shared their experiences of life in Mississippi from their different perspectives. "Let's talk and let's get to know each other," Baird proposed. "You tell me about your Christianity and about your life in Mississippi through your eyes and I will tell you as one who comes in from the outside as to how I see it."[30]

This is the story that Washington told Baird: he was born in Jackson on November 14, 1940. His father, Thomas Washington Sr., drove a truck for a freight line. Life for the young Washington revolved around two institutions of the black community: school and church. In Jackson, the strictly enforced segregation of the white churches made it difficult for him to view their members as serving the same savior he worshipped on Sundays.[31]

Witnessing the violent defense of Jim Crow by Jackson's whites only reinforced Washington's view of the white churches. In the spring and summer of 1963, Jackson's civil rights movement reached a crescendo of marches, sit-ins, and boycotts.[32] The state responded to the protests with mass arrests. Washington told Baird how he watched as the police arrested his brothers and sisters and took them away in garbage trucks to a makeshift barbed-wire stockade at the state fairground. "They were arrested," he said, "for no other reason than walking down a street with an American flag singing 'We Shall Overcome.' "[33]

Called to be the assistant minister at historic Cade Chapel in 1964, Washington saw the freedom struggle play out from a position of leadership within the black community.[34] In 1970, following the shooting by the police of two Jackson State students, Washington, along with other African American ministers, helped to diffuse the potentially lethal standoff between angry protestors and armed policemen.[35]

James Baird's perspective on the role and responsibility of the church during the civil rights movement could not have been more different. During the 1960s, Baird, a young Presbyterian minister in Gadsden, Alabama, avoided any involvement in the movement. In 1965, with liberal clergy from all over the country rushing to Alabama to join Martin Luther King on the Selma to Montgomery March, Baird kept his distance.[36] Along with most conservative white clergy in the South, Baird condemned liberal Christians who supported the civil rights movement. He believed this support stemmed from their misguided belief in the "social gospel" and "had little to do with the kingdom of God or Christianity."[37] It was not only ignorance of the social implications of the gospel that held him back, he confessed to Washington, but also fear for his job. "You couldn't very well have a ministry in a conservative church and get all involved in the civil rights movement," he explained, "because you'd probably be asked to leave the church."[38]

After three or four meetings, Washington and Baird thought that other ministers might benefit from having similar conversations. Each invited two people to join the group, and Baird offered his church as a venue. The meetings, they agreed, would be low key and the conversations confidential. Over the period of five years, the group met monthly at First Presbyterian Church. Clergy drifted in and out of the group and meetings often had around fifteen ministers listening to each other's stories. In regular attendance with Washington and Baird were: Maurice Bingham, a Bishop in the Church of Christ (Holiness) U.S.A.; Ronnie Crudup, the pastor of New Horizons, a new independent Pentecostal church in South Jackson; and Joe Rightmeyer, a conservative white minister at Covenant Presbyterian Church.[39]

Crudup does not recall the term racial reconciliation ever being applied by the group to what went on at those monthly gatherings; instead, it was "just the ... sense that there needed to be some coming together for people to know one another."[40] Although this sounds like a modest enterprise, it was a radically new experience for many of the participants.[41] As trust grew, the group found they could share their views openly with each other and friendships deepened. "We would openly just discuss issues and be frank and honest about how we felt about them," Washington remembers; "but we did it in love, and we discovered that we had a whole lot of things in common."[42] It was through these informal monthly meetings with their changing cast of characters that a network of relationships built up between white, theologically conservative ministers and African American pastors in Jackson.

In 1990, the ministers in Washington and Baird's group started a weekly morning prayer meeting and invited members of their congregations to participate.[43] The faithful met in Jackson's Salvation Army building every Tuesday before the workday began. African American and white Christians prayed together for their city. "We prayed for Christian harmony," recalls Crudup, "[for] harmonious relationships between blacks and whites." As with the ministers meeting, the agenda did not appear radical. The very fact, however, that people were meeting across racial and denominational lines proved a significant move; "particularly," Crudup points out, "in a city and state with the reputation that Mississippi had had where people really didn't know one another."[44] With the formation of Mission Mississippi in 1993, this weekly prayer gathering provided the pattern and nucleus for the weekly Mission Mississippi prayer breakfasts.

Mission Mississippi's Kick-Off Rallies

Those who responded to Paris and Smith's invitation to attend the interest meeting at Primos Restaurant that day in November 1992 remember the emotion and conviction aroused among the guests as Skinner and Morley spoke of the impact a citywide campaign with racial unity at its core might have on Jackson.[45] The meeting motivated enough of those present to form a steering committee who, at their first meeting on December 7, 1992, named the crusade Mission Mississippi.[46]

Over the next ten months, with guidance from Patrick Morley Ministries, the committee laid plans for a stadium crusade. The fledgling organization, with its emphasis on bringing people together, decided not to have a fixed number of people on the steering committee; any minister or church representative could join. By October 1993, there were 224 people listed as members of the steering committee. Although such a large body demonstrated the wide support for Mission Mississippi, it was clearly far too unwieldy to be a decision-making body. The solution was the formation of a small executive committee of around twelve members. With Lee Paris as the chair, the steering committee chose the other members of the executive committee evenly from among the African American and white church communities.[47]

Evangelistic crusades claiming to unite churches and even races were nothing new to Mississippi; for most of the twentieth century, Jackson had been a regular stop on the circuit for traveling revival preachers and their crusades. For three weeks during the warm May evenings of 1922, crowds flocked to Poindexter Park to hear the noted evangelist Gypsy Smith.[48] Invited by the Presbyterian minister J. B. Hutton, the tent in the park hosted the "campaign to make Jackson a better city."[49] This citywide campaign received the support of a number of Jackson's churches and was a point of reference when the Billy Graham Crusade rolled into town for the first time in 1952.

Working through a coalition of local churches, the Billy Graham Crusade found the City Auditorium too small for their purposes and so they held their revival meetings—with the congregation strictly segregated—from June 15 through July 11, 1952, in Tiger Stadium of Bailey Junior School on North State Street. With church choir members from white churches across the city singing together in the mass choir, the parochial and sectarian tendencies of Jackson's faithful gave way to a vision of greater denominational unity. On the final Sunday of the crusade, Calvary Baptist Church, one of the largest Baptist churches in the city, cancelled its evening service so that its members could attend. "This was the first time in the church's history," their church historian noted, "that an evening worship service had given way to another service."[50]

Dramatic events demand dramatic statistics and the crusade counted 362,000 people attending the four-week revival, 5,927 of whom made "decisions."[51]

Following the 1954 *Brown v. Board of Education* decision, Billy Graham began refusing to preach to segregated audiences.[52] When Graham's representative, Grady Wilson, returned to Jackson in 1964, Jackson's white church leaders viewed this policy with suspicion. Wilson proposed a crusade be held in the Jackson Coliseum, but the committee of church and laymen feared that the "leading businessmen of the city would not support an integrated meeting" and so withheld an invitation.[53] The absence of Billy Graham did not dampen the desire for a crusade. Throughout the second week of July 1968, the less controversial evangelist Dr. Paul M. Stevens, the president of the Southern Baptist Radio and Television Commission, presided over the segregated Greater Jackson Crusade in the Coliseum.[54]

When Billy Graham finally returned to the state capitol in 1975, public attitudes to race were markedly different. Held in the Mississippi Veterans Memorial Stadium—the same venue Mission Mississippi would use eighteen years later—Graham pulled together local resources from across the traditional racial and denominational lines. The crusade's platform reflected this new spirit of interracial possibilities; Johnny Cash and June Carter Cash rubbed shoulders with gospel star Andrae Crouch. Participating churches considered the 1975 crusade a success, both by the traditional statistical measurements—281,000 attended over eight days with 7,335 inquirers or decisions—and by the new possibilities for interracial cooperation between black and white ministers.[55]

Mass demonstrations of Christian solidarity offer a compelling witness to the "unsaved"—so the participants believe—because they demonstrate that churches worship a God who transcends denominational and racial strife. This evangelistic strategy became a standard feature of even the most unlikely crusades. In 1981, the controversial TV evangelist James Robison held a week-long crusade in the Mississippi Memorial Stadium in Jackson. With his outspoken right-wing politics and sensationalist preaching style, Robison failed to garner support from the large "first" churches in Jackson—including First Presbyterian Church and First Baptist Church—however enough churches, both white and black, supported him to raise his $75,000 budget. Robison emphasized the ecumenical and interracial nature of his crusade's support stating repentance would not be preached "for whites only."[56] That same year ministers, some of whom would later be among the founders of Mission Mississippi, organized the expressly interracial Mid-Mississippi Crusade for Christ led by African American evangelist Tony Evans.[57] After these crusades left town, little seemed to change in Jackson; eleven o'clock on Sunday morning remained the most segregated and sectarian hour of the week. The skeptic could be forgiven his suspicion that Mission Mississippi's crusade would leave just as fleeting an impression on the city.

From the start, despite appearances to the contrary, Mission Mississippi was fundamentally different from a Billy Graham Crusade. Lee Paris and the steering committee quickly decided the stadium event was to be only the start of a sustained movement. In Mission Mississippi's first newsletter came the insistence: "Mission Mississippi is *not* an event. *Mission Mississippi is a movement of God's people toward unity*"[58] The name "Mission Mississippi," originally the title for a one-off event, was now the name of a movement. The planned three days in the stadium were now designated Mission Mississippi's "Kick-off Rallies."[59]

Lee Paris, the chair of the executive committee, recalls the seriousness of the moment when they made the commitment to transition from planning an event to participating in a movement:

> Somewhere in the ten months of putting all this together we realized we were going to have a great show, and it was going to make a fantastic article for the newspaper. And then by Tuesday everybody was going to go back and nothing was going to have really changed; and, that if we were serious about this it would be a lifetime commitment and not a weekend thing. So we... went around the table and said: Who's in this for a twenty-year commitment?[60]

Despite this commitment to become a movement, the popularity and success of Billy Graham-style evangelistic crusades provided the template for Mission Mississippi, influencing their planning and thinking.

Sociologist William Martin offers a succinct description of the preparation for a Billy Graham Crusade:

> Once an invitation has been accepted, representatives from the host city form a nonprofit corporation that will be responsible for financing the crusade and developing the necessary organization. Several months before a crusade begins, the Graham association sends members of its team to open an office in the host city and involve as many people as possible in various facets of the crusade. Committees, choruses, Bible classes, orientation sessions for ushers and counselors, prayer groups, and other activities arranged by the team involve thirty to forty thousand, and sometimes as many as eighty thousand people in various facets of a crusade.[61]

With Mission Mississippi established as a nonprofit organization, Pat Morley Ministries helped in the planning of a very similar style build-up to the stadium event. The steering committee created sub-committees to handle the logistics of a large stadium crusade. These committees were Publicity, Arrangements, Community Outreach and Follow-up, Finance, Music, Prayer, and Youth. Three of these committees (Publicity, Music, and Prayer) were co-chaired by African Americans and whites.[62]

The prayer committee encouraged people to attend the weekly prayer meetings held at 7 A.M. on Thursday mornings at different locations throughout the city. They also held monthly evening prayer rallies at different churches. As well as the ongoing schedule of prayer meetings, the committee organized special prayer events for pastors. In June at an overnight retreat named The Pastor's Prayer Gathering, ministers had the opportunity to spend time with the evangelists Skinner and Morley.[63]

Pat Morley and Tom Skinner made several visits to Jackson in 1993 before the rallies taking an active role in the preparation for the crusade. On January 22, they spoke to a pastor's luncheon at the Mississippi Agricultural and Forestry Museum Auditorium.[64] They returned in April for the Mayor's 22nd Annual Leadership Prayer Breakfast attended by 800 of Jackson's great and good citizens. That morning at the Coliseum Ramada Inn, the organization reported, "116 [attendees] committed to pray for Mission Mississippi and be involved in their weekly prayer gatherings."[65] Following the mayor's breakfast, Skinner and Morley spoke to students at Lanier High School. Skinner, concerned about the level of participation of African American ministers in Mission Mississippi, requested that Paris send him contact information for Jackson's black pastors so he could personally encourage them to get involved.[66] Every time that Skinner and Morley spoke, they challenged people to exchange their name, phone number, and address with someone of a different race, "preferably the same gender," and make a commitment to call.[67]

Mission Mississippi's emphasis on building personal relationships between African Americans and whites was a departure from the Billy Graham model. This distinctive focus was particularly evident in the decision to hold picnics in Smith Park in the run-up to the rallies. On Saturday, July 24, 1993, a new tradition started in the small park nestled between the Governor's mansion and the State Capitol. Organizers reported twelve hundred people in attendance, "complete with every food fantasy needed for a Mississippi picnic in the park"[68] In Mississippi, for both blacks and whites, the picnic—grilling at family reunions, pot luck dinners at church homecomings, and tailgating in the Grove before an Ole Miss football game—speaks powerfully of kinship, tradition, and shared history. Mission Mississippi hoped to demonstrate through the Smith Park picnics a new kinship and tradition not based in the divided and bloody racial history of Mississippi but in Christian unity.

A second picnic in Smith Park on Saturday October 9, just two weeks before the rallies, was the first of an intense flurry of events designed to take the Mission Mississippi message to the city. Skinner and Morley spoke at thirteen schools (city public schools and private white academies) and twelve churches in these two weeks.[69] With just five days to go before the opening night, the supporters of Mission Mississippi met on October 19 for a night of prayer in the City Auditorium. That same evening WLBT-TV, Jackson's NBC station—the same station that had once carried advertising for the Citizens' Council—aired for free a thirty-minute statewide telecast about Mission Mississippi and its message of unity in the body of Christ.[70] Viewers heard white Mississippian Randall Mooney speak of his commitment to forge new relationships with African Americans and his excitement at the opportunity Mission Mississippi afforded to change the country's perception of the state: "the nation...has pointed the finger at us and said, 'They are the ones that are racist.' And that is why it is so wonderful that God has decided, I believe, to choose that which is last to make it first."[71]

By Sunday, the day of the first rally, Mission Mississippi boasted the support of sixty-one of Jackson's churches. These ranged from the largest white downtown churches including First Baptist, First Presbyterian, Galloway United Methodist, and the Catholic and Episcopal Cathedrals to some of the most significant African American churches including Bishop Bingham's Christ Temple Church of Christ Holiness and Ronnie Crudup's New Horizons.[72]

Just as in 1922 when organizers dubbed Gypsy Smith's revival meetings a "campaign to make Jackson a better city," in 1993, Mission Mississippi boosted the social benefits of this latest crusade.[73] "Christian business people, religious leaders, and concerned citizens," declared the Clarion-Ledger, "have joined forces to combat racism, increasing crime, drug abuse and destruction of family values in a movement called Mission Mississippi."[74] This presentation of Mission Mississippi as a restorer of the social fabric of Jackson assisted the organization in raising funds for the event. Courting the sponsorship of the supermarket chain Jitney Jungle, Mission Mississippi pointed out that its aim "to bring about brotherhood and unity would greatly enhance life in our state both economically and spiritually."[75] In its first year, Mission Mississippi received significant donations from Deposit Guaranty National Bank, Trustmark National Bank, LDDS Communications McRaes, Inc, as well as South Central Bell and the state's power company, Mississippi Power & Light.[76] These contributions from big business, when added to the donations from individuals and churches, enabled Mission Mississippi to raise the quarter of a million dollars they needed.[77]

A utility company supporting Christian proselytizing might surprise many people unfamiliar with the culture of Mississippi. An incredulous reporter for the *Clarion-Ledger* investigated this relationship between businesses and Christianity in Jackson in 1996. He found a corporate culture that was likely to open the day with Bible study and its meetings with prayer. Bernie Ebbers, the now discredited chief executive and president of WorldCom and corporate donor to the Baptist Mississippi College, told the reporter, "I am thankful for my faith," explaining his Fortune 500 company was built by men "on their knees."[78]

With its origins in the Christian Business Men's Committee of Jackson, Mission Mississippi was a part of this Christian corporate world and their chairman spoke the language effortlessly. In 1995, Lee Paris (whose father, Henry Paris, was the chairman of the board of Union Planters Bank[79]) wrote to Union Planters Bank in Jackson explaining to them "our leading lending institutions have taken a strong interest in this work." He then suggested that, "with Union Planters becoming a major corporate citizen of our state, Mission Mississippi would greatly appreciate a contribution in the $5,000–10,000 range...toward building relationships toward the good of Mississippi."[80]

Mission Mississippi invited all of Jackson's churches to participate in the three-day event of music, speakers, and worship entitled "Bringing Down the Walls that Divide Us" with the subheading "Unity Through Christ." The kick-off rallies started on Sunday afternoon, October 24, with the "Worship and Unity Rally;" Monday evening was the Youth Musical Extravaganza, and Tuesday evening was "Bring Your Neighbor Night."[81] The crowd, filling the bottom tier of seats behind the stadium's end zone, gazed across the pitch at the temporary stage. The stadium dwarfed the event; with a capacity of sixty thousand, Mission Mississippi mustered an estimated twenty-four thousand over three days.[82]

The format of the rallies deviated little from a Billy Graham Crusade. Before the message and appeal, celebrities shared their testimonies from the platform interspersed with music from professional musicians and a mass choir. As with Graham's mission to Jackson in 1975, Mission Mississippi presented interracial Christian unity by balancing white and African American participation. Dave Dravecky, the white former pitcher for the San Francisco Giants, appeared high on the bill along with the five-time Grammy-winning gospel singer Larnelle Harris. Also featured were two former Miss Americas, (African American) Debbye Turner and (white) Cheryl Prewitt Salem.[83]

For such large-scale events to draw and hold their congregations evangelism must also be entertainment. To this end, the more lurid the testimony of the speakers and dramatic their tales of hardship conquered, the better. At Mission

Mississippi's rallies, Draveky the baseball pitcher shared how he "came back to play in the majors after undergoing surgery for cancer in his pitching arm," and how his faith survived its subsequent amputation. Tom Skinner told the youth assembled for Monday night's Youth Musical Extravaganza, "I ended up with twenty-two notches on the handle of my knife which meant my blade had gone into the bodies of twenty-two different people."[84]

Perhaps the most stunning example of dramatic testimony came when Cheryl Prewitt Salem, the white beauty queen, told the audience, "You know I was a cripple from a car wreck for six years of my life. I have been through three windshields, I have had over one hundred and fifty stitches in my face, I have never had any plastic surgery and yet I still won Miss America for God so he could be glorified!"[85]

The kick-off rallies also took a leaf out of Billy Graham's book in the way Mission Mississippi reassured local pastors that the participation of their congregation threatened neither their authority nor their church membership. "All new/renewed believers will be directed to their own Churches or to attend with their friends," Mission Mississippi's literature stated; and the minister's prestige would be safeguarded as, "All participating pastors will be seated on the platform at least once."[86]

All of the singing, testifying, and preaching at a Billy Graham crusade builds to the appeal for members of the congregation to commit their lives to Jesus. Without changing this familiar format of an evangelistic crusade, Mission Mississippi simply inserted a message of racial reconciliation at the appropriate places. On the second evening, as a pianist played the hymn *Just as I Am,* Morley intoned in a calm reassuring voice, "If you want to be an agent of change. If you want to make that decision...and you want to give your life to Jesus Christ...to be a person who will lead Mississippi back into a right relationship with God and right relationship with each other...stand up where you are now and come." As those who responded to the message slowly assembled on the pitch, Morley invited them to pray the sinner's prayer. As Morley dropped into the well-worn rhetorical groove of personal salvation in this ritual of missions, crusades and revivals as old as Billy Sunday and Gypsy Smith, the new language of racial reconciliation and social change disappeared:

> Lord Jesus I need you.
> Thank you for dying on the cross for my sins.
> I open the door of my life and receive you by faith as my Savior
>   and Lord.
> Thank you for forgiving my sins and for giving me eternal life.
> I now invite you to take control of my life and make me into the kind
>   of person you want me to be.[87]

While Morley lacked the theological imagination to integrate racial reconciliation with personal regeneration in his prayer, the appeal was not the
only symbolic focus of the rallies. During the planning, Paris had had "an
inspiration—a vision, an idea. He didn't know what to call it," that black and
white pastors would raise a large cross together.[88] Inspired by Jesus' promise
in the gospel of John, "when I am lifted up from the earth, I will draw all
men to myself," (John 12:32 [NIV]) Paris believed "If the races would demonstrate reconciliation at the cross, the city would see Jesus."[89] The steering
committee, following Paris's vision, planned the raising of a twenty-four-foot
cross during the rally. Thirty-one years earlier in the same stadium, Governor
Ross Barnett in front of a crowd of forty-one thousand cheering and screaming white Mississippians raised his fist and screamed his defiance to the
Kennedy administration and the forces of desegregation: "I love Mississippi! I
love her people! Our customs! I love and respect our heritage!"[90] Now, instead
of waving rebel flags and singing "Go Mississippi!" the crowd sang the great
hymn of mission and unity: *Lift High the Cross*. They watched as to the right of
the stage their pastors in their suits and blazers raised the cross (see figure 3.1).
It reminded one onlooker of marines raising the flag on Iwo Jima.[91]

FIGURE 3.1. Clergy raise the cross at Mission Mississippi's first stadium
rally, 1993. (Courtesy of Mission Mississippi)

The day after the final stadium event, organizers met at the Cabot Lodge Hotel to evaluate the past ten months of work. Those who had financially supported Mission Mississippi to the tune of $250,000 heard the hard calculus of the return on their investment. As Morley's newsletter explained to supporters, "Tom Skinner and Pat Morley spoke 50 times...to 80,000 people, presenting Christ to 40,000. 24,000 people attended three days of outdoor rallies." The numbers extended beyond the events in the stadium. "Pat & Tom spoke to 16,000 kids in public and private schools at which they were openly permitted to share Christ."[92] By the end of the rallies, Mission Mississippi had also received the support of sixty-seven churches from the Jackson area.[93] The event had received not only good regional media coverage, but *The Chicago Tribune* carried the story under the headline "Beating Racism, one friendship at a time." The subheading continued, "It sounds simple, maybe even simplistic, but in Mississippi it seems to be working."[94] Both Skinner and Morley were convinced of the importance of what they had been a part of and committed themselves to Mission Mississippi "on a long-term basis."[95] Morley left Jackson proclaiming, "Mission Mississippi is a ten year strategic plan to bring the entire city together around the person of Christ."[96] The steering committee left the meeting tired but determined to continue the weekly prayer meetings and plan further events.

Interestingly, the two things that received the most glowing endorsements that day at the Cabot Lodge were not the big budget items but the picnics that encouraged interaction between churches and the "black and white issues discussion."[97] The *Chicago Tribune* had it right in identifying the development of friendships as the key to Mission Mississippi's potential. At least one person that day wondered if holding further large-scale events was the way that Mission Mississippi should continue. Phil Reed of Voice of Calvary raised his concern at the apparent intention to continue holding large-scale events. In a letter to Paris he wrote, "It does not seem like good stewardship of resources to spend the larger part of a $265,000 budget for a three day rally...given all of the needs in Jackson, and given the shortage of funds among many of the local ministries meeting those needs."[98]

Reed's was not the first question raised from within Mission Mississippi's ranks about the wisdom of large rallies. Dan Hall, a white Baptist minister and co-chair of the prayer committee, had written a letter to Morley and Skinner nine months before the rallies concerned about "Big Eventism," which he explained, "cultivates relationships based on activity and thus terms success by energy levels achieved and events accomplished." Such a "high profile, mega-event hoopla...generates temporary relationships and commitments, but fails to maintain either one beyond whatever event is finally being produced."[99] This "Big-Eventism" threatened to undermine what Hall saw as Mission Mississippi's strengths: "long term commitment, painstaking relationships, and heart based responsiveness to the need of the gospel preached to every facet of our society."[100]

The question of whether Mission Mississippi should continue pouring energy and resources into producing and promoting large-scale events did not go away. In the fall of 1993, however, the executive committee ignored or overlooked Hall and Reed's concerns. This was, in part, because of the apparent success of the rally format and the association with Patrick Morley Ministries whose stated mission was, "To help bring about a spiritual awakening in America and the world by conducting large-scale evangelistic and church renewal missions in strategic cities."[101] The continued investment in large-scale evangelistic missions was also an issue of imagination; this was a very familiar format for the large evangelical churches and white evangelical businessmen. A large event with big name speaker was an easy sell, and the prize of soul winning a worthy investment. How could you generate the same level of support and excitement for picnics and small prayer meetings? Mission Mississippi had hit on a familiar and workable formula that it continued for four more years.

In 1994, Mission Mississippi planned a two-day Celebration of Reconciliation in Christ to take place on October 18 and 19 in the Mississippi Coliseum. In May, the executive committee hired Jarvis Ward, a young African American minister, as the full-time executive director for Mission Mississippi. A supporter of Mission Mississippi from the beginning (he had served on the original steering committee and the youth committee for the 1993 rallies), Ward left his job as the director of special ministries at New Lake Outreach Center, an inner-city ministry in Jackson to take the position.[102]

In June 1994, Mission Mississippi received the news that Tom Skinner had died of complications relating to acute leukemia.[103] His wife, Barbara Williams-Skinner, came to Jackson that October to appear on the platform with Pat Morley and support the main speaker Tony Evans.[104] The rallies followed a similar pattern to those of the previous year with the first night as the celebration and a youth rally on the second night. Evans preached a message of unity. Striking a militant tone, he told his listeners, "God is forming a coalition of black people, white people, red people, yellow people to take back this land that this madman, Satan, has tried to claim."[105] Paris made a statement to the city's newspaper that "Blacks and whites have come together once again from across the city to celebrate reconciliation in our Lord Jesus Christ."[106] However, they had not come in the hoped-for numbers. According to Mission Mississippi's press release, only nine thousand attended over the two nights.[107]

Each October for the next three years, Mission Mississippi produced big events with big name speakers. In 1995 Frank Pollard, the minister of Jackson's First Baptist Church, shared the billing with E. V. Hill, who the *Clarion-Ledger* pointed out was "one of the featured speakers for the National Promise Keepers men's rally."[108] Taking place in the shadow of the O. J. Simpson trial, thirteen thousand people attended over the two nights.[109] The following year, Bill "Coach" McCartney, the founder of Promise Keepers, came with his friend Phillip H. Porter, a bishop in the Church of God in Christ and the chairman of the Promise Keeper's board. The last of the big rallies came in 1997 when the First Baptist Church Mission Committee funded the international evangelist Josh McDowell's visit to Jackson.[110]

To see Mission Mississippi during this time as simply organizing large-scale evangelistic rallies is a mistake. As attendance at, and support for, the Coliseum events waned, the quieter business of building relationships across racial and denominational lines continued. It was in this field of relationship building that Mission Mississippi proved most creative. As well as the standard fare of businessmen's luncheons and mayor's prayer breakfasts, Mission Mississippi organized: "Two and Two" restaurant nights where local restaurants agreed to give 22 percent discounts to black and white couples who made a dinner date together;[111] church partnerships between black and white churches that extended from pulpit exchanges and shared services to building Habitat houses together; the annual "Picnic in the Park" where black and white churches partnered to out-do each other in down-home cooking; and all the while those attending the weekly morning prayer meetings kept praying together.

By 1996, the staff of Mission Mississippi consisted of three full-time and two part-time positions with additional volunteer staff. Despite the growing number of paid employees, there was an awareness that the involvement of churches in Jackson was waning.[112] The executive board concluded, "Only 2% of the Churches have caught the vision of Mission Mississippi."[113] Ward was all too aware of the problem. As he talked with different church leaders, he discovered them less inclined to support Mission Mississippi now that it was clearly an ongoing commitment not simply a one-off crusade.[114]

Organizers could not ignore the poor attendance at the 1996 rally featuring McCartney and Porter. "The sight of a huge coliseum and a formal program before a very sparse crowd has been discouraging" John Geary, Mission Mississippi's Director of Development, told Paris. The rallies, headlined by big names, failed to draw crowds. Geary noted pithily, "Publicity and advance work has been good. Attendance has not."[115]

The 1996 rally proved to be a watershed for Mission Mississippi. It marked the end of the pursuit of racial reconciliation through "Big Eventism" and a refocusing on the small group work that had always been a part of Mission Mississippi. Following the rally, the board held a special meeting with an outside facilitator to take stock of progress and the future. They created a committee of four members "to consolidate the discussions of the Board as to vision strategy, means and specific implementation." They reported to the board on January 7, 1997, with a document, "Mission Mississippi Vision 1997 and Beyond."[116] The document clearly showed a desire to develop Mission Mississippi at the state level, and while acknowledging, "Demonstrations of unity within the Body of Christ are the foundation of evangelism," the emphasis in the rhetoric shifted toward making unity, rather than evangelism, the focus of all activities. The committee now considered the weekly prayer meetings to be the most effective and "chief activity of Mission Mississippi," while the annual rallies should become celebrations "to demonstrate this unity."

The board decided that Mission Mississippi needed a new executive director to raise the money for, and implement, this new vision. Ward left Mission Mississippi in mid-November 1997.[117] "Your decision," he told Paris, "helped to confirm the direction the Lord had already led me in making...It is God's will and His timing."[118] Mission Mississippi announced Dolphus Weary, a former board member, would be its new Executive Director. With the hiring of Weary, Mission Mississippi secured its connection with its third key stream: John Perkins and Voice of Calvary.

Dolphus Weary

Dolphus Weary was born August 7, 1946, in Sandy Hook, Mississippi, on the southern Mississippi-Louisiana border, into a poor sharecropper's family. When Weary was two years old, the family moved to D'Lo, Mississippi, where his father abandoned his wife and eight children. D'Lo straddles Highway 49 just two miles north of Mendenhall, the town where in 1961 John Perkins started holding youth rallies, Bible camps, and revivals.[119] At the age of seventeen, Weary accepted an invitation to a tent revival run by Voice of Calvary.[120] That evening, Weary responded to the evangelist's message; "I realized I was a sinner, that I wanted His salvation, and that I accepted it as His gift to me."[121] In the weeks and months that followed, the young Weary spent time at Voice of Calvary attending Bible studies and learning from Perkins and other Christians.

Weary grew up experiencing the capricious paternalism of whites and the grinding poverty and injustice of the sharecropping system. With ambitions to be a teacher and evangelist, Weary determined to leave Mississippi never to return. In 1967, assisted by contacts made through VOC, he transferred from the local junior college on a basketball scholarship to Los Angeles

Baptist College (LABC). Weary, along with one other black Mississippian, were the first African Americans admitted at LABC. While there, he met a fellow African American student named Rosie Camper and they married in 1970. After completing his Bachelor's degree and a Master's degree in Christian education, Weary returned to Mendenhall to work with VOC. When Perkins left Mendenhall for Jackson in 1974, Weary took over as director of programs. In 1978, under his leadership, VOC in Mendenhall became autonomous from VOC Jackson. Weary became the President and Executive Director of the renamed Mendenhall Ministries.[122]

In appointing Weary as Executive Director, Mission Mississippi had exchanged a young charismatic evangelist with a heart for young people for a veteran of the Christian community development movement. Weary was also a gifted preacher grounded in the evangelical school of John Perkins that emphasized content over the more emotional style of preaching found in many African American churches. As John Perkins' successor at Mendenhall Ministries, Weary had experience of preaching from white pulpits and fund-raising in white evangelical churches and colleges across the country. Paris, who had met Weary through Mission Mississippi and read his autobiography, saw in his experience exactly what Mission Mississippi needed.[123] "He has been traveling around the United States delivering the message of reconciliation, which is also the message of Mission Mississippi," Paris told the *Clarion-Ledger*. "He is uniquely qualified to provide the leadership that will take Mission Mississippi into the 21st century."[124] Weary served on Mission Mississippi's board, and as a result was well aware of their desire to make Mission Mississippi a statewide organization.[125]

Before launching Mission Mississippi statewide, Weary took stock of the resources at his disposal. On his departure from Mission Mississippi, Jarvis Ward reported one hundred participating churches, but these churches often did little more than sign their name to the big events and host the prayer breakfast when it was their turn.[126] "I came here and found out there were less than twenty churches that actually were financially supporting Mission Mississippi," Weary remembers.[127]

The year 1998 was "a year of rest" and a time for regrouping.[128] John Geary departed and Jon Elder, a seasoned white youth worker with twenty years as an executive director of Youth for Christ, came on the staff as Assistant Director and Statewide Coordinator. For the first time in Mission Mississippi's short history, there was no rally; instead, a "Reconciliation Weekend" took place that October. Utilizing "local leaders and music," rather than importing Christian celebrities, the weekend was a time to "re-focus on our mission: *reconciliation through meaningful relationships*."[129] Mission Mississippi held a youth retreat over the Friday night and Saturday. On Sunday, October 26, designated "Reconciliation Sunday," Mission Mississippi encouraged churches to have "pulpit swaps, choir swaps and joint worship services." The weekend finished with a worship celebration on the Monday night with Weary's mentor, John Perkins, delivering the address.[130]

In 1999, Dolphus Weary set out the new agenda in his column in the Mission Mississippi newsletter. Mission Mississippi would now have a "four-fold focus." First: restructure the office; second: go statewide working with existing racial reconciliation organizations; third: continue in Jackson. Most significant was the fourth focus: building more relationships "at the grassroots level." This marked the major shift away from the rallies. "Rather than focusing on events," Weary told the ministry's supporters, "Mission Mississippi will begin to deal with deeper heart issues, encouraging all Christians in Jackson and across Mississippi to surrender to the Holy Spirit and the reconciling work He wants to do in our lives."[131] This met with the wholehearted approval of the chairman, Lee Paris, who declared, "We are past the infant, and child-hood stages of this ministry."[132] Weary now felt in a position to expand Mission Mississippi's horizons beyond Jackson.

In 2000, Weary launched Mission Mississippi as a statewide movement in a carefully prepared and well-publicized campaign called "The Grace is Greater than Race Tour." In the fall, Mission Mississippi held a series of meetings in ten cities across the state.[133] From Sunday, November 12, in Hattiesburg

FIGURE 3.2. Dolphus Weary, 2004. (Photo by author)

and Biloxi to Sunday, November 19, in Vicksburg and Jackson, Unity Rallies took place in black and white churches from the coast to the hill country and from the pine belt to the Delta. Weary preached at each service ending his sermons with a call for pastors and lay people to make "intentional commitments to have us come back to help them organize a Mission Mississippi chapter."[134] To help in this task, Weary encouraged participants to attend the 2001 Statewide Conference on Christian Unity taking place in Jackson that coming February. Despite the low turnout on the final evening's Unity Rally in Jackson's Smith-Wills Stadium where around three hundred people huddled in the stands as temperatures hovered just above freezing, Mission Mississippi declared the tour a success.[135] The Grace is Greater than Race Tour became an annual event with eleven cities included the following fall. By the end of 2001, Jon Elder was able to report to the board that, including Jackson, there were now eight Mission Mississippi chapters or affiliates with "leaders working to form a Chapter or an Affiliate" in eight other cities.[136]

Following the Grace is Greater than Race Statewide Christian Unity Conference in May of 2003, Weary shifted Mission Mississippi's emphasis again. Now, moving into its second decade, Mission Mississippi's watchword was "Going Deeper!" The Grace is Greater than Race Tour IV did not consist of rallies to celebrate unity; instead, there were a series of four regional "mini-conferences."[137] These conferences aimed to educate the members of Mission Mississippi's chapters and affiliates in the theology, practices, and lessons that Mission Mississippi had learned over ten years of work in Jackson.

Mission Mississippi's Theologies of Racial Reconciliation

Presenting a coherent and systematic picture of Mission Mississippi's theology is a difficult task. An ecumenical movement, Mission Mississippi avoids public pronouncements that might make member churches uncomfortable or even withdraw from the organization. With the single objective of bringing Christians together across racial and denominational lines, it is hard to discern which of Mission Mississippi's statements are rooted in political expediency and which form core beliefs of the organization. Because so many different churches with their different sets of practices and beliefs are involved in Mission Mississippi, one cannot talk about the organization having a single theology. There are within Mission Mississippi major theological themes that are often in tension with each other; it would be more accurate to talk of Mission Mississippi's *theologies* of racial reconciliation.

Political Expediency and Ecumenism

In tracing Mission Mississippi's theologies of racial reconciliation, it is necessary first to appreciate the constraints placed upon the movement by its goal of not only bringing Christians together across racial and denominational lines, but also keeping them there. This is particularly challenging in Mississippi's racially segregated and religiously sectarian society. "I am scared of Christians," explains Dolphus Weary. "I am just nervous when I get around Christians.... If you say the wrong stuff you get turned off."[138]

Weary has good reason to be nervous. Within months of launching, Mission Mississippi found it difficult to hold its ecumenical coalition together. At its start, Mission Mississippi received wholehearted support from the Roman Catholic Diocese of Mississippi. In April 1993, every priest in the Jackson area received a letter from Fr. Francis Cosgrove, the Vicar General of the diocese, encouraging their "participation and that of your parishioners in this important event of reconciliation." This came with the "wholehearted support of Bishop Houck." The endorsement came with Cosgrove's personal recommendation: "I have known Lee [Paris] for several years since he coordinated ecumenical activities as a student at Ole Miss."[139] Mission Mississippi also involved Roman Catholics in leadership: Fr. Richard Somers, the priest at St. Richard Church, Jackson, served on the executive committee.

Trouble was not long in coming. In an open letter sent in May 1993, Rev. Wayne Rogers, a Presbyterian Church in America (PCA) minister at St. Paul Presbyterian Church, stated:

> The official recognition and inclusion of Roman Catholics on the executive committee and holding meetings at their church calls into question what "Gospel" is being preached, and implies and identifies Roman Catholicism in the public and Christian community as an evangelical and Christian church. This is an abomination to anyone who knows the teaching of the Roman Catholic Church concerning the basis of salvation.[140]

Announcing his church's withdrawal from Mission Mississippi, Rogers went on to challenge his "Christian brothers in the PCA to consider their participation in a coalition that undermines the gospel it professes to proclaim."[141] Although Rogers objected to Mission Mississippi's ties to Catholicism, others took quite specific theological issue with its message: Riverwood Bible Church demanded clarification when they believed they detected a postmillennial flavor to Skinner and Morley's eschatology.[142]

Dolphus Weary and Mission Mississippi's caution when dealing with the plethora of churches involved in Mission Mississippi, and its desire not to "say the wrong stuff," means that some of its theologies remain implicit, whereas some explicit statements may simply reflect a politically expedient desire to placate certain constituents.

Sources

There is a wide range of sources to consider when exploring Mission Mississippi's explicit theologies. Director of Mission Mississippi since 1998, and President since 2005, Dolphus Weary is the spokesman for Mission Mississippi. He preaches in numerous pulpits, black and white, across the country.[143] In 2001 alone, he spoke on eighty-five occasions.[144] In Weary, Mission Mississippi has someone who articulates and develops its message of unity and reconciliation in Christ. His sermons and interviews are the first place to go to understand Mission Mississippi's theology; but they are not the only source. Others regularly speak in meetings and to the media as official voices for Mission Mississippi. These people include: Lee Paris, the chairman of the board from 1993 to 2007; Neddie Winters, long-time board member and executive director of Mission Mississippi since 2005; and Dan Hall, the former minister of Cornerstone Church in Jackson and challenger of the "Big Eventism" of the opening rally, who regularly appears as facilitator and speaker at Mission Mississippi's conferences.[145] In 2007, Winters and Hall joined with Weary in a preaching team that, according to Mission Mississippi's report on the year spoke in "85 different churches; 32 different cities and 20 different denominations."[146] In addition to these sermons, lectures, and workshops, there are over fifteen years of press interviews and Mission Mississippi's own publications to mine for emerging theological patterns and themes. As already noted, ecumenical and political pragmatism shape Mission Mississippi's explicit theologies but behind these public statements, publications, and sermons lies a set of implicit theologies. Considering these implicit theologies is a more difficult and more subjective task. It requires the observation and examination of Mission Mississippi's practices mindful of their context in the Closed Society.

The Evangelical Emphasis

The demographic characteristics peculiar to Mississippi influence the theologies and practices of Mission Mississippi. Mississippi has proportionally more African American residents than any other state in the Union. According to the 2000 U.S. Census, out of a total population of 2,844,658, 61.4 percent of Mississippians are white and 36.3 percent are black or African American. Statisticians also show that proportionately Mississippi is a state with one of the highest number of religious adherents: only 7 percent claim to have no religion at all.[147] The majority of these religious adherents subscribe to a socially conservative evangelical Protestantism.[148] As historian Randy Sparks notes, "The huge preponderance of evangelical Protestants among religious people in Mississippi" gives the state "the appearance of religious homogeneity."[149] This, however, is a bifurcated homogeneity with African American and white evangelicals attending separate churches. There are, it is important to realize, more Baptists in Mississippi than all of the other churchgoers put together. White Baptists make up 40.9 percent of Mississippi's churchgoers, 80 percent of whom are members of the conservative Southern Baptist Convention. The next two denominations in the league table are trailing far behind: Methodists claim 10 percent followed by Roman Catholics at 4.9 percent.[150]

Many of Mission Mississippi's founders and leaders come from the ranks of this conservative evangelical Protestant world.[151] Despite the participation of liberal Protestants and Catholics, from the start, Mission Mississippi did not reflect their presence in its official language or the aesthetic of its practices. When Mission Mississippi drew up its statement of faith, the steering committee adapted an evangelical statement of faith found in Chuck Colson's book *The Body*.[152] The document is a simple set of orthodox Christian creedal statements with an evangelical emphasis placed on "personal faith in and a personal relationship with Jesus Christ."[153] Paris was guilty of understatement when he said, "It almost looked like an evangelical statement of faith."[154]

White Southern evangelicalism dominates Mission Mississippi's choice of the language it uses to talk about racial reconciliation. From the start came an awareness that Mission Mississippi needed to be "careful about language" as racial reconciliation meant different things to different people and raised "suspicion."[155] In the Southern white evangelical world, the term racial reconciliation is far from a popular one. It has a liberal ring to it and Mississippi whites have a deep distrust of Northern liberals stretching back beyond the freedom riders and civil rights activists of the 1960s and the carpetbaggers of Reconstruction to the abolitionists of the early nineteenth century.[156] For the Southern white evangelical, talk of racial reconciliation (or even worse, diversity!) brings to mind the shallow "do-gooder" who wants everyone to "just all get together." As James Baird, the minister of Jackson's conservative white First Presbyterian Church explained, "The do-gooders for many conservatives, that's about the worst thing you can say about somebody."[157] Even more problematic than "racial reconciliation" is the word "ecumenical" which evangelicals associate with the National Council of Churches (NCC). The NCC, even before its strenuous efforts to overturn segregation and integrate churches in Mississippi during the civil rights movement, so offended evangelicals with its liberal theology that in 1942 they formed their own rival organization, the National Association of Evangelicals.[158]

Mission Mississippi had a problem: how to present an ecumenical movement for racial reconciliation to white evangelical churches where, as Weary stated, "If you say the wrong stuff you get turned off." It found the answer to this semantic problem by employing language already in use in evangelical literature. Mission Mississippi became not an ecumenical racial reconciliation movement but an organization for Christian unity with the slogan "Unifying the Body of Christ" at the top of its newsletter (see figure 3.3).[159]

The dominant influence of conservative evangelicals on Mission Mississippi is clearly visible in the choice of speakers at the rallies in the 1990s. Alongside Skinner and Morley, we find "Coach" McCartney, the founder of Promise Keepers, and the international evangelist Josh McDowell. Invited but unable to speak were the doyens of the moral majority: Chuck Colson founder of Prison Fellowship and Dr. James Dobson of Focus on the Family.[160]

Bringing Down the Walls That Divide Us...

FIGURE 3.3. Cartoon from Mission Mississippi's first stadium rally promotional newspaper, 1993. (Courtesy of Mission Mississippi)

In their activities since 1993, Mission Mississippi has demonstrated the influence of evangelicals in its particularly strong emphasis on strengthening and protecting "family values" and conservative gender roles.[161] Founded by men in 1992, Mission Mississippi has continued to appoint only men to positions of leadership within the organization. In April 1996, Mission Mississippi sponsored the City Wide Marriage Intimacy Conference and in 1997, it collaborated with the National Center for Fathering to hold a two-day "City Wide Seminar" on fathering.[162] This seminar came after a weekend retreat that February for pastors on "Fathering and Ministry" and another weekend in March entitled "Marriage and Ministry."[163] The executive committee decided to organize these events, which clearly stray outside of Mission Mississippi's purview, because they shared the concerns and worldview of the majority of Mississippians.[164] American Family Radio recognized Mission Mississippi's concern for "traditional families" and "family values" by sponsoring the Grace is Greater than Race tour in 2000.[165]

Exclusively Christian

Mission Mississippi presents its decision to work exclusively for reconciliation within the Christian church at times as a strategic decision, and at other times as a theological commitment. In the earliest planning meetings, the executive committee cast a pragmatic eye over the state's demographics. In trying to bring reconciliation across the racial divide in Jackson, organizers were aware that limiting Mission Mississippi's focus to the Christian community left many people out. In early discussions, after a meeting with a "Moslem brother," Morley and Skinner pointed out that Mission Mississippi would "have to dialogue with and include in the dialogue substantial influences in the city who do not know Jesus."[166] The inclusion of people from other faith communities was of particular concern to the chairman Lee Paris, whose father is Jewish. Struggling with his role in founding an organization that in its proposed constitution excluded members of his own family, Paris and his father visited his father's rabbi. Paris explained to the rabbi that Mission Mississippi was, "narrow in a sense theologically, but broad in the sense of representation of the population." The rabbi's answer came as a relief, "The rabbi was very wise and made the comment that if you bring together black and white in the state under the banner of Christianity that represents the vast majority of the citizens in Mississippi, then you have accomplished something that will bless everybody in the state."[167]

Paris combines a strategic pragmatism with the particularity characteristic of evangelical Christianity in his explanation of Mission Mississippi's choice to be a Christian organization rather than a more broadly faith-based movement. The steering committee, Paris recalls, believed they had the best chance "to reach both sides of the railroad tracks" with a "strong foundation in Christ." Although a less particular faith-based approach would have "a broader foundation," and might reach more people at first, to build Mission Mississippi as "a long lasting standing house, it needed to be on the foundation of Christ."[168]

It would be a mistake to think that Mission Mississippi decided to work exclusively with Christians based simply on a calculation of the overwhelming preponderance of Christians in the state. For Mission Mississippi's powerful evangelical constituents, "the foundation of Christ" that Paris believes grounds Mission Mississippi's work, is the reconciling work of Christ. "Scripture tells us," Paris elaborates, "that in Christ we are already reconciled and we are supposed to be celebrating our unity."[169]

Salvation and Racial Reconciliation

An evangelical theology of salvation profoundly shapes Mission Mississippi's understanding of racial reconciliation. Evangelicals emphasize the reconciliation between God and the individual through the saving work of Christ.[170] In its statement of beliefs, Mission Mississippi considers it important to distinguish between this reconciliation in Christ and the reconciliation of divisions between Christians. The third point in the statement of faith reads: "The way of true reconciliation to God is found through personal faith in and a personal relationship with Jesus Christ. True reconciliation with each other is found in obedience to His teachings."[171] Distinguishing between personal reconciliation and interpersonal reconciliation, one as the work of God the other as human responsibility, inevitably—though perhaps unintentionally—creates a hierarchy between the two. This hierarchy of personal salvation over reconciliation with the neighbor results in another inevitable hierarchy: the privileging of evangelism over racial reconciliation.

Some influential figures in Mission Mississippi maintain this difference between personal and interpersonal reconciliation with careful exegesis of biblical texts that do not seem to conflate this distinction. Neddie Winters, Mission Mississippi's Executive Director, explains that there is a tendency for people to speak of racial reconciliation using Paul's injunction for Christians to be ministers of reconciliation (2 Cor 5:18). "Well that's not what we are talking about," Winters insists. The ministry of reconciliation that Paul calls Christians to is one of evangelism: it is "now that you are a Christian go and make somebody else a Christian."[172] Once a person has become a Christian,

Winters believes, then they have grounds for reconciliation with their Christian brothers and sisters across racial, denominational, and even economic barriers. Rather than using the text from Second Corinthians, Winters finds support for Mission Mississippi's work of reconciliation in two other epistles: in the instruction in James not to show favoritism to the rich over the poor in church (James 2:1–9), and in Paul's insistence in Ephesians that God has abolished the dividing wall of hostility between gentiles and Jews (Eph 2:13–14).[173]

This division of reconciliation, and the consequential elevation of evangelism to the highest task of the Church, tends to make evangelicals understand racial reconciliation as simply serving this higher purpose. In other words, many evangelicals in Mission Mississippi believe the reason the Church should set its racially divided house in order is to better evangelize the lost world. Mission Mississippi succinctly expressed this position in its Vision Statement produced in 1997, stating: "Demonstrations of unity within the Body of Christ are the foundation of evangelism as outlined in John 17."[174] In the minds of evangelical Christians, this subordination of interpersonal reconciliation to evangelism inevitably relegates the importance of ministries focusing on racial reconciliation behind existing evangelistic and outreach ministries.

From the outset, Mission Mississippi recognized and struggled to redress this imbalance between evangelism and racial reconciliation. With the encouragement of Skinner and Morley, Mission Mississippi tried to present "a Biblically wholistic [sic] gospel as opposed to the traditional half gospel."[175] Despite this effort, Mission Mississippi Pastors' Meeting of January 31, 1994, still reported confusion as to whether Mission Mississippi's purpose "is evangelism or reconciliation."[176] If any of those pastors were present ten years later at Mission Mississippi's Statewide Unity Conference, they were probably still confused.

In 2004 at the Unity Conference, Dan Hall tried to impress on participants the necessity of interpersonal reconciliation for effective evangelism. "Mission Mississippi did not start as a racial reconciliation movement," Hall told the packed room, "It started as an evangelistic outreach to our community in which we realized we were divided. And, how can the gospel be presented by a divided church.... We will never be effective as a Church if we are divided. We will not reach the lost."[177] Hall then strove to correct the emphasis on evangelism *over* racial reconciliation by intensifying the significance of reconciliation *for* evangelism: "This is not about what music we listen to, this is not about what your favorite food is...this is about people who will spend eternity either in heaven or in hell."[178]

There is present in Mission Mississippi a second understanding of the reconciliation of Christ that does not divide personal and interpersonal reconciliation; this is the belief that the reconciling work of Christ heralds and inaugurates the kingdom of God in which neighbors are reconciled to each other and to God. Dolphus Weary learned this gospel from John Perkins when, as a young man, he attended Bible studies at Voice of Calvary. Perkins did not separate the gospel into "a salvation gospel and a social gospel." Instead, there is "one gospel—a gospel that reconciled people to God but at the same time reconciled people to each other."[179] This understanding of reconciliation, while coexisting with the more traditional privileging of evangelism, causes a certain degree of dissonance within Mission Mississippi.

Dan Hall, in the same address at the Statewide Unity Conference in 2004, affords an illustration of this second understanding of reconciliation. "I am not that committed to racial reconciliation," Hall announced to a rather bemused group of ministers and lay people. "I think it is inferior to stop at racial reconciliation. If our only issue is to figure out how to get blacks and whites to work together, we have missed the mark." The participants at the conference started to wonder if they had come to the right seminar. "What I am committed to," Hall explained, "is the kingdom of God, and the kingdom cannot be the Kingdom where racism exists."[180] In his talk of the kingdom, Hall elevated Mission Mississippi's project beyond that of simply fixing the Church to evangelize the lost. Hall was trying to inspire his listeners to catch a glimpse of that reality that Jürgen Moltmann calls "the eschatological horizon" that lies "beyond the apocalyptic horizons of our modern world to the new creation of all things in the kingdom of God."[181]

A hope rooted in the sacrifice of Christ that looks toward His coming Kingdom, Moltmann contends, turns a fearful, closed church serving itself into a church open to others.[182] Dan Hall drew similar conclusions: "Folks, this isn't just a church issue. If we are going to do kingdom, we have to do kingdom across the board. The cross of Christ equalized everyone," Hall expounded, "which is why we can love the lost and the saved. Someone doesn't have to be a Christian for us to say they deserve equality."[183]

Dan Hall, in presenting both understandings of reconciliation in the same address, demonstrates the tension present in Mission Mississippi between a kingdom theology of reconciliation, rooted in the reconciling work of Christ who "in his flesh . . . has broken down the . . . hostility between us" (Eph 2:14), and a theology that makes a sharp distinction between God's reconciliation with an individual through Christ and the reconciliation of a Christian with his neighbor.

A Movement of the Heart

Another clear influence of evangelical theology on Mission Mississippi is the belief that racial reconciliation requires God's Spirit to change the sinful and racist heart. Dolphus Weary insists that reconciliation must be "a movement of the heart."[184] Recalling the Apostle Paul's dilemma as to the fate of Onesimus the Christian convert and runaway slave, Weary wrote in the Mission Mississippi newsletter, "Paul simply could have told Philemon what he ought to do." Instead, Paul writes to Philemon, Onesimus's legal owner, "Therefore, although in Christ I could be bold and order you to do what you ought to do, yet I appeal to you on the basis of love" (Philemon 1:8–9a [NIV]). This leads Weary to conclude, "Only the Lord can change our hearts and get rid of our old historical attitudes about each other."[185]

Dolphus Weary understands that what afflicts the hearts of Mississippi Christians is the personal sin of racism fostered by the state's sinful history of injustice, oppression, and segregation. "Did you know that we have all been damaged by segregation and isolation?" Weary asked the congregation at the final rally of the 2000 Grace is Greater than Race Tour. Weary then answered his own question. Starting with the well-worn evangelical trope that everybody is a sinner and in need of salvation, he connected it to a wider social reality. "We've been damaged. Black folk been damaged. White folk been damaged," Weary told the crowd. "And as I go throughout the state and throughout the city and try to talk to black preachers and white preachers, I find that people can't get beyond their own selfish personal racism."[186]

At the rally in 2000, on a freezing night in Jackson at the Smith-Wills Stadium, the small crowd listened as Weary wrestled with the solution to a society whose hearts have been damaged by racism and infected with prejudice. Weary began with the solid evangelical assertion of forgiveness and regeneration in Christ. "In 2 Corinthians 5:17," he declared, "it says 'therefore if anyone is in Christ that person is a new creation.' "[187] Starting with evangelical theology, Weary went on to push its logic and reveal its deficiencies for racial reconciliation in Mississippi. The concluding challenge of Weary's sermon that night is worth quoting at length:

> Let me tell you I understand what it means when [the Bible] talks
>   about someone walking in sin;
> And now that they give their life to Jesus, they no longer walk in
>   that sin.
>
> I understand that a person who used to be a drunkard is not
>   drunkard anymore:
> A person who used to be a liar is not a liar anymore.
>
> I understand that to be new in Christ means that you have a new life
>   inside of you. My problem is I don't know what to do with the
>   old body.

I don't know what to do with my blackness.
I don't know what it means to be a new creation in Christ and still
   be black.
I don't understand.
I am still struggling with it.
I am still struggling with what does it mean to be a new creation in
   Christ Jesus.
Please hear me! I am struggling with that.

I think this tour wants to say to me, and wants to say to us:
There is no such thing as a white Christian.
There is no such thing as a black Christian;
It is only the fact that we are Christian, we happen to be black
   or white.

But the question is: do we really believe that?
Do we believe it?

When I come in contact with a white brother and I come in contact
   with a black person, which one am I gravitated to first?
Am I gravitated to my white brother because he is a child of the King
   and I am a child of the King?
Or, am I gravitated to a black person because his face is black?

I am struggling with it.
I am struggling with it, believers.
I am struggling with it.
What does it mean to be a part of a new creation?
I don't understand it, but I am struggling with it.

Am I a Christian first?
Am I a Christian above my denomination?
Am I a Christian above my blackness?

I believe that grace is greater than race.
I believe that being a child of the King is greater than my blackness,
But I have to tell you this: I need to learn how to practice,
And I ask you to practice with me.

I ask you to go back to your churches and practice that you are not a
black Christian; you are a Christian that happens to be black.
You are not a white Christian; you are a Christian that happens to be
white.
One day when we get to Glory, its not going to make any difference.
We need to start practicing that on this earth, right now, where
we are.[188]

Evangelicals traditionally hold rebirth in Christ as an answer to those lost
to the vices of drinking, gambling, and sex; however, what resources does this
"born again" gospel bring to bear on the sins of ethnocentrism and racism?
That cold November night in Jackson, Weary searched for the answer to this
question. He did not, as so many evangelicals do, turn to a colorblind gospel
that resolves to ignore ethnic identities; instead, he struggled with the reality
of racialized America in the hope of the Kingdom of God: he is a "child of the
King...on this earth, right now, where we are."[189] Weary drew these conclusions employing the rhetorical style of the African American preacher while
speaking firmly from within the evangelical tradition. He concluded with the
challenge to Christians that happen to be black or white to go back to their
churches and "practice" this new social reality. But what are the practices that
Mission Mississippi and Dolphus Weary suggest churches should engage in to
exercise and grow into this new identity in Christ?

Friendship and Intentional Relationships

From its genesis, Mission Mississippi stressed the importance of interracial
relationships for the process of racial reconciliation and encouraged practices
that facilitated these relationships. Pat Morley, as he guided the early direction
of Mission Mississippi, stressed in his literature, "The most powerful force in
the world is a relationship,"[190] and "We want to help 'redefine' relationships by
bringing the body together to pray for their cities."[191] On the TV special aired
before the first stadium rally, Morley challenged Mississippians to enter into
relationships: "racial reconciliation is not a group experience, it's a personal,
one-on-one kind of thing."[192] Morley reinforced this message by his public dem-
onstration of friendship with Tom Skinner. Skinner and Morley's friendship
was just one of the high profile interracial friendships that Mission Mississippi
held up in its early literature as an inspirational model for others to emulate.[193]
Mission Mississippi enshrined the importance of interracial relationships in
its slogan "Changing Mississippi one relationship at a time."

Although Mission Mississippi places great emphasis on the redeeming and reconciling work of Christ, and on exploring the implications of this theology of salvation for Christian unity, there is almost no equivalent attention paid to explicating the theological concept of *relationship* or *friend*. The importance of friendship in racial reconciliation for Mission Mississippi is not in question; however, one must deduce, or even construct, Mission Mississippi's theology of friendship from its practices rather than any explicit theological statements.

Mission Mississippi clearly differentiates between the friendships participants already have and those that they deliberately enter into across racial and denominational lines. Dolphus Weary calls these "intentional relationships" and talks of participants needing "intentionality" in maintaining practices that nurture these relationships.[194] Dan Hall explained that intentionality is required because, unlike the friends we make easily, "[interracial] relationships are just hard. They are bloody; they are difficult and lead to hard conversations."[195]

Perhaps Mission Mississippi's talk of intentional relationships rather than friendships comes from an unconscious recognition of the power that private friendships wield in a closed society.[196] The open friendship that Moltmann identifies as Christ's calling for his disciples "does not know the privacy and intimacy of modern friendship." Moltmann insists, "To live in [Christ's] friendship today requires... friendship be deprivatized. Friendship must once again receive the character of public protection of and public respect for others."[197] Mission Mississippi's use of the word "relationship" contains both the public and private senses of friendship—one can have business relationships and personal relationships—that Moltmann would have Christians reclaim.

Spencer Perkins and Chris Rice's book *More than Equals: Racial Healing for the Sake of the Gospel* provides support for the suggestion that Mission Mississippi avoids the term friendship.[198] Perkins (the son of John Perkins) and Rice, both members of VOC, lived with their families as part of an intentional interracial community in a large house in West Jackson. In their book, Rice and Perkins looked for language to express their relationship that they held up as a model of racial reconciliation. The term friend for them seemed insufficient. They wanted to talk of relationships that are "more than the fickle friendships that turn sour when one or other's feelings get hurt."[199] Searching for a way to describe their relationship with one another, the pair hit on the term *yokefellow* used by Paul in Philippians 4:3. Yokefellows are joined together in relationship for "the cause of the gospel, a gospel of reconciliation."[200] "Friendships can happen with very little effort," Rice and Perkins explained, "yokefellows are intentional."[201] Perkins and Rice's work was very influential for Mission Mississippi:[202] when their book was republished in 2000, after Spencer's death in 1998, Mission Mississippi printed a review stating *More than Equals,* "is one of the most valuable books ever published on racial reconciliation." The reviewer challenged the reader, "If you truly want to be a minister of reconciliation, I urge you to read this book. Then come and help us put these ideas into practice."[203]

Mission Mississippi's practice of forging intentional relationships that are, in some way, fundamentally different from the common understanding of friendship, has further parallels with Moltmann's open friendship. Moltmann insists the open friendship of Christ stands against churches that practice a closed friendship of segregation by doctrine, wealth, or ethnicity because "the closed circle of friendship among peers is broken in principle by Christ."[204] Employing similar language, Weary talks of Mission Mississippi's struggle to break this pattern of closed friendship in the churches of the closed society. "How do we draw a circle of inclusion rather than a circle of exclusion?" asks Weary. "Many times denominations draw circles of exclusions, but we are not a denomination; we are a movement of the body of Christ and so we are constantly trying to ask questions about how do we draw circles of inclusion."[205] Viewed this way, in its practice of fostering intentional personal relationships between people of different social, denominational, and ethnic backgrounds, Mission Mississippi is breaking the idol of closed peer relations that constituted Mississippi, the Closed Society. As Will Campbell predicted, this "conscious decision" to put the Church's "house in order" came not from the radical reformers of the liberal churches but from within conservative evangelical Christianity.[206]

The Question of Justice

In considering Mission Mississippi's theology of racial reconciliation, it is important to notice what is absent from the conversation. Running through Moltmann's theology is the understanding that a Christian hope in the resurrection makes the Christian dissatisfied with the present world and its oppression and injustice.[207] Extending open friendship must include the desire to see that friend receive justice. It is striking then that in Mission Mississippi's publications, statements, and official documents there is a deafening silence when it comes to the requirements of justice in the process of racial reconciliation. Accounting for this omission is the task of the next chapter.

4

Open Friendship and Justice

Justice, Jackson, and the Gospel of Reconciliation

The year of the first Grace is Greater than Race Tour, Oxford
University Press published a book with disturbing implications for
Mission Mississippi. Sociologists Michael O. Emerson and Christian
Smith presented what they themselves described as "a rather dismal
portrait of the realities of and prospect for positive race relations
among American Christians in the United States."[1] In their book
Divided by Faith: Evangelical Faith and the Problem of Race in America,
Emerson and Smith argued that despite a growing emphasis on racial
reconciliation, white evangelicals "do more to perpetuate the racial
divide than they do to tear it down."[2] They drew this conclusion after
conducting a nationwide telephone survey of two thousand people
and two hundred face-to-face interviews. The survey and interviews
showed that white evangelicals are unlikely to see systemic injustice
against minority groups. They are likely to see any ongoing racial
problems in America as the result of:

> (1) prejudiced individuals, resulting in bad relationships and
> sin, (2) other groups—usually African Americans—trying
> to make race problems a group issue when there is nothing
> more than individual problems, and (3) a fabrication of the
> self-interested—again often African Americans, but also the
> media, the government, or liberals.[3]

This blinkered perception, they argued, is because white evangelicals "are severely constrained by their religio-cultural tools."[4] Evangelicals' theological emphasis on an individual's repentance leading to personal salvation and a personal relationship with Jesus, inclines them to address sin at the level of the individual. "Thus, if race problems—poor relationships—result from sin, then race problems must largely be individually based."[5]

Emerson and Smith sketched the history of the evangelical racial reconciliation movement recognizing the influence on white evangelicals of a few key African American ministers—including John Perkins and Tom Skinner—who preached a gospel of reconciliation that "challenge[d] social systems of injustice and inequality."[6] Unfortunately, in the process of white evangelicals adopting and disseminating this message to the white mainstream, they tended to filter out the social critique embedded in the radicals' original call for racial reconciliation. Emerson and Smith summarized the content of this call for reconciliation devoid of a call for justice as, "individuals of different races should develop strong, committed relationships...[and] repent of individual prejudice."[7] This individualism runs deep in American society but "contemporary white American evangelicalism is perhaps the strongest carrier of this freewill-individualist tradition."[8]

White evangelicals' social isolation in "racially homogenous in-groups and the segmented market" compounds this "radical limitation of the white evangelical tool kit."[9] Put simply, white evangelicals go to church with other whites and tend to live in dominantly white worlds, leaving their worldview unchallenged.[10] The result is that economically and racially segregated churches—despite their best efforts—perpetuate economic and racial inequality.

From their survey, Smith and Emerson found that "when racial isolation was reduced," this inability of evangelicals to see systemic injustice was undermined[11] This finding would seem to legitimize evangelicals' emphasis on establishing interracial relationships to effect racial reconciliation, but in a chapter entitled "Let's be Friends" the two sociologists dismiss this strategy. Such friendships have "only minimal effects." Their statistics showed "changes to racial perspectives occur mainly in the context of interracial *networks* rather than by merely having an intimate friendship."[12] Compounding this discovery, their interviews revealed that for most evangelicals the emphasis on friendship "do[es] not require financial or cultural sacrifice."[13] Simply extending friendship to an African American is an attractive option compared to a more costly form of reconciliation.

Considering Emerson and Smith's description of white evangelicals' pursuit of racial reconciliation in terms of Moltmann's theology, we see white evangelicals attempting to embrace the gospel of open friendship without also calling for the reformation of the closed church. The closed white evangelical church of racial and economic homogeneous in-groups, in its dogmatic adherence to a gospel rooted in freewill-individualism, is too much at home in the larger closed society; there is in fact a significant correspondence between the worldview of the closed church and the closed society. A call for friendship cannot truly become the open friendship of Christ if its message is still limited by the orthodoxy of a closed society. Indeed, the closed church deracinates the social dimension of the gospel leaving a closed orthodoxy free from any demands beyond personal repentance and salvation. So successful are these closed churches in imposing this closed orthodoxy on their members that they render white evangelicals unable even to see structural issues of inequality and systemic sin. The prophets of a radical open friendship who cry in this wilderness are either marginalized or have their messages adulterated into an insipid gospel of cheap reconciliation.

Jackson, Mississippi, clearly faces systemic problems rooted in the state's history of white supremacy and the continuing social and geographic segregation of the two largest racial groups. The urban landscape of the city testifies to the history of Jackson and its current crisis. Back in the roaring twenties, the white city fathers wrote:

> We are confident that a closer acquaintance with our city and county
> will bring you to the conclusion that Jackson is one of those fortu-
> nate cities in the rapidly advancing south, where the Goddess of
> Beauty has laid her lavish hand and where nature and thrift have
> combined to build unusual business opportunities in a land of
> health and happiness.[14]

In 2004, the gothic Lamar Life building on East Capitol Street still spoke of their hopes for a prosperous future, but just down the street lay the King Edward Hotel derelict since 1967. This ten-story hotel stood like an elegant liner from a bygone era that struck an iceberg and refused to sink. Its gaping windows looked across the tracks and a cleared wasteland to the boarded-up Capitol Street United Methodist Church whose congregation fled the city as their streets transitioned from a white to African American neighborhood.[15] The story of so-called white flight lies at the heart of Jackson's problems.

Following Mississippi's reluctant acceptance of the 1968 federal open housing law, a steady flow of whites moved out of the city as African Americans moved into once all-white neighborhoods. The Census reveals the story. In 1970, the majority (60.2 percent) of Jackson's 153,968 citizens were white. The city continued to grow in size, peaking in the 1980 census at 202,895, by then whites made up only half (52.4 percent) of the city. The 1990 census revealed a significant change in Jackson's demography with African Americans now the majority (55.7 percent).[16] Politics accelerated the white flight. The city had been governed by a mayor and two commissioners elected citywide, but in 1984 this system was voted out in favor of a mayor and council with seven members elected from wards. This new political arrangement coupled with the new black majority in the city meant that by 1993 Jackson's governing body became majority African American.[17] By 2000, the census showed that African Americans now made up 70.6 percent of the city. The white population had dropped from 106,285 in 1970 to 51,208 (27.8 percent).[18]

The city's whites fled to suburbs in neighboring Madison and Rankin Counties. Their departure had a dramatic financial impact on the city, the results of which accelerated the out-migration. "A loss of 1,000 Jackson residents," the *Clarion-Ledger* reported, "has an estimated economic impact of more than $8 million a year, and a direct loss of more than $448,000 annually to city and county governments."[19] This loss of revenue affected all of the city's services and thus the city's ability to attract investment.

Whites cite the city's rising crime and struggling school system as the reasons for moving their families. Explanations given for leaving often boil down to this: now that Jackson is a majority African American city governed by African Americans, whites fear for their personal safety and the security of their possessions and believe their children will not receive a good or safe education in the city schools. Jackson does have a crime problem. In 2004, there were fifty-seven people murdered, giving the city a murder rate of 27.81 per 100,000, more than five times higher than the national average. This is mostly so-called black-on-black violence and there is a clear link with poverty, as 70 percent of the homicides occurred in low-income areas that surround the downtown.[20] However, quite apart from the crime, the situation of the city schools spurs many of the remaining whites to move. The white child whose parents send them to public school faces the prospect of being in a tiny minority.[21]

Thwarting the desegregation of the city schools, many whites chose to send their children to the "seg" academies such as Jackson Prep or Jackson Academy. Others, however, decided to stick with the public school system: some out of principle and some for economic reasons. Ralph Maisel, the father of three boys, chose not to take them out from the city system: "I think my first and earliest decision was that I didn't have the money....I couldn't put them all in at the same time at a private academy." In 1989, 20 percent of the students in Jackson city schools were white, but the impact of white flight reduced this minority and set up a rapid withdrawal of most of the remaining white students. Just twelve years later, white children in city schools were an endangered species: only 4 percent of the students in city schools were white.[22] The schools struggled not only from the loss of income but also from the loss of so many educated middle-class parents who formed the backbone of the schools' PTAs. Most of the African American students in the city schools come from poor families; in 2003, more than 70 percent of the 31,529 students were on the federal free-and-reduced meal program.[23]

The city's churches had to come to terms with the devastating demographic change precipitated by the abolition of Jim Crow and subsequent white flight. As Jackson expanded in the twentieth century, churches planted congregations in the new residential neighborhoods. At the turn of the century, the three largest white protestant churches started congregations in West Jackson: Calvary Baptist, Capitol Street Methodist and Central Presbyterian.[24] These became the "second" churches to the big downtown "first" congregations. In the late 1960s, African Americans started to move into West Jackson. The 2000 census confirmed what was obvious to the casual observer that West Jackson was now an 80–100 percent African American community.[25] The large white churches struggled to remain in the transitioning neighborhood. Central Presbyterian Church, whose membership in 1964 came to over a thousand, disbanded in 1993 followed three years later by Capitol Street Methodist, which had once had over twenty-five hundred members.[26] Today, only Calvary Baptist Church hangs on in one of Jackson's most depressed African American neighborhoods with the destitute and homeless on the street corners. It stands as the last marker of a once vibrant white community.

The large downtown "first" churches and cathedrals remain in place, held by their sense of history and place in the city. First Baptist Church, for example, has over half of its ninety-five hundred predominantly white members living outside Jackson city limits. Rev. Jim Baker, senior associate pastor at First Baptist, proudly told a reporter in 2003, "Some of our members live as far away as 20 miles." Instead of confessing his flock's culpability in white flight and the demise of Jackson he proudly stated, "We have a membership that's dedicated to continuing a Christian witness here in this city."[27] Baker's failure to connect the flight of his congregation with the city's woes fits neatly with Emerson and Smith's findings. First Baptist's primary responsibility to the city is faithfully to preach the message of personal salvation through Jesus Christ, urging the unconverted to repent and be baptized.[28] This is not to make light of the decision of these churches to stay. Concerned for the safety of their congregants and their automobiles, First Presbyterian Church and First Baptist Church have security guards (some of them armed) patrolling their buildings and parking lots.

Across the grounds of the State Capitol Building from the gothic First Baptist Church stand the imposing neoclassical columns of Galloway United Methodist Church. Galloway has moved a long way since 1964 when its congregation affirmed, "It is not un-Christian that we prefer to remain an all-white congregation. The practice of the separation of the races in Galloway Memorial Methodist Church is a time-honored tradition. We earnestly hope that the perpetuation of that tradition will never be impaired."[29] In 2004, at the urging of the Methodist Bishop of Mississippi, Galloway invited Ross Oliver to be their new pastor. Oliver, the white General Secretary of the Methodist Church of South Africa, came to Jackson commissioned to bring his twenty-four years experience of ministry in apartheid and postapartheid South Africa to bear on "racial reconciliation and combating economic disparity" in Mississippi.[30] Comparing post-Jim Crow Jackson with postapartheid South Africa, Oliver realized, "in the ten years from 1994 to 2004, the transition in South Africa has been far more systemically transformative than the past forty years in Mississippi since the civil rights era."[31] From his perspective as a minister, he reached conclusions similar to Emerson and Smith's: "My struggle here is that the church has abdicated its responsibility largely in terms of the fundamental social issues, those things that are deeply affecting life in Mississippi."[32]

One Sunday morning soon after his arrival, Oliver preached on the parable of the persistent widow, explaining, "[it is] the story of economic systems that exploit the poor." An unimposing figure with a goatee and bottle-lens glasses, the forty-nine-year-old Oliver is a dynamic and impassioned speaker. If the congregation remained ignorant of the "systemically transformative" nature of the gospel of Jesus Christ, it was not because he never mentioned it from the pulpit. That morning Oliver left the congregation in no doubt that "the widow represents an underclass of people who are without support, without resources, without connections," and the unjust judge stands for "those who have authority, those who have power, those who can make decisions that affect life for others and fear neither God nor have compassion for people."[33] "Contrary to all expectations," the widow prevails over the unjust judge because, as Jesus says in the parable, "will not God bring about justice for his chosen ones, who cry out to him day and night? Will he keep putting them off? I tell you, he will see that they get justice, and quickly" (Luke 18:7–8 [NIV]). "Justice," Oliver explained, is God's "purpose and design," and the Church is to cooperate in this grand design. He concluded his sermon with the challenge: "Which side does God find us on, the side of the judge or the side of the widow?"

On whose side does Mission Mississippi find itself: the widow or the judge? Does it openly call out for justice and the reformation of a society still shaped by the legacy of racism and segregation, or is it prevented from doing so by the "religio-cultural tools" of the white evangelical church? Does Mission Mississippi pass over systemic issues of injustice merely to concentrate on personal relationships in the context of a gospel of personal salvation? Ross Oliver's first impressions suggest that Emerson and Smith's critique of evangelicals' attempts at racial reconciliation hold true for Mission Mississippi:

> I have a fundamental problem with Mission Mississippi's approach
> in that it is not in any way addressing the systemic nature of racial
> separateness and therefore racial polarization. I mean, I admire the
> goodwill of focusing—let's do this one relationship at a time. I am
> not sure that it is working on any significant scale. I am not seeing
> churches partnering...for the amount of energy and money that
> goes into it, I actually think it is quite paltry that it is not systemic.
> It is not dealing with the fundamental socio-economic and political
> dimensions of it.[34]

These pointed observations of a newcomer to Jackson find support with those who have dedicated their lives to working with and on behalf of the poor in the city and state. John Perkins, one of the founding fathers of the evangelical racial reconciliation movement, does not hold back in his critique of Mission Mississippi's failure to address systemic issues of injustice. From his office in West Jackson, Perkins offered his comment on Mission Mississippi's slogan: changing Mississippi one relationship at a time. "One person at a time," he scoffed, "that's just...the element of this individualism." The problem, according to Perkins, is an institutional one. A pragmatic revolutionary, Perkins insisted that Mission Mississippi does not understand that individuals cannot change institutions, only institutions change institutions. What hope does that leave the poor for changing Mississippi? Perkins argued, "The institution that the poor have is their bodies. The institution that the poor have is their collective voice, their collective power to change that institution." This led him to conclude, "The Church is the institution that God left here on earth...It is God's force on earth, and that force is to challenge all other institutions."[35]

Down the road at VOC Ministries, its white director, Phil Reed, offered a similar, if more measured, assessment of the problem facing the church and his perceptions of Mission Mississippi's shortfall:

> The inequity in wealth; the inequity in employment; the inequity in
> politics; and power: we have to deal with all of those things. We have
> to deal with the systemic issues and that is the hard piece. There is

the piece that there is reluctance to even deal with and, if I might be so bold, even at Mission Mississippi, unless things have changed, there is a reluctance really to deal with that piece of it.[36]

As well as the absence of a call for justice from Mission Mississippi's rhetoric of reconciliation, Perkins and Reed had a second concern. "It seems the goal of Mission Mississippi is to have a predominantly white church and a predominantly black church fellowship together," explained Reed. He had heard Weary "state on more than one occasion that the goal for Mission Mississippi is not integrated churches." Although these statements are designed to allay the fears of both African American and white churches, this strategy worried Reed. "I am not saying every church has to be integrated in order to be a legitimate church; however, I am saying that given the fact that almost no church is integrated that's a problem."[37] Weary is well aware of the criticisms from his mentor and former colleagues from VOC. Perkins even confronted him directly over his strategy not to challenge churches to integrate in a Mission Mississippi board meeting.[38]

Surprisingly, Mission Mississippi's appointment of Dolphus Weary, a man who had dedicated his life to Perkins' "wholistic" gospel of personal and societal salvation, did not bring a shift in its emphasis to include the need for the Church to address systemic injustice as part of a process of reconciliation. It is vital to understand the forces that prevented this from happening. Initially, all the signs were that Weary would broaden Mission Mississippi's agenda. In his letter accepting the post of executive director, Weary explained to Lee Paris, "Once the bridge is built between us and God, there are other bridges that need to be built.... Three specifically that I'm concerned about are the bridge that crosses the race gap, the economic gap and the denomination gap."[39] Speaking three years after his appointment, however, Weary no longer pushed Mission Mississippi to build a bridge over the economic gap. "In my life prior to Mission Mississippi we did a lot of preaching in terms of trying to get reconciliation between the haves and the have-nots," explained Weary. Now, after "decipher[ing] from the board what their vision is.... My relationship with Mission Mississippi is more pointed—it is more specific. It has the boundary of the Christian community and it has the boundary of racial reconciliation and denominational reconciliation."[40]

The separation of justice from reconciliation is just as theologically problematic as trying to separate God's reconciliation with humans through Christ from reconciliation between humans. The South African theologian John De Gruchy, in his excellent book *Reconciliation, Restoring Justice,* shows how Paul's theology inextricably links reconciliation and justice in the redemptive work of Christ. De Gruchy shows how for Paul, "reconciliation is the controlling metaphor for expressing the gospel," but "[it] is only one of the words used by Paul to describe God's redemptive activity.... Apart from 'salvation,' 'redemption' and 'deliverance,' Paul also speaks frequently of 'justification,' which connects his understanding of reconciliation to God's justice."[41] Paul's understanding of God's justice is quite different from the justice meted out in most courts of law. God's justice, De Gruchy explains, is a restorative justice rather than a punitive justice. Thus, talking of God restoring God's reign of justice in Christ is the same as saying "God was reconciling the world in Christ."[42] The implications for Mission Mississippi are clear: involvement in the "ministry of reconciliation" (2 Cor. 5:18) is necessarily to be involved in working for restorative justice for the oppressed.

The resistance to a gospel of reconciliation that includes the demand for a restoration of God's justice as it pertains to economic systems is not surprising. As Desmond Tutu observes in reference to the whites that supported apartheid in South Africa, "It needed a big dollop of grace to reject a system that assured one so much privilege, so many benefits and advantages."[43] The tragedy is that white churches in Mississippi, despite believing that through Christ they have received an immeasurably big dollop of grace, are still resistant to the demands of restorative justice. Eric Stringfellow, an African American columnist for Jackson's *Clarion-Ledger* and board member of Mission Mississippi believes that "real racial reconciliation in the context of Mississippi has to do with economics." He finds, however, that talking about this to whites, even on Mission Mississippi's board, "makes people uncomfortable."[44]

Phil Reed of VOC finds this discomfort at the inclusion of justice in a racial reconciliation agenda is easy to explain. "Getting to know a black person doesn't cost me anything, In fact it is great. But when it starts getting down to: I have to start looking at the way I use my money and dealing with systemic issues, it is very costly and people don't want to have to pay a cost."[45] As Smith and Emerson pointed out, "those in positions of power... rarely come to church to have their social and economic positions altered."[46]

Weary, in downplaying justice in his call for racial reconciliation in Mississippi, brought his message into line with the will of those on the board uncomfortable with such an economic critique. Lee Paris, as chairman of the board from 1993 to 2007, was the most influential person in shaping that vision. When asked explicitly why the language of justice is absent from Mission Mississippi's call for reconciliation across racial and denominational lines Paris answered:

> I don't remember a big discussion of that in Mission Mississippi—
> and I know there have probably been people that have wanted to
> tie the two together. For me justice is God's job and the laws of our

land's job and...I guess that's not a calling on my life to seek justice. That's God's job and the law's, and that is not a buzz word to me.[47]

What is one to make of Paris's understanding that reconciliation and justice are utterly separate matters? He is neither racially isolated nor simply concerned to embrace a gospel free from personal sacrifice. To appreciate his answer, one must listen to Paris's story and consider the history of the closed society and closed institutions that shaped his theology.

Lee Paris and First Presbyterian Church, Jackson, Mississippi

LeRoy "Lee" Henry Paris II is, on first impression, an unlikely candidate to be fighting the battle for racial reconciliation in Jackson, Mississippi. With shoulder-length hair brushed back and a youthful face, Paris looks more like a music executive from Nashville than a businessman from Jackson. Ole Miss memorabilia line the walls of his office; a framed photograph of the cheerleaders in the 1950s running onto the field with the largest Rebel flag ever made sits by his desk. His cell phone rings to the tune of Dixie; one of his dogs is called Dixie; and a Colonel Reb' banner hangs over the front door of his white columned mansion—he added the columns after purchasing the house. Paris is not exaggerating when he says, "I have always enjoyed my Southern Heritage."[48] He hardly seems the sort of person of whom Pat Morley, speaking at Mission Mississippi's tenth anniversary celebrations, would say, "I truly believe that when the history books are written a hundred years from now that history will record that one of the great men in the history of this state is Lee Paris."[49]

Raised in Indianola in the heart of the Mississippi Delta, Paris grew up in a family and society shaped by this agricultural region's main crop: cotton.[50] His father, LeRoy Henry Paris, worked in the successful family business, Lewis Grocer Company.[51] The company, started in 1896 by Jewish immigrants from Poland, grew quickly supplying the needs of the prosperous Delta. Through the 1920s and 30s, the Lewis Grocer Company profited through the region's system of sharecropping. They "furnished" groceries to plantation stores on credit, which in turn "furnished" the goods to their laborers who, paid only in plantation "script," were unable to shop at any other stores.[52] By the 1960s, the company operated in four states as the Lewis Grocer Company, Sunflower Food Stores, and Super Valu, with their distribution center and offices still in Indianola.[53]

While a student at Ole Miss, Lee's father met and fell in love with fellow student Rose Marie Leonard. Although a very successful and popular student—Ole Miss students elected him as a cheerleader and Colonel

Rebel—as a Jew, Paris was an outsider in the Closed Society. When LeRoy and Rose announced their engagement, they found that the marriage of a Jew and a Presbyterian ran counter to the mores of Mississippi's white Protestant society: the Presbyterian Church in Rose's home of Kosciusko would not bless the marriage. Instead of a church, the couple held their wedding service in the Delta Gamma sorority house on the Ole Miss campus.[54]

Looking back on his childhood, Lee Paris does not remember any social awkwardness resulting from his father's religion. With his father a former Colonel Rebel, his family tracing their roots in Mississippi back six generations, and his great-great-grandfather a Confederate veteran, Paris felt a part of the white Mississippi world. "Everybody knew my family," he recalls, "and [we] had a very good name and [I] never felt one ounce of not fitting in at the highest and most accepted levels of society."[55]

The eldest of three children, Paris spent his youth in the close-knit community studied by sociologists in the 1930s as the classic "Cottonville" and "Southerntown."[56] The Indianola they described, strictly bound by caste and class, had changed little by Paris's childhood thirty years later. "I had the privilege of growing up in a very privileged world. We had black house servants and yardmen and people that worked for us in many different capacities."[57] His parents and society taught the young boy his station appropriate to his white caste and wealthy business class. Paris recalls one maid called Magnolia: "I loved her very similar to the way I loved my own mother." His new perspective on race clouds this fond memory. "Now thinking back on it," Paris said shaking his head, "Magnolia served us probably thousands of meals and yet did not sit at the table with us."[58]

Paris grew up in a devout household with "family prayer gatherings every night."[59] The parents had reached an understanding regarding the spiritual formation of their children. "When my parents...decided to get married, they made vows to each other that they would not try to convert each other and that my dad would assist my mom [with] whatever children the Lord blessed them with in raising them as Christians."[60] His father attended the small synagogue in Lexington founded by his grandfather in 1904, while his mother took the children to Indianola's First Presbyterian Church.[61] As a young child, he took little notice of the difference in his parents' faith, "The culture I grew in—I don't think I knew anybody that didn't go to church. But there were several families in town where the mom went to one church and the dad the other...and so that is the way I pigeon-holed my family's religion."[62]

At the Presbyterian Church, the young Paris recalls, "I sat under the teaching of some incredibly godly women, particularly, Sunday school teachers and good pastors and was taught the Word from a very early age." He has, he explains, "one of those wonderful but boring testimonies.... I don't remember a day that I didn't know the Lord.... God has just always been near to me and I haven't strayed too far from his calling."[63] This Christian education extended from the church to his school. Paris attended Indianola Academy, a new all-white private school whose principal was also a member of the First Presbyterian Church.[64] He was there for four years before desegregation in 1970 caused the school to grow "exponentially overnight." When he graduated in 1975, Paris had never been to school with an African American, nor had he had any social contact with an African American that extended beyond the bounds of an employer/employee relationship.[65]

Despite the dramatic integration of Mississippi's flagship University in 1962, when the young Paris came onto the campus in 1975, there were only just over six hundred African American students enrolled at Ole Miss.[66] He studied history and business before moving on to the law school. The African Americans he met at the university did not trouble his "white world." "There were a few [African Americans] and it was fine. The ones I encountered, other than their skin color, [were] just like everybody else at Ole Miss."[67]

Although his college years did not revolutionize the young Paris's views on race, his commitment to his faith and theological tradition deepened. He helped start the University of Mississippi chapter of Reformed University Fellowship (RUF), serving on their core-group steering committee and as their first treasurer.[68] RUF was the student ministry of the newly formed Presbyterian Church in America (PCA). On graduating in 1982 and moving to Jackson with his new wife Lisa, it seemed an obvious choice to join First Presbyterian Church, the largest PCA church in the city.

In the nine years between moving to Jackson and the start of Mission Mississippi, Lee Paris says of himself: "I was a busy, ambitious, young man, making my mark in the world, raising my family." In 1983, he went to work as general council for the real estate firm Mississippi Properties; he acquired the company in 1986 with the help of a partner. Alongside his business commitments, Paris enjoyed his involvement as a deacon at First Presbyterian Church and his participation in the Christian Businessmen's Committee. All of these worlds in which he moved—work, family, church—were white. The few African Americans he related to were those who by dint of education and business acumen caused minimal disturbance to the cultural homogeneity of the closed white world.

> I came to Jackson and continued pretty much exclusively in a white
> world. I had during those next ten years a few encounters with
> African Americans. You could probably count them on one hand.

FIGURE 4.1. Lee Paris, 2004. (Photo by author)

I remember having my first social lunch with an African American
at the University club. Again, the few encounters that I had were
blacks that were on such a level that they were just no different from
me. It wasn't a stretch.[69]

It was in this closed white world of church and business that Paris
responded to the challenge of Pat Morley and Tom Skinner. Praying over
Morley's suggestion to have a citywide crusade, Paris believed he heard the call
of God on his life. Initially this call made little sense to a man steeped in white
Mississippi culture and without an African American to call a friend: "I think
in the beginning...I was just amazed that God would call me to do something
like this. I mean, given my background."[70] He now considers his background
a strength for his work starting Mission Mississippi:

If somebody from a more liberal school of theology would start
it then obviously the more conservative element would just not
have been involved. Had I been from Minnesota and moved

down here: well that's just somebody trying to cram their ways down on us again. Had I been from here but gone off north to school: well look what he learned up there and coming down here.... Had I been of another political party, well you know there's that stuff. I was culturally "one of us."[71]

Rather like Paul's boast "in the flesh" that he is a "Hebrew of the Hebrews" (Phil. 3:4–6), Paris repeatedly references how he is just, "a typical guy from the Delta interested in Southern Heritage, Ole Miss, [his] fraternity, [a] Republican."[72] He tells how he has six generations of Mississippians on both sides and his daughter is the fifth generation to graduate from Ole Miss. He also boasts of his Presbyterian credentials and love for First Presbyterian Church, Jackson.

Paris now claims his Christian identity trumps his identity rooted in Southern Presbyterian tradition and white Southern heritage. This was not always the case. The turning point came, Paris recounts, one New Year's Eve shortly before the start of Mission Mississippi. Sitting in his pew at First Presbyterian Church, Paris listened to the preaching of his pastor, Dr. Baird. It was, he recalls, "one of the most powerful sermons I have ever heard in my life." The message that night was about "the difference in biblical thinking and traditional thinking and that how at First Pres we are so tied to our traditions in such a powerful way." Baird challenged the congregation that night that they were in danger of "embracing tradition over and above what...God had called us to do." Paris felt convicted that his own life and that of the congregation stood "at a crossroads" of tradition and the gospel.

Of all the churches supporting Mission Mississippi's first stadium rally, First Presbyterian Church made the largest contribution. In 1993, the church with its membership of around thirty-five hundred people—described by their minister as "an affluent, transient congregation that has second and third houses and jets around the world,"—contributed $12,000 to Mission Mississippi. In addition to the church's donation, seventy family units gave money.[73] The church's membership also lent significant leadership to the new organization: thirty people served on Mission Mississippi's committees; in 1993 church members chaired or co-chaired four of the seven working committees; and three members (Baird, Paris, and Smith) were on the executive board.

Paris's enthusiasm and Baird's influence explains the disproportionate commitment of First Presbyterian Church to Mission Mississippi when compared with other churches.[74] Baird considers his high profile support of Mission Mississippi—he served on the first board and his picture appeared in the *Clarion-Ledger* at the launch of Mission Mississippi—"probably not the smoothest thing for me to do at First Presbyterian Church."[75] Most ministers, Baird contends, especially in such "a conservative bastion...would rather have their own ministry...which they [could] control." Mission Mississippi was not a small sub-ministry of the congregation; it demanded cooperation. "With Mission Mississippi you can't control it. You can take part in something and what you are doing is trusting. You are trusting the blacks."[76]

Before Mission Mississippi, First Presbyterian Church did not have a reputation for "trusting the blacks" or supporting ministries run by African Americans. Dolphus Weary recalls that while he was the Executive Director of Mendenhall Ministries he asked First Presbyterian Church to help support, and be involved with, Mendenhall Ministries. Weary found the church's response exasperating: "They said to me, 'We support a black ministry in Canton, do you want us to stop supporting them and support you?'"[77] Weary considered First Presbyterian Church's response unjust: "Now they support one hundred and fifty to two hundred white ministries, but they were going to put it on me, put the weight on me, 'Do you want us to stop supporting this other ministry and support you?' And I looked at them and said, 'No, I just want to encourage you to keep on supporting them,' and I left."[78]

Given Weary's experience, it seems amazing that the church ever supported Mission Mississippi. Credit for eliciting First Presbyterian Church's initial support must go to Baird's negotiation of the cultural crossroads facing his congregation. Baird adopted the classic Southern approach of gradualism that he dubbed "patience": he claims never to have preached on the subject of race from the pulpit.[79] Baird's cautious way of showing that the gospel trumps tradition seemed frustratingly circumspect to Paris; the issue of race, Baird tried to explained to Paris, "was a powder keg within the congregation."[80] The way to handle this delicate situation was through a nonconfrontational style of leadership. "We don't push," he told Paris, "we demonstrate. Just demonstrate. We don't ask for anything. We provide good leadership for Mission Mississippi. [If we do this] our people will come along." An alternative approach might not achieve the desired ends. "If we have to ram it down their throats and if you're going to make a big issue out of it," he warned Paris, "there will be some strong resistance."[81] Initially, Baird's gentle approach bore fruit. For the first year, the congregation seemed happy hosting Mission Mississippi's prayer breakfasts and even having Tom Skinner preach at an evening service.[82] Despite all of Baird's caution, however, there were those within First Presbyterian Church who wished to set a spark to the powder keg of race and tradition.

In the final days of 1993, the ministers and the elders of First Presbyterian Church received an anonymous letter. Its author claimed, "Mission Mississippi obviously is a means of forcing social integregation [sic] on the congregation of

First Presbyterian Church." The advocates for Mission Mississippi within the congregation: "Jim Baird, Lee Paris, Victor Smith, and the ruling clique of the Session: Bob Cannada, Gene McRoberts, John Crawford, Steve Rosenblatt and Jim Moore" had fallen, "for the social restructuring ruses now in wide vogue and use."[83] This letter came as the session of First Presbyterian Church considered Mission Mississippi's request for the church to continue their significant financial contribution for 1994.[84]

The author conceded that "red and yellow, black and white [are] equal in His sight." However, in language echoing the rhetoric of the 1950s, the author of the letter stated that the notion of equality "does not require us to emulate the Blacks' forms of worship, or to take a negro home for dinner in order to prove ourselves Christians." The writer's position denied the possibility that the gospel of Jesus Christ requires anything resembling Moltmann's open friendship. "We can do justice to all men and women," he contended, "and still select our intimates for whatever reasons strike our fancy."[85] The letter ended with a warning shot across Baird's bows: "If you are concerned about Mission Mississippi, consider cutting your church pledge and your payment of monies to 1st Pres."[86]

The church responded to the warning in classic Presbyterian style: the management committee appointed a sub-committee to investigate Mission Mississippi's purpose and the content and sources of its theology.[87] The evidence of Mission Mississippi's sound doctrine, vision, and fiscal responsibility satisfied the committee and its chairman Calvin Wells, who passed on their findings to the Session. Paris hoped his church would finally wholeheartedly endorse Mission Mississippi. While the Session's resolution, passed on March 14, allowed that "Mission Mississippi may continue to show during the year 1994 that First Presbyterian Church…is a supporting church," the Session also tried to mollify those opposed to the organization. "In view of the fact that…some members of this congregation have objected to using budgeted funds to support Mission Mississippi, it is the decision of this Session that no part of the 1994 budgeted funds be used to support Mission Mississippi."[88] Instead, the church created a fund for Mission Mississippi into which church members could make contributions "over and above what the individual gives directly to Mission Mississippi."[89]

The Session's creative attempt to avoid conflict, far from sweeping the matter of racial reconciliation back under the Presbyterian carpet, precipitated a series of events that threatened to polarize the congregation. On Friday, April 8, 1994, every member of First Presbyterian Church received a letter in the mail.[90] The recipients recognized the familiar dot matrix printing on the address labels from official church mailings, but there was nothing familiar about the contents. The anonymous author of December's threatening letter had written a response to the Session's decision. Typed and photocopied on legal size paper and bearing the title "Concerning MISSION MISSISSIPPI," the letter included a clipping of the Session's resolution and a copy of the December 29, 1993 letter.[91] Along with the appeal to members to "stop making pledges to 1st Pres, or cut them drastically," came a series of new allegations against the Session and Mission Mississippi. "First Pres" had "deliberately abandon[ed] its primary mission of preaching only the pure gospel of Jesus"; instead, they had been "snuckered-in" to following the "Social Gospel." Pat Morley and Tom Skinner had fooled the church into contributing toward "'honorariums' or payments of at least $13,500 *plus* unnamed expenses for preaching a sermon or two on reconciliation of blacks & whites." In one sentence, the author demonstrated his contempt for any attempts at racial reconciliation, his disdain for Mission Mississippi's motives and theology, and crude stereotyping of African Americans: "An astoundingly good business Skinner & Morley have, a black man and a white man peddling to white preachers and laymen, scared by constant Black violence, the promise of peace between the races by man's reconciliation, not God's.[92]

The most outrageous statement in that mailing came in a paragraph in the reprinted first letter:

> Blacks in this country claim they are furious because of the wrongs historically done their forefathers: lynchings and other murders, and therefore WE now are required to placate this fury by groveling to the blacks and acceding to their every present demand. No matter that neither we nor our forefathers in this church ever did any of the injustices complained of. Should we now refuse to somehow placate these Black resentments, we are labeled as being Prejudiced and Non-christian.[93]

Here the author absolved himself and his ancestors—and all three thousand members of the church and their forbears—from participation in *any* acts of injustice that African Americans suffered. However, the members of First Presbyterian Church were in fact deeply involved in the "wrongs historically done" African Americans, if only through their complicity in a society built first on slave, then on exploited black labor. The struggle to hold onto the economic and social privileges afforded by the perpetuation of these "wrongs historically done" profoundly shaped the culture, doctrine and history of First Presbyterian Church, Jackson.

Slavery, Segregation, and the Spirituality of the Church

When Paris insists "justice is God's job and the laws of our land's job," he is reiterating a distinctive theological position articulated in a particularly sophisticated form by Southern Presbyterians. Called *the spirituality of the church,* this doctrine was formulated in its most distinct and influential form in the nineteenth century by Southern Presbyterians to defend the privileged and powerful from the intrusion of abolitionist morality into their religion. It became a trusty doctrinal bulwark against the continued intrusion of carpetbaggers, scallywags, liberals, ecumenists, and civil rights activists into the Southern way of life.[94] To understand both the form Mission Mississippi has taken and the challenge it faces in engaging white churches, one must understand the historical forces at work in the Closed Society and its closed churches that birthed, shaped, and institutionalized this theology. Specifically, one must consider the history and influence of Paris's denomination and congregation: First Presbyterian Church, Jackson, Mississippi.

Presbyterians, Abolitionists, and Antebellum Jackson, 1837–1865

On April 8, 1837, seven Presbyterians organized the first Presbyterian congregation in Jackson, Mississippi. They held their services in the State House, a simple two-story brick building measuring thirty by forty feet.[95] It was an inauspicious start in an inauspicious city. Jackson, only fifteen years old, was a rough-and-ready frontier town in comparison with the antebellum grandeur of the older river towns of Vicksburg and Natchez. Following the ceding of five million acres of land to the federal government by the Choctaw at the treaty of Doaks Stand, the General Assembly of the state of Mississippi formed Hinds County in 1821. At the same time, they commissioned Thomas Hinds, James Patton, and William Lattimore to locate the site for the state capital within twenty miles of the "true centre of the state."[96] They recommended land on the west bank of the Pearl River called Le Fleur's Bluff. On December 23, 1822, the sixth session of the state's General Assembly opened in Jackson in a patch of wilderness ambitiously demarked with an elegant checkerboard street plan along lines suggested by Thomas Jefferson.[97]

The new capital, named for President Andrew Jackson, did not flourish. For the ten or eleven months the Assembly was not in session, the town emptied of people: in 1830, the Hinds County tax rolls show only three lots in Jackson on which taxes were assessed.[98] Public displays of piety were not a feature of this frontier town; one citizen recalls of those early years:

> Our old State House…was rarely used as a house of worship; for in
> the first place there were hardly enough people to constitute a
> congregation, had all been inclined to attend; and secondly, there
> were so many who cherished a deep-rooted aversion to such
> assemblies that a wandering divine would have been obliged to
> declaim to empty benches.[99]

It was not until 1836 that the Methodists organized a congregation and started holding the first regular Christian worship in Jackson.[100] T. J. Wharton, who became a judge in the city, remembered the state of Jackson when he arrived in 1837. Hoping to find the "metropolis of the great cotton-growing, slaveholding aristocracy of this proud commonwealth," he was deeply disappointed to find "the population did not exceed 900." The morality of the capital did not impress him either. From the State House "where," Wharton noted, "the Methodists and all other congregations worshipped at that time, there was a plank walk three or four feet wide elevated above the ground and extending from the back door to a side door of a saloon or 'dram shop'" over which "a human stream was continually pouring, day and night, during the session of the legislature."[101]

Jackson's hope for improvement lay in the in the state's economic development; and in 1837, slave labor powered the economy. Wealthy planters had only just started establishing plantations in the Delta, and they needed their slaves to continue the work.[102] Slaves cleared and drained the swampy wilderness exposing the fertile earth for the planting of cotton. Cotton, a labor-intensive crop, required slave labor to plant, chop the weeds, and pick the bolls. The growing abolitionist movement in the North threatened the planters' investment in land and slaves and jeopardized Jackson's future.

In May 1837, the month following the foundation of the church in Jackson, the Presbyterian Church's General Assembly meeting in Philadelphia succeeded in quashing the abolitionist movement in the denomination. In order to accomplish this, the defenders of slavery formed an unholy alliance with traditional Calvinists: a partnership that established the close connection between white supremacy and conservative theology in the Southern Presbyterian Church for the next 150 years.

By the third decade of the nineteenth century, much to the alarm of Presbyterians from slaveholding states, supporters of the abolition of slavery were on the verge of gaining enough support to pass a resolution in the General Assembly declaring slaveholding a sin. In 1836, a committee charged with investigating slavery delivered an unequivocal condemnation of the practice: "[Slavery is] an institution, contrary to nature—unsanctioned by the divine law of love. The authority it claims is usurpation, and the subjection it demands is unreasonable. The whole system is at war with the divine institutions. It is therefore *sin—essentially* SIN—and all its claims are founded in injustice."[103] The committee proposed the General Assembly pass a resolution declaring, "That the buying, selling, or holding of a human being as property, is, in the sight of God, a heinous sin, and ought to subject the doer of it to censure of the church."[104] If the General Assembly were to pass such a resolution then church discipline would require congregations to excommunicate slaveholders. Readmission to the communion table could only occur if the sinner chose "to renounce their sins, and [was] determined to lead a holy and godly life."[105] For a slaveholder this act of repentance would be both apparent and costly: it would require that he free all his slaves. Moderates desiring church unity and Southern delegates wishing to protect their region's economic interests managed to stall the resolution.[106] They returned to Philadelphia the following year with new alliances and a plan to excise the abolitionists from their church. An understanding of how they succeeded requires a brief description of the political and theological fault lines within the Presbyterian church of the 1830s.

The Church was actually a union of the Congregationalists of New England and the Presbyterian Church. The two churches had joined in 1801 to pool their resources better to compete with the Methodists and the Baptists in evangelizing the expanding frontier.[107] As the nineteenth century progressed, the Congregationalists increasingly came under the influence of Unitarian theology and a distinctive "New School" or "New Divinity" developed that brought into question the orthodox Calvinist beliefs in original sin.[108] The New School, embracing the evolutionary optimism of the day, wished to promote the possibility of human agency and responsibility. In doing so, they reacted against the traditional doctrine of original sin and the total depravity of man that seemed to threaten their hopes of reforming society and building a nation with a Christian character.[109] Nathaniel W. Taylor, the chair of didactic theology at Yale, became the chief proponent of New School or "New Haven" theology. In 1828, he preached a sermon that rejected original sin in the sense that man inherits "any disposition or tendency to sin, which is the cause of all sin."[110] Through his revivals in the Northeast, the evangelist and abolitionist Charles G. Finney popularized this gospel firmly wedding New School theology with abolitionist reforming zeal.[111]

The increasing influence in the General Assembly of this New School theology with its abolitionist commitments alarmed both the orthodox or "Old School" Presbyterians and those who wished to preserve slavery. Abolitionism was not inconsistent with the Old School position; however, the inherently conservative stance of the Old School, as the historian Irving Stoddard Kull observed, meant they were "no more disposed to tamper with the social order than with true doctrine."[112] These overlapping concerns and commitments formed the ground for an alliance: the Old School agreed to leave the subject of slavery completely alone if they received Southern support in ousting the New School.[113] With Southern delegates voting as a block in support of Old School motions, the enemies of New School theology and abolitionism passed a motion that declared the Plan of Union of 1801, "was originally an unconstitutional act on the part of the Assembly."[114] This meant that the four synods brought into being after 1801 under the Plan of Union simply ceased to exist and the General Assembly discounted their delegates' votes.[115] This maneuvering led the following year to the New School delegates forming an alternative Assembly.

The schism of 1837–1838 left the Old School with its conservative Calvinism in control of the Presbyterian Church in the United States of America and removed any danger that its General Assembly would declare slaveholding a sin.[116] With the removal of the Congregationalists accomplished, the Presbyterian Church now proclaimed the benefits of slavery. A pastoral letter, "Narrative of the State of Religion," included in the minutes for the assembly for 1837, postulated the benefits of slavery for the church's mission: "To what source so promising can we turn for missionaries to traverse the sands of Africa, as to this numerous people? They are providentially placed among us." The letter continued with a reminder that freedom for slaves lay in the private sphere of personal salvation rather than the political sphere of emancipation: "The prayer of every benevolent heart should ascend to God for their best interests, and especially that all classes of them may be delivered from that worst of bondage, the thralldom of sin and Satan."[117]

The General Assembly's decision that Presbyterians could continue as slaveholders was good news for the newly formed congregation in Jackson, Mississippi, some of whose members were undoubtedly slave owners themselves. The records of the congregation show on April 1, 1842, there were twenty-seven white and twelve black members who were almost certainly slaves owned by white members of the church.[118] This small band met in the Methodist church and the Baptist Church before holding the first service in their own building on February 1, 1846.[119] The church, located on the northwest corner of Yazoo and State streets, could accommodate nearly a thousand congregants.[120]

The congregation had difficulty recruiting and retaining ministers: the church had eight ministers in its first twenty-one years.[121] Part of the problem was that Jackson was not the most desirable of places to live. Although the city itself was set up on high ground on the west bank of the Pearl River, to the east lay swampy land. Residents complained of mosquitoes "so numerous and hungry that we all look as if we had small pox."[122] Consequently, malaria and the dreaded yellow fever blighted the city.[123] Epidemics of yellow fever, or "the yellow jack," swept the city between 1852 and 1855.[124] In 1855, the disease caused families to flee the city and the churches to close their doors.[125] Stability came to the Presbyterian Church in Jackson in 1858 with the appointment of the Reverend John Hunter.[126] Hunter, an Irishman by birth, served as the pastor for thirty-eight years.[127] At the time of his appointment, the greatest threat facing Jackson and Mississippi was not yellow fever but war.

James Henley Thornwell, Providence, and Slavery

From the 1830s until the Civil War, the abolitionists took an increasingly militant position: where once they had advocated—with some success—voluntary emancipation, they now demanded immediate abolition.[128] Abolitionists had a persuasive moral case but their opponents attempted to rise to the intellectual challenge to counter this threat to private property and ecclesial harmony. The Presbyterian Church, through the work of men such as James Henley Thornwell of South Carolina, produced perhaps the most sophisticated theological arguments in defense of slavery.[129]

Thornwell was a conservative Calvinist of the Old School; one of his contemporaries joked that he "would brand the Apostles themselves . . . as apostates, if they did not subscribe to the Westminster Catechism."[130] As a good Calvinist, Thornwell believed himself to be a part of the covenant community of God, a continuation of the covenant that God established with Abraham. The covenant, originally marked by circumcision, now by baptism, extended to the children of the covenant community. Thornwell, in a long article with the euphemistic title "The Baptism of Servants," extended the covenant still further to include "the household" of the patriarch. Just as Abraham had to circumcise his entire household, so, Thornwell believed, Christian slaveholders should baptize their slaves.[131] In a later sermon, *The Rights and Duties of Masters*, he attempted to demonstrate how the abolitionists' criticisms of slavery were in fact not arguments for emancipation; rather, they were arguments against the abuses of slavery with which, he explained, he was in full agreement. Instead of calling for the abolition of slavery, Thornwell urged Christian slave masters to reform, not abolish, the institution.[132] Slavery was, after all an institution that God, in his "inscrutable Providence" had arranged for the enslaved Africans' "moral progress." The condition of slavery would not suit the temperament of white Americans, Thornwell explained to his white audience; however, "subjugation to a master, [is] the state in which the African is most effectually trained to the moral end of his being." Thornwell concluded, "Slavery may be a good, or to speak more accurately, a condition, though founded in a curse, from which the Providence of God extracts a blessing."[133]

For Thornwell, and those who shared his view of slavery as an instrument of God's providence, the abolitionists had an "awful temerity to tamper" with this divine scheme.[134] It was both blasphemous and futile, Thornwell maintained, to try to abolish slavery as both scripture and "the universal custom of mankind" supported the place of slavery in a divinely ordered society.[135] International condemnation merely confirmed Thornwell's worldview for, "God has not permitted such a remarkable phenomenon as the unanimity of the civilized world, in its execration of slavery, to take place without design.... God will vindicate the appointments of His Providence...we can receive the assault of the civilized world."[136]

On January 9, 1861, Mississippi set itself to receive "the assault of the civilized world" when the upper house of the state legislature, following the prayers of William C. Crane, the rector of St. Andrews, Jackson, voted to secede from the Union.[137] The assault came to Jackson in the summer of 1863. In May, General Sherman took the city, destroying the railroad tracks and any public property deemed to be aiding the war effort. His troops rampaged through the city. They burned the Roman Catholic Church, two hospitals, a bank, and a block between City Hall and the State House.[138] Sherman took the city again in July. In his report he noted, "The city with the destruction committed by ourselves in May last and by the enemy during this siege, is one mass of charred ruins."[139] The correspondent for the *Chicago Times* with the Union forces reported, "The entire business portion of the city is in ruins except a few old frame buildings."[140] Jackson's smoldering ruins earned the city the name "Chimneyville."[141] The war wreaked a terrible toll on Mississippi. By the end of the conflict in 1865, Mississippi's cities were in ruins; the economy was shattered; and a quarter of the state's white men who were of military age in 1860, were dead.[142]

The Civil War left lasting scars on Southern Presbyterian theology and fractured the national denomination into two regional churches. In May 1861, with all but two of the Southern states having seceded from the Union, the General Assembly of the Presbyterian Church (Old School) met in Philadelphia and pledged its allegiance to the Federal Government. The Southern delegates withdrew from the Assembly and called for a meeting in Augusta, Georgia. On December 4, 1861, the representatives of forty-seven Southern presbyteries formed the Assembly of the Presbyterian Church in the Confederate States of America (PCCSA).[143] Thornwell endorsed the new church in an address to its first assembly entitled "To all the Churches of Jesus Christ throughout the

Earth." Slavery, Thornwell recognized, was at the heart of the split: "[it is the] one difference which so radically and fundamentally distinguishes the North and the South, that it is becoming everyday more apparent that the religious, as well as the secular interests of both will be effectively promoted by complete and lasting separation."[144]

The regrettable split in the church, Thornwell believed, had been precipitated by Northern Presbyterians. Their fault had been in insisting that the church take sides on the issue of slavery. In making his case, Thornwell laid the groundwork for what would become the doctrine of the spirituality of the church:

> The provinces of the Church and State are perfectly distinct, and the one has no right to usurp the jurisdiction of the other. The State is a natural institute, founded in the constitution of man as moral and social, and designed to realize the idea of justice. It is the society of rights. The Church is a supernatural institution, founded on the facts of redemption, and is designed to realize the idea of grace. It is the society of the redeemed. The State aims at social order; the Church at spiritual holiness. The state looks to the visible and outward; the Church is concerned for the invisible and inward.... They are as planets moving in different orbits.[145]

As the historian Jack P. Maddex demonstrates, Thornwell never intended this to mean that churches could not "address the state and to endorse or condemn societies' programs."[146] However, following the Civil War, this is exactly how Southern Presbyterians came to understand Thornwell's position. With the crushing defeat of the Confederacy—the cause so many Southerners believed ordained by Providence—Presbyterians were less inclined to proclaim divine sanction for human politics. The Southern Church's General Assembly of 1865 drew the conclusion that only as "a spiritual kingdom" independent of politics could the church survive the fall of earthly regimes.[147] Selectively drawing on the writings of Thornwell, his pupils, the influential postbellum divines Robert L. Dabney and Benjamin M. Palmer, established the spirituality of the church as one of the Southern church's key doctrines.[148]

Jim Crow and the Church, 1865–1896

With the end of the war came a new relationship between whites and blacks in Mississippi. The occupying federal troops organized the registration of eligible voters, which included the freed slaves. Before the election of 1867, 79,176 blacks and 58,385 whites registered to vote. Many whites stayed away from the polls in protest and the Republicans, with the support of freed slaves, won decisively. Their victory led to the inclusion of the Fourteenth and Fifteenth Amendments against voter discrimination in the state's new constitution.[149] Learning their lesson, in 1868, the Democrats started to intimidate black voters: they recorded the names of black voters at the polls, threatening to have them sacked from their jobs if they voted Republican.[150] In 1875, W. Calvin Wells, the secretary of the Democratic campaign committee for Hinds County and future elder at First Presbyterian Church, Jackson, helped coordinate a strategy to defeat the Republicans. Known as the "Mississippi Plan," Wells' scheme included intimidation, bribery, deception, and fraud.[151] "We were *forced* to a choice between the evils of Negro rule and the evils of the questionable practices to overthrow it," Wells wrote thirty years later. "We chose what we thought to be the lesser evil, and it is now not to be regretted."[152] The methods proved so effective that by 1876 the Democrats had regained control of every branch of the state's government.[153]

The political turmoil only briefly slowed the state's economic development. In the 1880s, railroad companies drove tracks through the fast disappearing wilderness of the Delta. Towns sprang up along the lines and planters and loggers could now move their cotton and timber to market with ease.[154] By 1884, Jackson had become a transport hub with seven railroad lines coming into the city. The railway lines brought raw materials and people to the city's fledgling industries and processing plants.[155] The Presbyterian Church, under the leadership of John Hunter, now had a congregation of around two hundred. With the population of Jackson increasing every year and new wealth starting to banish the privations, if not the memory, of the Civil War, the congregation decided to build a new church at a cost of around $18,000. They held their last service in the old building on July 19, 1891, and on May 14, 1893, they moved into what the *Clarion-Ledger* reported approvingly as, "a handsome, Gothic structure."[156]

Presbyterians in Jackson built their new church as the architects of white supremacy secured the foundations of segregation in Mississippi. In 1890, the state legislature passed a new constitution disenfranchising African American citizens of the state for the next seventy-four years.[157] The new constitution included the "Understanding Clause" requiring a person registering to vote to be able to read and give "a reasonable interpretation" of a section of the constitution and the payment of poll tax for two years before registering.[158]

The constitution of 1890 was just one more step in legalizing the new codes of social and political exclusion that had replaced the old slave codes in Mississippi. For the first two decades after the war, these new codes were informal in nature, though almost universally understood by whites and African

Americans. African Americans found themselves increasingly denied access to restaurants, parks, theatres, railway cars and steamboat salons.[159] Mississippi, along with other Southern states, gradually formalized these discriminatory practices in what became know as the Jim Crow laws. In 1888, the state legislature passed a law requiring separate accommodations on railroads.[160] The Federal Supreme Court offered no opposition to the growing number of Jim Crow laws when in the infamous 1896 case, *Plessy v. Ferguson,* the justices ruled that separation of the two races did not mean they were any less equal under the law.[161]

The PCUS had embraced the new Southern custom of segregation long before the Supreme Court ruled in Jim Crow's favor. In 1869, the General Assembly adopted measures anticipating separate denominations for white and African American Presbyterians. In 1874, they approved the establishment of Stillman College in Tuscaloosa, Alabama, "an institution for the training of the colored ministry."[162] Next, the General Assembly's Committee on Home Missions formed Presbyteries specifically for African American congregations including Ethel Presbytery in Mississippi. By 1898, the General Assembly felt the time had come for African American Presbyterians to form their own denomination. The Afro-American Presbyterian Church, however, failed to thrive, and so in 1915 the Afro-American presbyteries organized into a constituent synod of the PCUS called the Snedecor Memorial Synod.[163]

The distinctive attitude of Southern white society towards race hampered attempts to reunite the PCUS with the Northern Presbyterian Church (PCUSA). Often talked about, the General Assembly first seriously considered union with the Northern church in 1918 when it appointed a committee to look into organic union.[164] Delegate John M. Wells of the First Presbyterian Church, Jackson opposed union on the floor of the Assembly on three grounds: doctrinal differences, the differing attitude toward "the Negroes," and "the continuing political deliverances by the Northern Church."[165] Of particular concern to him was the difference over the doctrine of the spirituality of the church.

Since the beginning of the century, Southern Presbyterians considered the spirituality of the church a distinctive doctrine of their denomination.[166] In 1901, Thomas Cary Johnson, a professor at Union Theological Seminary in Richmond, Virginia, listed the "spirituality of the church, both in practice as well as theory" in his five distinctives of the PCUS.[167] The areas of disagreement between the Northern and Southern church of doctrine, race, and the spirituality of the church intertwine and thread through Southern Presbyterian debates. As the twentieth century progressed, political, theological, and ecumenical developments in the church and the country amplified these themes until they exploded in acrimonious schism.

Race and the Rise of Fundamentalism, 1896–1954

When Dr. James Buchanan Hutton succeeded Dr. Hunter at First Presbyterian Church in 1896, there were no inklings of the impending crises that would rupture the fabric of the region and church. An earnest man, throughout his ministry Hutton worked for moral regeneration and Sabbath observance in Jackson; his obituary memorialized his fight against "the traffic in the virtue of women, in liquor, and in gambling."[168] Serving the church for nearly forty-four years, Hutton saw the impact of modernity on both the city of Jackson and the Southern Presbyterian Church.

At the start of Hutton's ministry, Jackson, with a population of around six thousand, was still only the fourth largest city in the state. The growth in industry made possible by the railroads meant that by 1920, the city numbered 21,262, and by Hutton's death in 1940, the census recorded Jackson's population at 62,107.[169] Continuity in the city's political and social structures aided this period of prosperity. Between 1917 and 1945, the city's Commissioners remained unchanged. These three white men boasted of their "harmony ... [with] the business interests of the city."[170] The churches expanded to meet the needs of the growing population. First Presbyterian Church under Hutton planted three churches in the new suburbs: Central (1898), Power Memorial (1924), and Fondren (1930).[171]

While the city grew as a bifurcated community, divided socially and geographically by Jim Crow laws, churchgoing whites did concern themselves with the welfare of African Americans. They saw the matter of race relations in paternalistic terms, assisting Negro institutions in the work of advancing their race. Presbyterians were particularly notable in their support of education. Throughout the 1930s, Jackson College struggled financially after the Baptist Home Mission had withdrawn its funding of the African American college.[172] The College tried to secure state institution status and funding, but the legislature turned down their requests in 1936, and again in 1938. Worthy white churchgoers formed the Religious Conference Groups with the aim "that if sufficient evidence of all-out co-operation, regardless of differences, could be shown to the authorities, then there was every hope that sympathy and a strong positive belief of a successful future could eventually persuade the Powers-that-Be to act." These groups, noted B. Baldwin Dansby, the college president, were "over-all Presbyterian."[173]

Despite such acts of paternalistic concern, white Mississippians were aware that their Jim Crow laws, ideology of white supremacy, and record of lynchings garnered criticism from much of the nation. During the 1930s, the NAACP shone a harsh light on Mississippi during its unsuccessful attempts to pass federal antilynching legislation.[174] Dansby, the president of Jackson College, took note of the apparent contradiction between the external criticism of Jim Crow Mississippi and the piety of her white Citizens:

> The State of Mississippi was always before the gaze of the nation, but regardless of what were the recurrent defects, politically, socially or otherwise, defects that persisted in the creation of a negative atmosphere as far as the rest of the country was concerned, her devotion to the church and her insistence upon functional religion were well established.[175]

Mississippi's conservative equilibrium shaped by white supremacy and "devotion to the church" faced internal as well as external challenges. In the 1920s, conservative Presbyterians grew increasingly concerned at the rise of the liberal German school of biblical criticism in their denomination's seminaries. This modern trend in biblical scholarship wished to demythologize the text of the Bible and throw into question the historicity of the miracles, virgin birth, and physical resurrection of Christ. These conservative Presbyterians became part of the fundamentalist movement that, according to historian George Marsden, "opposed both modernism in theology and the cultural changes that modernism endorsed."[176] In 1923, J. Gresham Machen, a professor at Princeton and vigorous proponent of Old School theology, published an attack on modern theological trends. In his book *Christianity and Liberalism,* Machen rejected modernism in favor of the fundamentals of the Christian faith enshrined in the traditional Calvinist doctrines of the faith and supported by the inerrant words of scripture.[177] Resigning from Princeton Seminary in 1929, Machen founded Westminster Theological Seminary in Philadelphia, and in 1936 left the PCUSA to form a new denomination called the Orthodox Presbyterian Church (OPC).[178]

Although Machen's conflicts took place in the Northern Church, Southern Presbyterians watched developments with a keen interest. Machen's denunciation of the PCUSA for departing from traditional doctrines lent ammunition to those opposed to union with the Northern Presbyterians. Machen and Westminster Seminary found strong support in Mississippi. During the 1930s, both Machen and Cornelius Van Til, Westminster Seminary's professor of apologetics, spoke at Synod of Mississippi youth conferences.[179] J. B Hutton, the minister at First Presbyterian Church, Jackson and editor of *Mississippi Visitor,* publicly backed the Northern Conservatives. With his encouragement, churches in the Central Mississippi Presbytery called Westminster Seminary graduates to fill their pulpits.[180] The fundamentalism of Westminster Seminary gave energy and resources to conservative Southern Presbyterians at a time when progressives within their denomination were attacking their traditional defense against social change: the spirituality of the church.[181]

Between the wars, the influence of the social gospel movement and the widespread hardships of the depression caused many Southern Presbyterians to reassess their traditional view of the Church as a strictly spiritual entity. In 1934, the General Assembly established the Permanent Committee on Moral and Social Welfare. The following year, the General Assembly adopted its report without debate. The report refuted the denomination's "historic position…that the power of the church is exclusively spiritual"; instead, "the Church must interpret and present Christ's ideal for the individual and society." The Church, therefore, has a responsibility to "deal with those actual evils in the individual life, and in the social order which threaten man's moral and spiritual development, which hinder the progress of God's Kingdom here on earth, and which produce needless suffering."[182] No one had to wait long to find out which "actual evils" the Committee felt were most pressing. In 1936, the committee presented a report highlighting the plight of the "Negroes in the South."[183]

The desire of the progressive members of the PCUS to address social injustice and race relations came with an accompanying push towards ecumenism and doctrinal reform. All three of these areas would need to change if a union with the Northern church could ever be possible. Although those in favor of change described this as a movement toward "spiritual" and "ethical maturity," the traditionalists saw this as a dangerous departure from the distinctive doctrines of the denomination.[184]

To understand the role race played in the ensuing struggle, it is essential to realize the inextricable interconnection at this time between: liberal theology with its use of sociology and biblical criticism; the ecumenical movement and the Federal Council of Churches' social pronouncements; and the movement to reunite the Presbyterian churches with the doctrinal and social compromises required to make this possible. These progressive movements threatened the ordered worldview of their traditionalist opponents. Fighting to be true to their religion and received social hierarchy of caste and class, Southern conservatives felt it imperative to hold their ground on the inerrancy of scripture and a rigid subscription to the Westminster Confession of Faith. In the battle to resist the erosion of religious and social traditions, the spirituality of the church formed the wall of the conservative's bastion. To extend the metaphor, the besiegers tried to breach the wall at its most vulnerable point: segregation. The defenders managed to hold on to segregation for a protracted siege of thirty years using the weapons of tradition, doctrine, and theology.

In 1942, Dr. L. Nelson Bell, a former missionary and father-in-law to Billy Graham, started publishing *Southern Presbyterian Journal*.[185] Founded in response to the PCUS's reentry into the Federal Council of Churches (FCC) and the growing momentum towards union with the PCUSA, the journal promoted fundamentalist theology and supported segregation.[186] The journal became the mouthpiece for a conservative group within the PCUS calling themselves the Continuing Church Movement. The Synod of Mississippi threw its weight behind the movement to stop the union and the attendant reforms of doctrine and social policy. In 1944, W. Calvin Wells, grandson of the W. Calvin Wells of Reconstruction fame, elder at First Presbyterian Church, and the Synod of Mississippi's representative on the General Assembly's Committee on Cooperation and Union, issued a public challenge in the pages of the *Southern Presbyterian Journal*.[187] Union, Wells believed, would result in a terrible compromise of orthodox Presbyterian Christianity. After outlining the extent of liberal belief in the Northern church, Wells concluded that union would lead to "those who believe the Bible is verily God's Word, which teaches the doctrines as set forth in our Confession of Faith and the Larger and Shorter Catechisms," being, "ridiculed, overwhelmed with votes to the contrary, and...expelled or excommunicated."[188]

The Synod of Mississippi, and the First Presbyterian Church in Jackson in particular, gained a reputation as a stronghold of opposition to the changes taking place in the PCUS. Through the 1940s, the church grew under the leadership of R. Girard Lowe, remembered fondly as a "consecrated, spiritually-minded, conservative man of God."[189] Lowe's death in 1951, just months before the completion of a new church building on North State Street, left the elders casting about for a suitably conservative candidate for the pulpit in the new sanctuary.[190] They found John Reed Miller, a professor at Belhaven College and minister at the new Trinity Presbyterian Church on Northside Drive.[191]

John Reed Miller was a powerful preacher and an ardent conservative Calvinist of the Machen school. A native of Pittsburgh and formerly professor at the all-black Knoxville College, he found an eager audience in Mississippi for his ultraconservative brand of theology. Miller's militant stand against theological liberalism in the PCUS formed a symbiotic relationship of conservative resistance with the First Church's militant social conservatism. As the PCUS continued its move towards union, the conservatives started to prepare for the day that they might have to leave the denomination. Miller advised members of his church against going to any of the PCUS's liberal seminaries, directing them instead to the OPC's Westminster Seminary in Philadelphia.[192] Westminster Seminary in turn recommended its graduates consider pulpits in Mississippi, describing it as "one particular bright spot in the Southern church."[193] In 1957, the liberal PCUS journal *The Presbyterian Outlook* ran an investigative exposé of churches in Mississippi apparently preparing to leave the PCUS to join the OPC. The article entitled "Infiltration—To What End?" identified Miller and a professor at Belhaven College called Morton Smith as the architects of the OPC "infiltration."[194] Historians of the subsequent split in the PCUS support the findings of the article and point to Miller's significant influence on churches in Mississippi and to his connections with Westminster Seminary.[195]

By the time the General Assembly met in 1954, conservatives and liberals were warring on the two fronts of segregation and union in their battle for the PCUS. The Assembly approved a plan of union and sent it to the presbyteries for their decision. Conservatives, led by Bell, through vigorous campaigning, managed to stop the plan from receiving the support of the three quarters of the presbyteries it required to proceed.

At the same Assembly, the Council on Christian Relations presented a report on segregation. Condemning segregation as "discrimination which is out of harmony with Christian theology and ethics," they recommended, "the church, in its relationship to cultural patterns, should lead rather than follow."[196] The acceptance of the report led to the Assembly issuing "*A Statement to Southern Christians*" declaring support for the recent Supreme Court's Decision in the school desegregation case *Brown vs. Board of Education of Topeka, Kansas.*[197]

The Spirituality of the Closed Church

Massive Resistance, 1954–1964

In the summer of 1954, First Presbyterian Church, Jackson stood with Mississippi's state legislature and the newly organized Citizens' Councils in their determination to challenge the federal ruling and defend white supremacy. First Presbyterian Church, Jackson distinguished itself by having one of two church sessions in the PCUS that *unanimously* dissented from the denomination's support of *Brown vs. Board.*[198] Its elders issued a statement denouncing the Assembly's recommendation as wrong to claim that segregation of the races was discrimination. Such a suggestion threatened "the peace and purity of the church"; consequently, First Presbyterian Church would "maintain its traditional practice of distinct separation of the races."[199] The church received the support of the Synod of Mississippi, which sent an overture to the next General Assembly asking them to rescind the statement and "to redefine the functions of the... Council on Christian Relations."[200]

Those Presbyterians wishing to be convinced of the necessity of segregation and white supremacy could find eminent and intellectual members of
their own community to reassure them. Dr. Guy T. Gillespie, the retired president of Jackson's Belhaven College and architect of the synod's dissenting overture, presented an intellectual argument for the segregation of the races. In an
address, later printed and widely circulated both by the Citizens' Councils and
by the liberal *Presbyterian Outlook,* Gillespie set out his case. America faced a
choice between "the Anglo Saxon ideal of racial integrity . . . and the Communist
goal of amalgamation." The weight of his argument rested on his observation that segregation is "one of nature's universal laws" and is a "time-tested
national policy." Segregation's proponents, he maintained, engaged in "racial
pride" not "race prejudice."[201] Gillespie was careful to acknowledge, "The Bible
contains no clear mandate for or against segregation;" however, he argued,
"valid inferences can be drawn in support of the general principle of segregation as an important feature of the divine plan throughout the ages."[202]

No matter how erudite the arguments for segregation, and there were
many, the strongest case against the Presbyterian church's denunciation of
segregation still rested not in theological cases for segregation but in an appeal
to the spirituality of the church. In 1957, in a carefully worded response to further pronouncements by the Council on Christian Relations, First Presbyterian
Church set out its case against the church's interference in the political issue
of segregation:

> The Session does not feel that the Presbyterian Church in the United
> States should take any action with reference to current social, politi-
> cal and economic problems . . . an organized church should exist only
> for the purpose of stimulating and strengthening its members and
> for coordinating and implementing their activities in bringing others
> to know Him and serve Him.[203]

The individual Christian should "seek to correct injustices and defects in our
social, political and economic order" but exactly what constitutes an injustice
should remain a "private judgment in all secular matters."[204] Published in
the pages of *The Southern Presbyterian Journal,* the statement objected to the
General Assembly's condemnation of severe literary tests as requirements for
voting, segregated schools, and the Citizen's Councils. It also strongly con-
tested the notion that "freedom of fellowship" should extend to "an unnatural
association of people."[205]

Members of First Presbyterian Church, who included some of the most
powerful and influential men in Jackson, tended to use their "private judgment
in all secular matters" to defend the existing social, political, and economic

order.[206] The church itself encouraged its members in their participation in the Citizens' Councils: in the 1957 statement the Session declared, "There are numerous citizen's councils and groups throughout the South which are composed of Christian citizens of the highest type."[207] Elders of First Presbyterian Church were involved at the highest level in the Citizens' Council. Two attorneys and highly regarded elders in the church, Robert C. Cannada and Erskine Wells (another descendent of W. Calvin Wells), served as directors of Jackson's Citizens' Council.[208] Civil rights activists were well aware of the church's support for the organization Hodding Carter called the "Uptown Klan" and labeled its minister, John Reid Miller, "chaplain of the white Citizens' Council of Mississippi."[209]

Robert C. Cannada, in his professional capacity as attorney for the city, had a grandstand view of the changes that activists backed by federal legislation were trying to bring to Mississippi: he defended the City of Jackson when the NAACP field secretary Medgar Evers brought a case against the city's segregated public schools.[210] Leon F. Hendrick was another elder at First Presbyterian Church whose private judgement in secular matters defended segregation.[211] A circuit court judge during the civil rights movement, Hendrick signed off on the order that allowed police arresting Freedom Riders in Jackson to transfer them straight to Parchman, the state penitentiary.[212] Hendrick also presided over the two farcical trials of Byron de la Beckwith—Medgar Evers' assassin.[213] In 1962, the civil rights movement placed Hendrick on the other side of the bench when, as the Chairman of Jackson's Library board, he found himself a defendant in a case brought by two African American students from Tougaloo College. Police had arrested the students the previous year during a "read-in" at the city's municipal library.[214]

These students were part of a coordinated civil rights campaign in Jackson that, in addition to challenging segregation in waiting rooms, lunch counters, and libraries, also targeted the segregationist policies of the city's white churches. On Sunday, June 9, 1963, Ed King, the new chaplain of Tougaloo College, started a "pray-in" campaign in which groups of black and white students sought admission to worship services at Jackson's white downtown congregations.[215] Three days later Jackson's citizens woke up to the news of Medgar Evers' assassination. That next Sunday, First Presbyterian Church, First Baptist Church and Galloway United Methodist Church turned away groups of Tougaloo students, their numbers swelled by out-of-town visitors for Evers' funeral.[216] St. Andrews Episcopal Cathedral, however, admitted one of the groups. The news flashed across the wire, but the other churches, including First Presbyterian Church, continued to keep their doors firmly closed to racially integrated worship.[217]

A month later, John Reid Miller received word from a Methodist minister from New Haven, Connecticut, that he would be visiting First Presbyterian Church on Sunday, July 28, with a group of black and white students currently attending a World Council of Churches' work camp at Tougaloo College. While policemen hovered nearby in case of trouble, ushers barred nine white and two black students from entering the church.[218] Ed King recalled, "There had been no arrests at Presbyterian churches...although the doors were closed and the police guards were always present and often threatened visiting groups."[219] Jackson's Citizens' Council shared First Presbyterian Church's resolve to "maintain its traditional practice of distinct separation of the races."[220] In late September, with the church's elders Erskine Wells and Robert C. Cannada serving as directors, Jackson's press reported, "Jackson Citizens' Council...would develop a plan to eliminate integration in local churches."[221]

Accommodation in Society and Secession in the Church, 1964–1973

As activists beat on the doors of the Closed Society and marshaled the force of the courts, Presbyterians like Cannada realized that change would come to Mississippi; the doctrine of the spirituality of the church informed their response to this change. Thornwell had insisted the divinely ordained role of the state is "to realize the idea of justice" to ensure "social order."[222] Therefore, the Christian of good conscience must obey the law and work to bring about a peaceful social order. As Massive Resistance gave way to strategic accommodation, Cannada agreed to serve as a director of Jackson's Citizens' Council from 1963 to 1965 because he understood it to be his civic responsibility. He believed that for Mississippi to avoid violence and a breakdown in law and order during this difficult time, responsible and respectable Christian citizens needed to guide the process and shape the outcome.[223]

Paul Johnson's election as governor in 1964 marked the move from "bitter-end" resistance to desegregation in Mississippi.[224] In his inaugural address, Johnson announced, "If I must fight, it will not be a rearguard defense of yesterday...it will be an all-out assault for our share of tomorrow."[225] The Citizens' Councils also changed their tune: they abandoned the strategy of resistance to desegregation of public schools, adopting instead a strategy of starting private whites-only schools. In August 1964, Jackson's Citizens' Council, with Cannada on the board, announced the opening of Council School No. 1 in Jackson. The September issue of *The Citizen* was entirely devoted to "How to Start a Private School" that would better "teach the importance of racial integrity."[226] The school opened late in November with only twenty-two pupils in six grades. Undaunted, they relaunched the school with greater success in

1965. By 1966, the Citizens' Councils of America announced, "promotion of segregated private education is the major project of the Citizens' Councils."[227] As a legal and peaceful way of thwarting the intention of federal legislation, the plan was brilliant. It was not until 1970 that Mississippi, under federal pressure, finally had to stop running a segregated school system. In the meantime, Cannada, the attorney for the Jackson Municipal School District, joined the Public School District Lawyers' Committee. Formed in 1966 by the Mississippi State Bar, the Committee gave legal advice to support school districts fighting desegregation lawsuits.[228]

In 1965, First Presbyterian Church opened a day school operating from the church buildings on North State Street. Cannada, with his expertise and insight into the future of the city's school system, was one of the originators of the idea to start a school. Forty years after the school opened, Cannada claimed that the church simply desired to provide a particular type of Christian education, not thwart school desegregation.[229] Historian Joseph Crespino points out that "whites could and did distinguish between white-flight private schools—or 'segregation academies'—and schools founded by Christian parents trying to provide a holistic religious orientation for their child's education."[230] However, as in the case of First Presbyterian Church Day School, the definition between the two is not always clear. Certainly, the timing of the decision to start the school is a little difficult to overlook. Whether intentional or not, First Presbyterian Church Day School opened its doors as the Citizens' Council's campaign to preserve racial integrity shifted to opening private schools.

Applying the logic of the spirituality of the church, one might think that operating a school meant that First Presbyterian Church was straying outside its spiritual mission. But this was not how the church session understood the matter. According to Thornwell, the state's concern is the lawful preservation of public order; "the Church is a supernatural institution, founded on the facts of redemption, and is designed to realize the idea of grace" whose "provinces" are "perfectly distinct" from the State.[231] Put simply, the state defends the peace while the church holds fast to the truth. According to this view, accommodation to liberal demands is a possible course of action for the State, but the Church can never compromise the truth. If starting a school provided the church's children with an education built on "the facts of redemption," then it easily fell within the province of the Church as set out by Thornwell. From the perspective of the leadership of First Presbyterian Church, the imminent desegregation of the city schools was simply another symptom of the wave of liberalism that the church was duty-bound to resist.

Just as First Presbyterian Church countered the liberal influence in the public school system by founding the day school, they resisted the liberal turn in the PCUS by starting their own seminary. John Reid Miller and his colleagues in the Central Mississippi Presbytery had for some time been unhappy sending students to any of the denomination's seminaries. First Presbyterian Church had supported the OPC's Westminster seminary, and in June 1960, the church offered a large gift to the PCUS's Columbia Seminary with the condition that the seminary place theological restrictions on professors and maintain a whites-only enrollment policy. Columbia refused the gift.[232] In the early 1960s, Miller, who had already started a winter theological institute at First Presbyterian Church, pushed for the foundation of a seminary.[233] Among the key individuals in the movement to start a seminary were Robert Cannada and Erskine Wells, both of whom were attorneys, First Presbyterian Church elders and Citizens' Council directors.[234] With financial support in place for a seminary, there was debate over where it should be located; the founders were reluctant to start the seminary in Jackson in the midst of the racial unrest in the city. They were, however, left with no choice when, according to Cannada's son, it transpired that Jackson "was [in] the only presbytery in the old Southern Presbyterian Church that would support this new independent conservative seminary and let its ministers teach in that seminary."[235]

In 1964, Reformed Theological Seminary (RTS) opened in Jackson, Mississippi. Designed to resist any liberal interference from the PCUS, RTS was free from any denominational affiliation and its board consisted entirely of laymen.[236] Teachers had to stand by the "absolute inerrancy" of the Bible and subscribe to "the Westminster Confession of Faith...as originally adopted by the Presbyterian Church in the United States."[237] The seminary had such strong links with First Presbyterian Church that thirty-five years later the church's minister could joke, "We are RTS and RTS is us."[238] Cannada personified this connection as a ruling elder at First Presbyterian Church, chairman of the RTS Board of Trustees, and chairman of the Executive Committee of the Board for thirty-four years. His son, Robert C. "Rick" Cannada served as Executive Vice President of RTS.[239] While claiming neutrality, RTS produced ministers who opposed the moves towards union in the PCUS and considered the progressive social pronouncements and activism within the main denomination a betrayal of the distinctive doctrine of the spirituality of the church. Many of these RTS graduates became instrumental in leading their congregations out of the PCUS.[240]

Although whites in Mississippi and across the South grudgingly ceded the public sphere to federal demands for desegregation, the battle against the liberals' incursion into the Closed Society now raged in the private sphere of the Church: in that sphere, they were determined there would be no compromise. In 1973, following a decade of increasingly acrimonious debate and political maneuvering, the Presbyterian Church in America (PCA) split from the PCUS.[241] Throughout the 1960s, an ecumenical and civil rights agenda, to the horror of the conservatives, had driven much of the denomination's proceedings. In 1963, the World Council of Churches, with delegates from the PCUS, designated Mississippi a mission field on account of the state's poverty and racism. The PCUS's contributions to the National Council of Churches went in part to the Delta Ministry established in Mississippi in 1964, just in time to support SNCC's Freedom Summer.[242] The Central Mississippi Presbytery protested: in a resolution adopted on April 16, 1964, they refused to recognize the World or National Council of Churches and objected in the strongest terms to the Delta Ministry. "The preaching of the word of God would be seriously hindered," they insisted, "and relations between the races would be disrupted." The text, reported in the Jackson papers, continued in prose that civil rights activists interpreted as a threat: "[We protest] all those agencies cooperating with them in this project which will promote lawlessness and the flagrant violation of the inherent right of all citizens of the state of Mississippi. We insist such action will certainly result in violence, bloodshed, and possible death."[243]

That same year, following the General Assembly's failure to endorse civil rights legislation, liberal Presbyterians formed the Fellowship of Concern, a group dedicated to moving the PCUS General Assembly toward racial reconciliation.[244] In response to this group, the conservative Continuing Church Committee formed the Concerned Presbyterians to put forward the opposing position.[245] As momentum grew toward a final showdown, various other conservative groups formed. One of the most significant was Presbyterian Churchmen United, whose founders included Morton Smith and Donald Patterson, soon to be called as the minister to First Presbyterian Church.[246]

Along with their main concerns over the ascendancy of liberal theology, support for the civil rights movement, and ecumenism, as the 1960s progressed, the conservatives increasingly voiced their concern at the growing influence of feminism, the antiwar movement and a change in teaching on personal sexual morality and abortion. One of the movements own apologists explained, "One of our most disturbing concerns was the determined effort being made by many liberal leaders to undermine not only the faith of our children and grandchildren but also their morals."[247]

By the beginning of the 1970s, the conservatives decided their future lay apart from the PCUS. On August 11, 1971, they announced the formation of a steering committee for the Continuing Presbyterian Church to be headed by Donald Patterson, the minister of First Presbyterian Church (he had succeeded Miller in 1969).[248] Moreton Smith, now a lecturer at RTS, wrote a book—bearing the obtuse title *How is the Gold Become Dim!*—setting out the case for the Continuing Presbyterian Church movement.[249]

Morton Smith's book demonstrates the continuing importance of the "spirituality" argument as the cornerstone for the conservatives' case and the connection between this doctrinal position and social conservatism. In the longest chapter in the book, Smith details the erosion of doctrine of the spirituality of the church and conservative Calvinism in the PCUS. In a point-by-point refutation of the 1954 General Assembly's document "The Church and Segregation," Smith appeals to the doctrine of limited atonement. The General Assembly was wrong to base their support for equal rights on "the infinite value of every person...demonstrated in the sacrificial death of Jesus Christ." For Smith, "[they] have departed from the Confession's view that the sacrifice of Christ is limited to the elect only."[250] The report is also wrong, contended Smith, to claim that the church's duty is to oppose segregation. Smith used arguments similar to those put forward by Gillespie nineteen years earlier. Because, Smith believed, the Bible neither explicitly endorses nor condemns segregation, "It is debatable as to whether the Church should get into the matter of trying to change that particular cultural pattern, and branding one form of culture sinful as opposed to another."[251]

Smith's book also demonstrates how, by 1973, new issues had joined the concern to preserve racial integrity voiced by Gillespie in 1954. Smith was outraged by a slew of liberal pronouncements from the General Assembly on social issues ranging from capital punishment, the war in Vietnam, equal opportunity housing, gun control, and abortion to changes in the Book of Church Order allowing women to serve as teaching and ruling elders and deacons in the Church.[252]

The split from the PCUS initially consisted of nearly forty-one thousand communicants in 260 churches. The strongholds of this new denomination were in the deep Southern states of Mississippi, Alabama and South Carolina.[253] On July 19, 1973, at First Presbyterian Church, thirty-eight of Central Mississippi Presbytery's seventy-three churches left the PCUS to form the Mississippi Valley Presbytery; joined by ten more congregations in the succeeding months, this meant that more churches left the PCUS in this presbytery than in any other.[254] First Presbyterian Church's influential presence in the old Central Mississippi Presbytery was the main cause for this flood of congregations supporting the schism.[255] The schism proved extremely traumatic for those on both sides. In a sermon delivered at the opening of their first General Assembly, the convener Jack Wilson said, "This separation has forced division among families, friends, and local congregations. It has been heartrending with many tears....[The] separation from fellow Christian friends is traumatic."[256]

Pride in their Presbyterian and Confederate heritage marked the new denomination. "The Reformed Faith as it has been embraced by Presbyterians," boasted Morton Smith, "is the purest form in which the Gospel has been manifested since the days of the Apostles, [and] the PCUS in its earlier years represented one of the greatest Churches ever to exist."[257] Calling themselves the National Presbyterian Church in America, they held their first General Assembly on December 4, 1973, at Briarwood Presbyterian Church in Birmingham, Alabama, one hundred and twelve years to the day after the PCCSA split from the National Church.[258] In 1861, the PCCSA had issued a statement by Thornwell entitled "To all the Churches of Jesus Christ throughout the Earth"; now in 1973 the new denomination issued a five-page declaration entitled "Message to all churches of Jesus Christ throughout the World." This document consciously echoed Thornwell in content as well as title. Seemingly unconcerned that Thornwell's argument for separation of the spheres of State and Church was rooted in the defense of slavery, the 1973 document reiterated his position: "We believe the church is a spiritual organism. It is our duty to set forth what God has given in His Word and to not devise our own message or legislate our own laws."[259]

Mission Mississippi and the Spirituality of the Church

In 1992, as Mission Mississippi took shape, James Baird and Lee Paris sought approval and advice from the elders at First Presbyterian Church; they invited the influential Robert C. Cannada to the first meeting at Primos in November 1992. Cannada was particularly close to Paris, and considered himself a mentor to the young Presbyterian businessman. As Paris worked founding Mission Mississippi, Cannada counseled him to make sure the organization stayed true to a traditional Southern Presbyterian understanding of the spiritual mission of the church and avoid having any political or economic objectives. Cannada was pleased with Mission Mississippi's "spiritual" emphasis on unity in the Church rather than any "political" call for the integration of the races and he offered his full support to the organization.[260]

When Baird and some elders at First Presbyterian Church received the first anonymous letter in December of 1993 condemning Mission Mississippi, Cannada tried to support Paris and Baird and calm the waters at the session by pointing out the solely spiritual nature of the organization. Cannada also drew up the resolution for the session that would still enable First Presbyterian Church to say they supported Mission Mississippi without any money coming from their budget. His effort to quash the dissent within the session clearly failed with the appearance of the second widely circulated letter in April 1994.

The second letter found a number of supporters in the congregation. "I would have calls at home well into the night with folks voicing their objections [to Mission Mississippi]," recalls Paris.[261] Although graciously appreciating the cultural legacy that prompted Mission Mississippi's detractors, Paris occasionally found himself caught off guard:

> "I had one lady tell me that she had known me all my life and known my family, and my grandmother would be turning over in her grave if she knew what was going on. And I told her that I could take all of her remarks but not that one. That, if I told my grandmother that I was doing…God's will…[then] my grandmother would be supportive of me.[262]

The Session, rather than dismissing the accusations as an echo from a darker time, afforded them almost unbelievable gravity. Despite James Baird's robust denunciation to the whole session of the charges leveled against the church and Mission Mississippi,[263] the elders formed the Mission Mississippi Ad-Hoc Committee to examine the charges in detail. Paris described what happened: "There were some very wise men on the session that were assigned to kick the tires in a way that I don't know if anything has been kicked—before or since—so hard."[264]

The committee canvassed church members for written responses to the question of First Presbyterian Church's involvement with Mission Mississippi. The Ad-Hoc Committee presented the session with a summary of the responses, noting in the introduction that of the thirty-five responses received by January 5, 1995, nearly a third were against the church continuing its support of Mission Mississippi. The collection of quotes from "Pro" respondents demonstrated an incredulity that anyone could object to Mission Mississippi given the urgent problems facing Jackson. Although harder to categorize, excerpts from the "Con" letters revealed a desire to maintain the purity of First Presbyterian Church's worship. Respondents feared that involvement with African American churches would lead to a contamination from such things as emotional and charismatic worship and political preaching on matters of race and economics.[265]

Following the Ad-Hoc Committee's report, in February 1995, the Session ratified their previous decision to support Mission Mississippi in name only. In addition, "the Session continues to decline recommending any particular action by…any group representing itself to be a part of the First Presbyterian Church." This prohibition included "Sunday School classes, members of the church staff, Women in the Church, church committees, organized choir, or other unit." If anyone wanted to be involved in a Mission Mississippi activity representing First Presbyterian Church then they must "request approval from the Session of such contemplated action."[266]

In a letter to a member of the session, Paris made clear his disappointment and distress that the church that had nurtured him in the faith could not support what he believed to be a ministry with a clear biblical mandate. "As you know, for the past two years I have poured my heart into this effort," Paris wrote. "It has been a heavy cross for me to bear not feeling the full support of the Church I love and serve as I labored for the Lord as He has called me."[267] Those on the Session who prolonged the deliberations on Mission Mississippi demonstrated their distrust of James Baird's judgment. With the resolution of the Session in February 1995 to support Mission Mississippi in name only, Baird must have been relieved the matter had reached some conclusion; however, following his retirement that December, the Session recalled the Ad-Hoc Committee to reopen their investigation of Mission Mississippi. Paris, with evident exasperation, wrote to the committee:

> That some would have doubts that Christ is at the center of His ministry of Mission Mississippi is difficult to comprehend. I would surmise that these men have had little personal experience of us....As to the question of causing disagreement within our particular church body...I would respectfully offer that decisions seeking to obey Christ have and always will meet opposition. It is not my place but our Session's call to determine the will of Christ for our Church. In doing so, I pray that *His* response is the only consideration.[268]

After months of continued deliberations, the committee could not fault Mission Mississippi. "Some godly men on that committee I think really tried to find every reason in the world that they could recommend back to the session not to support Mission Mississippi,"[269] explained Paris. "It was always the social gospel problem....They just could not believe that that's not what this is about."[270] Finally, after two years of investigation and withholding contributions, the Session reinstated Mission Mississippi as a ministry supported by the church. First Presbyterian Church's new level of financial support was, however, now only a quarter of the amount given by the church in 1993.[271]

Lee Paris continued to worship at First Presbyterian Church and worked to move the congregation he loved closer to his understanding of unity in the body of Christ that transcends racial and denominational lines. Through his friendship with African American minister Thomas Jenkins, First Presbyterian Church partnered with Jenkins' New Lake Church of Christ (Holiness) USA to run a summer day camp program.[272] On Sunday November 15, 1998, Dolphus Weary, Mission Mississippi's newly appointed executive director, preached at First Presbyterian Church. As this was only the second time an African American had spoken from the pulpit, Paris invited Mission Mississippi's board to attend the service.[273]

Conclusions

Lee Paris's journey into racial reconciliation and his relationship with his church and his culture is a story that reveals the new boundaries of the Closed Society. His story, considered in its historical context, also shows the profound ways in which Mississippi's white churches were and are complicit in maintaining, defending, and reconfiguring the Closed Society.

In his book *A Stone of Hope,* the historian David L. Chappell argues the success of the civil rights movement came from the strength of the black churches' prophetic challenge to Jim Crow and the corresponding failure of the Southern white churches to provide a united front in support of segregation. According to Chappell, the white churches split over the race question ("a split...that never became formalized"), and "failed in any meaningful way to join the anti-civil rights movement."[274] Chappell acknowledges the majority of white Southerners did not need to be persuaded to join the segregationist cause; but, he argues, white ministers did not try to inspire their congregations to militant resistance of the Supreme Court's decision. The role the ministers played came from "the urge to appear moderate and reasonable while proving their segregationism."[275]

Chappell rightly points out that lacking a convincing biblical case for segregation, pro-segregationist ministers' arguments "coalesced around opposition to social and political preaching."[276] However, by ending his account of white resistance in the 1960s, Chappell makes an extraordinary and dangerous error. Although the fire-breathing segregationists might have wished for more dramatic public support from white churches, as federal courts stripped the Closed Society of legal segregation, the white churches acted as the bastions of the Closed Society. Through the white churches' sponsorship of Christian "seg" academies, the Closed Society, not the Supreme Court, won the battle over school desegregation.[277] Only by taking a chronologically truncated view of the African American struggle for freedom is it possible for Chappell to state so categorically that the white church "failed in any meaningful way to join the anti-civil rights movement."[278]

Chappell makes a second fundamental error in his assessment of white churches' contribution to the defense of the Closed Society. The different demands placed on religion by the powerful and the powerless apparently eludes Chappell. Excited by his personal discovery of a robust prophetic religion in the African American church, and failing to find a corresponding prophetic religion in the white church "to inspire solidarity and self-sacrificial devotion to their cause," Chappell concludes that this is the reason why, "for one fleeting but decisive moment," whites failed successfully to counter the civil rights movement.[279] He fails to appreciate that while the powerless need prophetic religion to challenge the institutions that oppress them, the powerful—who wish to maintain these institutions—need a religion that quietly goes about its spiritual business allowing them to do as they please in the world they run. This religion of the powerful did not founder on the rocks of prophetic religion, but sailed through the storm of the civil rights movement and continued on course. Masquerading as one of the great doctrines of Southern Presbyterianism, the spirituality of the church is in fact the time tested political strategy of powerful men to perpetuate an unjust *status quo* free from moral censure.

Although Jim Silver's Closed Society is gone, his student, Governor William Winter, sees an unbroken continuity between the state today and the Mississippi his teacher described:

> There is still a tendency in the South, in Mississippi, to establish
> a certain orthodoxy in terms of what is politically and socially and
> racially desirable. It is much more subtle, it is much more under-
> stated, much more sophisticated, but there is a subtle conformist
> pressure that exists for people to maintain a certain Southern way of
> life—different from the old Southern way of life but still a Southern
> way of life, however you want to define that. Churches play a major
> [role] in maintaining, not only the religious orthodoxy, but the politi-
> cal orthodoxy which goes along with the religious orthodoxy, and
> that is a devil's brew.[280]

Today, nearly forty years after the "end" of the civil rights movement, hundreds of thousands of white Mississippians gather on Sunday to worship in all white congregations. The boundaries of the Closed Society have retreated and grown tighter around the bastions of the private sphere. To call into question the rightness of these racially closed private spheres is to challenge the heart of this new Closed Society. This explains the vehemence of the reaction to Mission Mississippi from within First Presbyterian Church when, by Emerson and Smith's account, there should have been little protest in an evangelical church to a call for racial reconciliation stripped of a systemic or economic critique. It is, however, no small thing in the resegregated world of contemporary Mississippi when the color line is broken in what Spencer Perkins and Chris Rice called, "the most intimate arenas of friendship, family, social life, neighborhood and church."[281] When Mission Mississippi threatened to do just this within First Presbyterian Church, Jackson, those determined to repel the invaders and patch the breach invoked the trusty doctrine of the spirituality of the church to defend these closed societies of the private sphere.

The doctrine of the spirituality of the church is a sophisticated theological resistance to systemic change: it is not an innocent doctrine misused. The development of the doctrine, as this chapter has shown in detail, is inextricably embedded in the history of maintaining first slavery, then white supremacy and segregation. The doctrine continues to be conservative Presbyterian's best weapon in their culture war with the liberals. "We are in a war; we are in a battle. And the quicker we realize we are in a battle, the better," preached First Presbyterian Church's Ligon Duncan, and the first line of defense in this war "entails believing right doctrine."[282]

This marriage of reactionary conservative politics and dogmatic theology makes sense when viewed in the light of Jürgen Moltmann's diagnosis that a closed society fears the future. Fear of the future causes a society to close ranks in homogenous groups resistant to change. Churches that fear the future become increasingly obsessed with purity of doctrine and morality as a way of resisting the ambiguity that openness to future possibility requires. Moltmann wrote that, "Such a faith tries to protect its 'sacred things,' God, Christ, doctrine and morality, because it clearly no longer believes these are sufficiently powerful to maintain themselves."[283] Paris, in suggesting his church should be open to other Christians of a different race, precipitated a fearful defense of the distinctively Southern Presbyterian "sacred things." Moltmann's description of a closed church predicts the outcome of actions such as this: "When 'the religion of fear' finds its way into the Christian church, those who regard themselves as the most vigilant guardians of the faith do violence to faith and smother it."[284]

Ed King, the civil rights activist and Methodist minister, wrote a reflection on white Mississippians in the 1960s that could serve as a commentary on Paris's experience at First Presbyterian Church:

> [They] have a terrible fear of the unknown, of the future, of change.
> Uncertainty is intolerable; doubting is dangerous. Any man who

doubts that the present order is the best possible arrangement of things...is a dangerous man. Any man who would risk the good of the present for the uncertainty of the future—just because he...doubts the present order is such a threat to his fellow man that in the state some see him as a traitor; in the church some see him as a heretic.[285]

Lee Paris is, by his own admission, a reluctant as well as an unlikely prophet to his own people:

I didn't like fighting my culture. I was uncomfortable doing that but I am one hundred percent sure that it was a very clear calling from God. I mean, just as sure as I am sitting here talking to you, He called me to do this. And so it was a question of whether I was going to be obedient or not and He made it clear it was not going to be easy and it was not going to be short and I didn't have a choice in the matter.[286]

As much as Paris challenges his own church, he is still a creature of his culture and firmly believes the Church must avoid political or economic matters and stay true to its "spiritual" mission. This is why, for Paris, justice remains none of Mission Mississippi's business.

Paris and Baird, with the advice and support of men such as Robert Cannada, prevented Mission Mississippi from even including the word justice in the literature: not out of some strategic desire to keep whites at the table but from a deep-seated belief that God requires the Church to concern itself solely with spiritual matters. This doctrine, forged by generations of powerful men, works very well for those with political and economic power; however, it does not work so well for the powerless who lack any political voice. For the powerless, their church is perhaps the only institution that can speak truth to power. The religion of the power-holders should not tell the church of the powerless to refrain from speaking against injustice.

To fully participate in Christ's ministry of reconciliation, Mission Mississippi must take the side of the widow and not the judge: that is, to become a participant in Christ's ministry of restorative justice. Hindering this ministry are the unconscious constraints of what sociologists Emerson and Smith describe as the evangelical's "religio-cultural tools" of the "freewill individualist tradition."[287] There are also, as we have seen, explicit limits placed on reconciliation by those who subscribe to the doctrine of the spirituality of the church. Dolphus Weary and those among his colleagues at Mission Mississippi who believe churches should challenge systemic racial inequality and injustice in Mississippi and America place an audacious hope in the power of Open Friendship in the Closed Society. They believe that intentional relationships across racial and denominational lines can open the eyes of the socially blind and undermine doctrines founded in fear. They hope to change Mississippi one relationship at a time.

5

Reconciliation 101:
Opening Friendship

Mission Mississippi's claim to be "changing Mississippi one relationship at a time" is both a pragmatic strategy and a theological statement of hope for social and systemic change in the state. This relationship-driven approach to racial reconciliation is acceptable to white evangelicals who wish to keep their personal religion free from the taint of the social gospel. At the same time, for the African American leaders of the movement with a commitment to grassroots community development, "one relationship at a time" is the first step in a strategy to access and mobilize the economic and social capital of the white church.

Dolphus Weary, the president of Mission Mississippi, calls this first step *Reconciliation 101*. For Weary, Mission Mississippi is only the entry-level class in a program that will move its students on to address issues of justice. Such advanced classes in reconciliation lie beyond Mission Mississippi's remit. Mission Mississippi's clear and limited objective is to bring Christians together to form intentional relationships across racial and denominational lines.[1] Weary considers John Perkins' teaching on reconciliation and economic development part of a more advanced curriculum: "I tend to call that Reconciliation 202 or Reconciliation 303 that people need to be led to."[2] According to Weary, the reason that justice is not on the syllabus for Mission Mississippi is that its inclusion would cause some constituents to withdraw from the dialogue. "It's called Reconciliation 101," Weary explains, "because there are so many people who are waiting to hear the right word to jump off the boat; who are waiting to hear the right phrase to justify why they shouldn't be involved. Waiting to hear stuff like: If we are truly reconciled racially then we ought to do something about the justice issues."[3]

Weary does not see this as capitulating to the demands of the unjust; rather, he believes if such people will stay long enough to develop relationships across racial lines, then the possibility exists for them to change. He outlines the way people, awakened to the Christian call to reconciliation through Mission Mississippi, might advance to these tougher lessons. "[Once] they've got to know some people...now they are ready to go deeper in their racial attitudes and some discussion groups and some planning time to really deal with issues like justice and economic development."[4] Reconciliation 101 is, however, more than a pragmatic starting point for a social program. For Weary and his colleagues, it is essentially a theological position: any possibility of "changing Mississippi" *starts* with individuals intentionally establishing personal relationships motivated *primarily* by the desire for reconciliation. It is the individual's belief in their reconciliation in Christ that demands such intentionality in reaching out across seemingly insurmountable barriers of race, denomination, and tradition. This theology of Reconciliation 101 places the call for intentional relationship before the demands for justice in the belief that as Christ-centered, reconciling friendships develop, both parties will see the need to address issues of justice in their society.

Reconciliation 101 is both a contextual theology and a strategy shaped by the fears, desires, and traditions of Mission Mississippi's various constituents. This chapter considers this theology in light of contemporary scholarship on theologies of reconciliation, particularly the work of Miroslav Volf. There follows an assessment of the outworking of Mission Mississippi's project using the stories of key participants and the history of two programs: the church partnerships and the Monthly Businessmen's Prayer Luncheon. The chapter concludes by locating instances of Volf's concept of "double vision" resulting from Mission Mississippi's Reconciliation 101.

Volf and the Theology of Embrace

The contemporary theologian Miroslav Volf has written extensively on reconciliation and its relationship to forgiveness and the demands of justice. This theology finds its fullest expression in his 1996 book *Exclusion and Embrace.*[5] Volf formulated his theology of reconciliation a long way from Jackson, Mississippi, in a crucible of bitter sectarianism and deadly ethnic division. Born in 1956 in Croatia—then a part of communist Yugoslavia—Volf grew up the son of a Pentecostal minister in the Serbian town of Novi Sad.[6] As a boy, he witnessed the hostility of Tito's communist government to the church: the secret police regularly harassed his father who, as a preacher, they considered an enemy of socialism.[7] The only professing Christian among the thirty-five hundred students at his high school, he was singled out by his teachers. Volf traces his calling as a theologian back to having to find answers for his fellow students when they challenged and questioned his religious faith.[8] During his year of national service in the army, he came under the scrutiny of the military police. Accused of being an enemy of the people and a spy, and threatened with eight years in prison, he withstood months of interrogation before the police finally released him without charge.[9]

Volf left school and studied theology at the new evangelical seminary in Osijek, Croatia. After graduating, he took the opportunity to go to Fuller Theological Seminary in California. There, one of the professors recommended Volf to Jürgen Moltmann in Tübingen as a doctoral student. A Pentecostal evangelical, Volf worried that the German theologian would not accept him as a student. Volf recalls that Moltmann, the advocate of Christ's open friendship, "accepted me for who I was."[10]

While studying under Moltmann, Volf taught at his old seminary in Osijek. In the summer of 1991, tanks rolled through the streets of Osijek forcing the faculty and students to flee the seminary. The faculty and students relocated a hundred miles away in a Reformed parsonage in Slovenia and Volf became a refugee professor in a makeshift seminary. The television brought them news of the progress of the war and the destruction of their homes.[11]

Volf did not stay long at this seminary in exile. That same year he took a position on the other side of the world as a lecturer back at Fuller Theological Seminary. Safely in the United States, Volf started working on a paper giving his theological response to the fierce ethnic conflict in his home country.[12] Setting about the task, Volf found that the theological tools he had to hand were inadequate. "I tried to apply liberation theology to the situation," Volf explains. "It didn't work. Both parties saw themselves as oppressed, and both saw themselves as engaged in the struggle for liberation. So the main categories of liberation theology, oppression and liberation, serve to justify the struggle rather than lead to peace."[13]

Volf needed a theology of reconciliation that would bring the hope of peace to these warring factions. He saw two poles in the existing practices of reconciliation in the church. On the one hand, he saw an approach to forgiveness and reconciliation *outside* justice and, on the other, forgiveness and reconciliation *after* justice.[14] Forgiveness and reconciliation outside justice is a form of reconciliation made possible by the ignoring of past and ongoing injustices.

The oppressor will be reconciled to the victim only if the slate of past wrongs is ignored and the victim makes no demands for justice and reparation. Volf calls this reconciliation outside of justice "cheap reconciliation."[15] This cheap reconciliation excises what he calls the social dimension from the doctrine of reconciliation. "The retreat from social responsibility," laments Volf, "is more than a failure to take seriously the traditions of Jesus and the prophets. It presupposes an inadequate understanding of reconciliation."[16] Alternately, those engaged in struggles for liberation reject all such attempts at cheap reconciliation demanding instead that justice be done as a prerequisite to reconciliation. They demand "strict justice"—that everything be made right—before extending forgiveness and reconciliation.[17]

Both the approaches of strict justice and cheap grace are problematic. John De Gruchy, the South African Reformed churchman and theologian, meditating on this problem after his country's Truth and Reconciliation hearings, concluded that, "the single-minded pursuit of justice can lead to destructive vengeance, just as the pursuit of reconciliation without justice perpetuates evil."[18] Volf makes a bolder claim using milder language: neither justice *after* nor justice *outside* forgiveness and reconciliation is Christian because "in both cases it is to treat the offender as if he had not committed the offense or as if it were not his." Both cases, for Volf, deny the central Christian doctrine that everybody is in need of forgiveness.[19]

The search for an alternative understanding of reconciliation, forgiveness, and justice took Volf to the parable of the Prodigal Son in Luke's Gospel. In the parable, the father, seeing the returning son, does not wait for the son's confession and repentance; instead, "while he was still far off, his father saw him and was filled with compassion; he ran and put his arms around him and kissed him"(15:20). Volf notices that the father did not demand a confession of guilt from the errant son before he embraced him because their relationship "did not rest on moral performance."[20] Volf reads this embrace of the father as God's embrace of all creation. He finds this embrace key to an understanding of the cross and atonement where "God does not abandon the godless to their evil but gives the divine self for them in order to receive them into divine communion."[21] The connection that Volf makes between the parable and the cross finds poetic expression in the Anglican Eucharistic liturgy when the priest prays: "Father of all, we give you thanks and praise, that when we were still far off you met us in your Son and brought us home. Dying and living, he declared your love, gave us grace, and opened the gate of glory."[22]

Delivering his paper in the winter of 1993 on the metaphor of embrace as a theological response to the trouble in Yugoslavia, Volf argued that Christians were required to extend the same embrace to their enemies. Volf supported his injunction with Paul's exhortation in his letter to the Romans: "Welcome one another, therefore, just as Christ has welcomed you, for the glory of God" (15:7). Christians are called to have this same "will to embrace" toward their enemies.

Following the lecture, Jürgen Moltmann asked his student a question: "But can you embrace a ĉetnik?"[23] Ĉetniks were Serbian fighters notorious for inflicting terrible atrocities on the civilian population in Croatia—crimes still being committed against Volf's own people at the time he delivered his lecture. Volf paused before answering. "No, I cannot—but as a follower of Christ I think I should be able to."[24] Volf's development of a theology of embrace, he would later write, "is a product of the struggle between the truth of my argument and the force of Moltmann's objection...between the demand to bring about justice and the call to embrace the perpetrator."[25]

The key to understanding Volf's theology of embrace is his distinction between the will to embrace and the embrace itself. "The *will* to embrace," writes Volf, "is indiscriminate, the *embrace* itself is conditional."[26] This careful differentiation enables Volf to negotiate a third way between the two polls of cheap reconciliation and strict justice, because, as he explains, "*the embrace itself*—full reconciliation—cannot take place until the truth has been said and justice done."[27] Truth and justice occur in what Volf calls the "overarching framework" of the will to embrace.[28] This framework—the will to embrace the other within the embrace of the triune God—reconfigures our very notion of justice.[29] In fact, argues Volf, "There can be no justice without the will to embrace."[30]

Full embrace—the embrace of reconciled equals—is never fully achievable in our present world shot through with "pervasive inequality and manifest evil."[31] Our will to embrace only finds fulfillment in the glorious eschatological moment of reconciliation when says Volf, quoting from the book of Revelations, "the first things have passed away" and "the home of God is established among mortals."[32] Volf's insistence on the eschatological fulfillment of embrace does not lessen the Church's responsibility to seek truth and justice in the hope of embrace. As a student of Moltmann, Volf understands that an eschatological horizon of embrace does not lead to an otherworldly postponement of justice; rather, it intensifies the will for embrace and the desire to seek just and truthful reconciliation in the present. Such reconciliation in the here-and-now is always "nonfinal reconciliation," and those who desire reconciliation engage in the practice of clumsy, exploited, or even rebuffed embraces.[33]

Volf's experience of the Yugoslavian war informs his view that in situations of conflict and injustice a simple binary division between oppressor and oppressed rarely applies. Both sides come with their own grievances and demands for justice and truth. Volf resists the postmodern notion that there are many truths by reasserting the classic Christian and monotheistic belief in God's universal justice and the christological title of the truth claimed by Jesus in the gospel of John. However, Volf warns, "our commitment to Jesus Christ who is the truth does not therefore translate into the claim that we possess the absolute truth."[34] We are sinful humans seeking to embrace other sinful humans; therefore, "If we believe rightly in Jesus Christ who unconditionally embraced us, the godless perpetrators, our hearts will be open to receive others, even enemies, and our eyes will be open to see from their perspective."[35]

Volf insists that this expansion of vision to include the perspective of the other is essential for reconciliation. The embrace requires a reflexive truth-telling that he calls "double vision."[36] Double vision describes the process whereby an individual must seek to hear and understand the other's truth and then seek to see themselves and their claims to justice and truth from this new perspective.[37] For Volf, this pursuit of double vision is the practical work demanded by the will to embrace because it requires the participant accept the notion that "the self of the other matters more than my truth."[38] Without a commitment to create the space in oneself for the other's truth and justice, the embrace is a charade that can mask continued exploitation and injustice.

Mission Mississippi and the "Will to Embrace"

The message of Mission Mississippi, clearly articulated at every meeting is: the healing of historical divisions and wounds starts with individual Christians sitting down with the desire to get to know another person of a different ethnicity or denomination. Mission Mississippi challenges participants to be intentional and deliberate about this often awkward practice of making space to meet the other person and hear their story. Here is the practical outworking of the Christian impulse that Volf calls "the will to embrace" and that his teacher Jürgen Moltmann calls "open friendship." Mission Mississippi, then, presents an opportunity to see how, in this particular context, issues of social justice manifest in this framework of the will to embrace.

In the minds of many of its residents, the legacies of slavery, segregation, and the civil rights movement shape Mississippi's race relations into a binary ethnic confrontation between the black oppressed and the white oppressors. Many black churches and white activists demand—to use Volf's categories—justice *before* there can be reconciliation and forgiveness. Because of this, Mission Mississippi has run into considerable criticism for their call that both sides need to participate in seeking reconciliation based on their common unity in Christ.

Dolphus Weary who expected resistance from white churches was surprised by the response Mission Mississippi received from African American churches: "We anticipated that the black church was ready for racial reconciliation," Weary confesses, "and what I discovered was that because of so much historical pain, the Black Church is no more ready than the White Church. It's been hard to even get [churches] to put it on their agenda." What Weary found is that whites tend toward cheap reconciliation, whereas African Americans desire the safeguard of strict justice against the possibility of further exploitation. "White people don't want to give up their position of power that whiteness brings," he explains, "and black people are afraid that the little power they do have is going to be lost."[39]

Mission Mississippi, in asking the oppressed to extend reconciling friendship to their oppressors is, in the view of its organizers, following the example of Jesus. Jesus' choice of friends shocked the respectable religious world of his day not simply because it included prostitutes, those transgressors of personal morality and threat to family values, but also tax collectors (Luke 7:34). In befriending tax collectors, Jesus entered into relationship with those who, using the threat of state-sanctioned violence, had financially exploited his neighbors and himself. When Mission Mississippi asks African American churches to be reconciled to their white brothers and sisters, they are asking them to befriend those who have benefited from their economic exploitation for years—they are asking them to embrace their tax collectors.[40]

As well as a power imbalance between the African American and white community in Mississippi, there is also a knowledge imbalance. At the risk of generalizing, asking a white Mississippian to enter a relationship with an African American neighbor is asking them to engage with a person from a world about which they know next to nothing. Lee Paris is typical of many whites when he says that before Mission Mississippi he lived "pretty much exclusively in a white world" and "the few encounters that I had were [with] blacks that were on such a level that they were just no different from me."[41] Ronnie Crudup, an African American minister and Mission Mississippi board member, describes the imbalance in knowledge from the other side of the racial divide. He says, "Our livelihoods, our safety, the whole nine yards, depend on us entering the white world and knowing how to navigate the white world, whereas [whites] had no need to enter the black world, to know black people."[42] In this context, African Americans find Mission Mississippi's appeal for them to enter into relationships with whites strange. Neddie Winters, Mission Mississippi's executive director, explains, "We have been figuring out how to relate to you guys all our lives. We have been careful about what we could say and what we couldn't say all our lives, so it is not a big issue for us to relate to you."[43] Here Winters is describing a relationship based not on a desire for friendship and embrace but on economic necessity and delineated by fear and exploitation.

Central to both Mission Mississippi's Reconciliation 101 and Volf's embrace is the creating of safe space in which truth can be told and stories graciously heard. Speaking to a group of black and white college students, Dolphus Weary stressed the important lessons of reconciliation learned by Mission Mississippi. Essential to intentional relationship is *a conversation of understanding, not a conversation of convincing.*"[44] Such a conversation of understanding requires the participants accept, as Volf states, that "the self of the other matters more than my truth."[45] Weary explained to the students how this attitude has to affect relationships in the highly charged sectarian atmosphere of Mississippi: "We are not trying to change people's theology. What we are trying to do is say we need to get to know each other because when we know each other we can talk about our differences in theology."[46]

The will to embrace—to make space in oneself to understand the other's truth, not to convince them of your own rightness—carries with it an understanding that this will mean a change within one's own self and identity. To enter into an embrace on the common ground of unity in Christ is to have to renegotiate one's own cultural and ethnic identity.[47] In a world where these identities are entrenched, this is no easy charge. Weary, in his sermon at the final rally of the Grace is Greater than Race Tour in 2000, publicly wrestled with this challenge. "What does it mean to be a part of a new creation?" he asked. "Am I a Christian first? Am I a Christian above my denomination? Am I a Christian above my blackness?" Volf faced a similar challenge at the height of the Balkan conflict. He posed a question to himself and his seminary students in exile, "Who is closer to you, your Croatian neighbor who's not a Christian, or your Serbian brother or sister in Christ? It was not at all clear how the answer would go."[48] Most participants in Mission Mississippi are considering for the first time how to engage in racial reconciliation. They are only just beginning to face Volf and Weary's dilemma of how to renegotiate their own cultural and ethnic identity.

Memory, Forgiveness, and Justice

When African Americans and whites sit down and start conversations of understanding in Mississippi, the participants have to navigate the burdens of memory and the legacy of tradition. Former Governor William Winter expressed it well when he told a reporter, "White folks can't continue to live in the pre-1860s. Black folks can't continue to live in the pre-1960s. We've come too far now to let the old scars continue to haunt us."[49] As Jarvis Ward, the first executive director of Mission Mississippi, watched black and white Christians come together for the first time, he recalled the lines from Longfellow's poem *Hiawatha*: "There are feuds yet unforgotten, Wounds that ache and still may open!"[50] How participants articulate the memory of these wounds and how they receive the memories of other's wounds determines if the healing continues or if the wounds rip open again. These conversations are the practice of confronting the issues of justice and forgiveness in the framework of the will to embrace.

James Turner is a regular at Mission Mississippi events in Jackson. Turner, like so many African Americans in Mississippi, lives with memories that are *wounds that ache and still may open*. As a minister, Turner feels a responsibility to pursue a resolution to his haunted and hurt memories: "It is important for me to be able to espouse and know that there is healing when you have had hurt...if I want to try to preach it, if I want to try to teach it, I should also be living it."[51] In Mission Mississippi, Turner has found a place to fulfill his pastoral obligation to seek his own healing. "Mission Mississippi," reflects Turner, "[affords] the opportunity to come together, the opportunity to pray together, the opportunity to work together. [It] is a continuous healing process."[52] He has pastored congregations in the Church of Christ Holiness (USA) for twenty-five years. One morning at a Mission Mississippi prayer breakfast, he met Stephen Edwards, an elder at First Presbyterian Church, Jackson. Edwards was also a board member of the Neighborhood Christian Center—a church-based after-school program for African American children in the city sponsored by First Presbyterian Church. A friendship developed between the two men, leading to Edwards recruiting Turner as the Neighborhood Christian Center's new executive director.

In his conversations with Edwards, Turner found that even though they were both professing Christians, they came from such radically different worlds that they saw Mississippi in very different ways:

> Steve has grown up...not so much a person who has had almost everything he has wanted, but he has been blessed in certain things and so it means there are certain things he has not been exposed to, [that] he has not seen. In my case, I was born in Utica, Mississippi on Mr Simmond's place—my parents and grandparents were sharecroppers. Steve did not really have any exposure to blacks until...college.

And my situation: I [grew up] in an environment where if I worked
[then it was] for somebody who was white.[53]

During the 1960s, Turner attended Holy Ghost High School, a Roman
Catholic high school for African Americans in Jackson; after graduating high
school he went to Tougaloo College. As a high school and then a college student, Turner participated in civil rights demonstrations and voter registration
drives. What he witnessed haunts him to this day. "We were involved with voter
registration drives in Canton...we went in the [county] recruiting and bringing people to register." The students brought the would-be registrants to the
courthouse in Canton. Surrounded by lawns, the courthouse sat in the middle
of a picturesque Southern square with stores and shaded sidewalks on each
side.[54] Waiting for the students and the registrants were officers of Canton's
police department. Knowing the policemen's record of intimidation, violence
and arbitrary arrests of African Americans who demanded their civil rights,
the students gathered around the courthouse as witnesses to afford the brave
registrants some protection.[55] "It was just confrontational," Turner remembers.
"You don't have the right to know who is in this vehicle," the officers barked at
the students as they tried to watch the proceedings. "You don't need to observe."
When this failed to deter the teenagers, the police started shoving the students
and shouting words that haunt Turner to this day: "Y'all get on out of the way
or we'll stomp you and beat you."[56] These were not idle threats; Turner witnessed acts of police brutality toward his fellow students. "[Now] each time I go
to Canton," Turner confesses, "I remember that the Sheriff...would stomp us
into the concrete and do different things to us and all those kind of things. And
those kind of memories come up and I have to continuously work at moving
past those things."[57] Even language triggers these memories. "It is the words
and things that really sticks with me," explains Turner. "Somebody [will] say a
certain word and it keys a memory....[Words like] 'beating' and 'stomping'—I
don't think I even use the word[s]. But when other people say 'stomp' it causes,
I guess, more of a fear."[58]

Turner has cautiously shared these memories with Edwards and some
other whites involved with Mission Mississippi from his desire to "move past
those things." He states simply, "It has been helpful." Turner's caution comes
from his experience of white Christians responding to African Americans'
stories of oppression from a position informed by a theology of reconciliation outside of justice: "I have had to understand that some people say: Well
I wasn't involved, I didn't do it."[59] Despite this type of response, Turner continues to pursue relationships with whites from his belief in the unity of the
Church in Christ and his own need for healing. "I have to work on the healing

process...otherwise I would be going the opposite direction and that's not where it's at, because Christ prayed for us to be one and we can't be one when we are continually being divided."[60]

Turner talks of the "healing" of his memories, but this expression might seem to validate those whites who believe African Americans should simply "get over" their grievances as it suggests that those memories have been cured and are no longer there. With his experience of the Truth and Reconciliation Commission, John De Gruchy argues that in order for there to be forgiveness between people, they must remember the past "in ways that heal relationships, build community and thus anticipate a new future."[61] This remembering does not involve glossing over or discounting past injustice to avoid upsetting the offender. "Genuine forgiveness," de Gruchy argues, "does not mean brushing aside and regarding injustice lightly, but on knowing how to remember rightly."[62] Avoiding the suggestion that the wrongdoers are correct in encouraging the victims to forget and move on, what language might be more helpful to talk about the healing of the victim's memory? A better phrase might be *the healing of remembering*; for, the healing required is neither an amputation of a painful past nor the amnesia of a divine anesthetic but rather the transformation and redemption of memory that enables reconciliation and forgiveness. The memories are necessary and need to continue; they are not to be left behind on some psychic operating table with the victim discharged back into the world as an amputee. True healing of remembering comes, Volf believes, when the victim's "memory of wrongdoing [is] framed by the memory and hope of reconciliation between the wrongdoer and the wronged."[63] This hope is rooted in the Christian Church's memory of Christ's Passion that "anticipates...the *formation of a reconciled community even out of deadly enemies*."[64]

The reason the victim must continue to "remember rightly" is that it extends the hope of reconciliation to the oppressor—the possibility that they will listen with understanding and change their worldview. Jürgen Moltmann, speaking from his position of white privilege, explains the importance for whites of listening "seriously to the stories of the blacks," for their own redemption. "The person who has incurred guilt can no doubt admit his guilt," Moltmann observes, "but only his victims know what suffering his injustice has caused." It is therefore necessary for whites to listen to African Americans and to learn to, as Moltmann says, "see ourselves through the eyes of our victims."[65]

Weary predicates Mission Mississippi's strategy and theology on the belief that, as Moltmann suggests, whites will listen to their African American brothers and sisters and develop double vision. Their new perspective, he hopes, will cause them to "go deeper" into racial reconciliation. Phil Reed of Voice of

Calvary Ministries in Jackson explains how this relational model of reconciliation can move to address systemic issues of injustice:

> In Jackson 85 percent of the people living below the poverty level are African Americans. And that's the statistic. But, when you develop this kind of friendship, then it is no longer a statistic. This is my friend that can't find a decent job, that doesn't have a decent place to stay.... It is not a statistic anymore; it is my friend. And so, it starts with friendships.[66]

Those who believe that Mission Mississippi will change Mississippi one relationship at a time place their hope in friendship.

Among those convinced of the importance of Mission Mississippi's strategy are a group of African American pastors active not only in Mission Mississippi's leadership but also in church-initiated community development projects in Jackson. A critic who would dismiss Mission Mississippi as simply an exercise in racial civility to assuage white guilt must explain these men's earnest and continuing support of the organization. The fact that these African American leaders in Mission Mississippi have an impressive record in grassroots economic community development lends significant credibility to Dolphus Weary's insistence that Mission Mississippi is the starting point for moving Christians to a deeper commitment to a reconciliation that includes social justice (see figure 5.1).

Thomas Jenkins, the pastor of New Dimensions Ministries in Jackson, has been involved with Mission Mississippi since he served on the original steering committee for the first stadium event in 1993.[67] A prominent figure at most Mission Mississippi functions, he has a public friendship with Lee Paris.[68] Jenkins came under the influence of John Perkins while majoring in accounting at Jackson State University in the early 1970s. Perkins had Jenkins keep the books for Voice of Calvary (VOC). "John was mentoring me...telling me all these things about what the black church ought to be doing. What the Church ought to be doing period,"[69] recalls Jenkins. When Jenkins graduated, Perkins, always keen to develop African American leadership and economic development, connected him with an African American priest in Louisiana named Father Albert J. McKnight, who had started the Southern Cooperative Development Fund.[70] Jenkins returned to Jackson to work out of an office in Perkins' building as the regional director of the Southern Cooperative Development Fund for Mississippi, Kentucky, South Carolina and Alabama. Perkins took full advantage of such easy access to his protégé and the Development Fund. "We were able to help Voice of Calvary buy houses, [and] renovate houses," remembers Jenkins, "and where we could get capital to

FIGURE 5.1. These juxtaposed images from a Mission Mississippi publication demonstrate both the organization's high-profile displays of reconciliation and the connection with Voice of Calvary Ministries with its commitment to grassroots community development work. *The Messenger*, 15 (January 2004), 8. (Courtesy of Mission Mississippi)

them—capital to the Mendenhall ministry—[we] did a lot of stuff...not only with them but with a lot of people because of his contacts."[71]

The numerous connections between the radical VOC and Mission Mississippi are striking. Thomas Jenkins, Neddie Winters (Mission Mississippi's Executive Director), and Ronnie Crudup (Vice Chairman of Mission Mississippi's Executive Board) have all served as chair of the board of Voice of Calvary Ministries.[72] In 2008, Winters served as an interim pastor for Voice of Calvary Fellowship; the congregation installed him as its pastor on January 1, 2009. These men—Crudup, Jenkins, and Winters—were also all involved in Hope Community Credit Union, a very significant and quite remarkable piece of economic development work.

In 1999, Hope Community Credit Union, a small credit union founded in 1995 by members of Anderson United Methodist Church, was struggling and about to close. The church asked various groups for assistance including the Fellowship of Hope Ministries, a group of some fifteen congregations that included Voice of Calvary and New Horizons.[73] The Fellowship of Hope took over the credit union's charter appointing VOC's Phil Reed as the chair of the board.[74] Ronnie Crudup, pastor of New Horizons, suggested Neddie Winters as the first manager. Winters, with a background in business, gave up his job as a full-time pastor and served as the Credit Union's manager for three years. In that time, Winters remembers, "We started with $165,000...and we moved that to something like a $10 million credit union."[75] In 2008, Hope Community Credit Union boasted they had "generated over $300 million in financing and brought economic opportunities to more than 30,000 people in economically distressed areas."[76]

Another example of the commitment of Mission Mississippi's leaders to church based community development is Thomas Jenkins' New Dimensions Development Foundation.[77] On the corner of Farish Street and Monument Street in the heart of Jackson's old African American business district stands a large, white, windowless, corrugated iron barn. On the end wall, a sign with a large red cross proclaims in the best Elizabethan English, "Come unto me all ye that labour and are heavy laden and I will give you rest." Surrounded by empty lots and derelict and burned out buildings, in 2005 this was the home of the Church in the City, a church plant of Thomas Jenkins' New Dimensions Ministries, Inc., pastored at that time by Neddie Winters (the congregation now goes by the name of Greater Grace Tabernacle of Deliverance). The building also serves as the center of operations for New Dimensions Development Foundation.[78] The ground floor contains classrooms for tutoring and skills training, storerooms for a food program, and a small factory for a business manufacturing choir and clergy robes, and custom-made draperies. At the back of the building, stairs lead up into the attic and a warren of windowless bedrooms, lounges, and a kitchen for the New Dimensions shelter for homeless women and their children.

The physical proximity of these different responses to the chronic needs of this African American community in Jackson is symbolic of the insepa-rability for Jenkins and Winters of charity, housing, economic development, skills training, job creation, evangelism, and Christian worship. Church in the City's vision statement demonstrated the progression from individual relationships to systemic change to which Winters, Jenkins, Weary, and Crudup all subscribe. It read, "The deplorable conditions of our communities are changed through relationships one person, one family, one block, one neighborhood, one community, one city at a time."[79]

Jenkins, Winters, Crudup, and Weary are passionately committed to moving Christians to recognize and address these deplorable conditions. "But," Weary points out, "If people won't walk into the room, and if people won't hear it, and if [reconciliation] is not on the agenda, then how in the world can you move people?" This explains these men's commitment to Mission Mississippi whose main goal—Reconciliation 101—is to facilitate the coming together of African American and white Christians in the same room with reconciliation on their agenda. Although Mission Mississippi directly organizes a range of events—picnics, prayer breakfasts and luncheons, and conferences—to bring people together, they hope that participants will generate their own programs and projects. "The state is so big and the communities are so dysfunctional," explains Weary, "that we need to go and try and help motivate those communities to start something."[80]

Church Partnerships

Mission Mississippi's central strategy is the formation of church partnerships between historically white and historically African American congregations that will, it is hoped, create a momentum that moves these communities past simple acquaintance and deeper into a reconciliation that names and addresses injustice. In 1995, when Cade Chapel, the oldest African American congregation in Jackson, and Crossgates Baptist Church in Brandon worshipped together, Mission Mississippi declared the service "a wonderful example of Mission Mississippi's vision."[81] Weary, however, expects much more from church partnerships than the occasional pulpit swap or shared service: "What we'd really like to do is put a New Horizon and a Trinity together and let the leadership say: How do we go deeper with our church relationships?"[82]

Weary is referring to the relationship between New Horizons Ministry and Trinity Presbyterian Church; Mission Mississippi has often cited these two churches as an example of a church partnership.[83] New Horizons is a large vibrant congregation in South Jackson based in a collection of buildings that more resemble a school than a church. The sanctuary, which holds around four hundred people, fills to overflowing for the two Sunday morning services. Their minister, Ronnie Crudup, bathed in the bright television lights, preaches a charismatic gospel of affirmation and personal development to his almost exclusively African American flock.[84] The worship is passionately led at high volume by the accomplished band and singers. Trinity Presbyterian Church, for most of the partnership, worshipped in their church of sandy brick, white columns and a white steeple on Northside Drive.[85] A conservative Presbyterian congregation averaging around four hundred on a Sunday morning, they sit in the wooden pews in a plain and tastefully appointed sanctuary singing the great hymns accompanied by a pipe organ. The minister, Mike Ross, delivers long academic sermons that would be at home in a seminary classroom.[86]

The partnership began with a joint Easter Service held on neutral ground at Belhaven College a year before the start of Mission Mississippi. The relationship came about through contacts made between men involved in their respective church's prison ministries.[87] Trinity and New Horizons continue to hold Easter Day sunrise services and conduct pulpit swaps twice a year. Both congregations have benefited from the link. Trinity's connections with international mission work enabled New Horizons to join with them in running joint mission trips to Malawi and South Africa; and Crudup and his team advised Trinity on their community outreach programs in the transitioning neighborhood around their church. "They helped us in knowing how to interface with, and relate to, and reach African Americans," recounts Ross. "And they said, 'Because of your preaching style and your worship and just the reputation of white Presbyterians...you're not going to reach a whole lot of adults. What you've got to aim at is the youth.'"[88] This advice resulted in Trinity's thriving after-school program.

The elders of Trinity Presbyterian, part of the Presbyterian Church in America, fiercely guard their order of worship and doctrines from adulteration. Crudup believes it was his training at the white, theologically conservative Reformed Theological Seminary (RTS) that allayed fears at Trinity that the partnership would compromise its doctrinal and theological purity.[89] It was Gordon Reid, one of Crudup's teachers at RTS and interim pastor at Trinity, who helped to establish the link.[90]

Mission Mississippi's touting of the New Horizons/Trinity partnership as a model is problematic. The same impulse to doctrinal purity that makes Crudup acceptable in Trinity's eyes works against Trinity's participation in Mission Mississippi. Trinity Presbyterian Church withdrew its support from Mission Mississippi soon after the first stadium event. Happy to go along with reconciliation across racial lines, crossing denominational lines proved less attractive. Ross explains that following the appointment of Roman Catholics to the board of Mission Mississippi, Trinity's session, "wrote to them and said we feel this is contrary to the gospel and to the direction of Mission Mississippi." The inclusion of Roman Catholics signaled to the elders at Trinity that Mission Mississippi was now an ecumenical rather than an evangelical organization, and as Ross explains, "We are not in favor of that."[91]

A second church partnership publicized by Mission Mississippi exists between Neddie Winters' Church in the City and St. Peter's by-the-Lake Episcopal Church. Unlike New Horizon's and Trinity, Mission Mississippi instigated this partnership. In 1997, Barry Cotter, the priest at St. Peter's, following his attendance at a Promise Keeper's rally, called Mission Mississippi asking for his church to be connected with a black church. They put Cotter in touch with Neddie Winters, then pastor of Hope Springs Missionary Baptist Church. The two men started meeting together to talk and pray and quickly developed a mutual respect. This friendship led to the two congregations coming together over a "covered-dish dinner." Encouraged by this success, the congregations joined together feeding the hungry and homeless in inner-city Jackson on Thanksgiving morning. The partnership progressed to a point at which the congregations regularly held joint services of worship.[92]

Unlike the New Horizon/Trinity partnership, in this case people were crossing racial and theological lines. The Baptists from Hope Springs were suspicious of the Episcopalian's liturgy and Eucharistic emphasis that all came out of a prayer book. The white Episcopalians found the spontaneity and level of congregational participation uncomfortable. Despite awkwardness, the experience brought some healing to old wounds and laid the foundations for lasting friendships. One elderly African American woman found the significance of everyone drinking from the same communion cup deeply moving. Neddie Winters remembers:

> One lady, she went to her grave just blessed as she could be with peace and with everything within her heart after being there with them [and] to be all drinking out of the chalice and not out of the little cups. She said, "Being there with them white folks and I used to work for these people and I have seen them mistreat my people. And to be there and to be in a setting like that where I can be in contentment and be at peace."[93]

The strategy of church partnerships moves Mission Mississippi's focus from relationships between individuals to relationships between institutions; however, these institutional relationships gain their strength and form from individual friendships. The partnership between St. Peters by-the-Lake Episcopal Church and Hope Springs MB Church gained its strength and focus from the friendship between Winters and Cotter. When Winters left Hope Springs MB Church and became pastor of the Church in the City, St. Peter's switched its partnership to Winters' new congregation. These two congregations signed a covenant stating: "God has established the relationship between the...congregations to function in the Body of Christ as a community of believers gathered together to be extensively involved in the work of racial reconciliation."[94] The departure of Cotter from St. Peter's again underscored the reliance of this partnership upon the personal friendship of the two ministers. The partnership now struggles to maintain momentum. The two churches joined in bringing food to Mission Mississippi's 2004 Partnership Picnic in the Park, but only one family from St. Peter's by-the-Lake attended.

Despite all its efforts to establish significant and lasting church partnerships, examination of the two examples Mission Mississippi most often gives does not reveal the sort of ongoing and deepening relationships for which it strives. It does reveal, however, the energy required to move congregations beyond their closed boundaries of denomination and race. It also shows that it is the establishment of personal friendships between church leaders that generates this necessary energy.

Reconciliation and Economic Opportunity

Mission Mississippi has a second strategy that more directly connects the will to embrace with systemic issues of economic access and investment in Mississippi's struggling communities. With its origins in the Christian Businessmen's Committee of Jackson (CBMC), Mission Mississippi has consistently held events targeting the business community. On October 15, 1993, at the Ramada Coliseum, over five hundred men gathered for a Businessmen's Luncheon that, in turn, led to a much smaller group meeting monthly for breakfast.[95] Mission Mississippi continues to host a businessmen's prayer breakfast at Jackson's University Club on the third Wednesday of every month. Through relationships formed at these meetings, Mission Mississippi hopes to influence the state's economic landscape. As one regular attendee explains:

> This is where networking happens and you build up a relation-
> ship with somebody. That is what they do when they go out on
> the golf course. They are trying to build relationships and get the
> jobs—[the prayer breakfasts are] the same thing—it is a networking
> opportunity.[96]

Mission Mississippi is creating a networking opportunity for African American businessmen who traditionally have little access to the powerful and informal white business networks of the Closed Society: the networks of club, church, and family.

It is difficult to assess the extent to which business opportunities and investment in the African American community stem from these contacts. Two examples of "success stories" repeatedly offered by both African American and white participants in Mission Mississippi are Charles Doty and Lextron, and Kenneth Leaks and his New Deal Supermarkets. Considering these two examples illuminates the way Mission Mississippi believes relationships, founded on the will to embrace, may change the distribution of wealth and the economic future of the state.

In 1992, at the birth of Mission Mississippi, Tom Skinner issued a challenge that Victor Smith, the white businessman who along with Lee Paris helped start Mission Mississippi, took to heart: "Tom Skinner asked us all: would you be willing to have a black friend?" Smith remembers. "And I prayed that day: God I would be willing if you give me a friend."[97] Smith served on the board of Jackson's Habitat for Humanity with Doty Smith, a young African American businessman; following Skinner's challenge, Smith invited Doty to have lunch with him. Smith, with his years of business experience, heard about Doty's difficulties launching his electrical assemblies manufacturing company called Lextron. Doty told an interviewer in 2002, "[Smith] helped me in the financial community when I didn't have those relationships established."[98] The help Smith provided was to act as guarantor for the bank loans Doty needed to purchase materials. "He had some credit problems with the bank and he needed better credit," recalls Smith. "I took him over to another bank and the banker said: well we will agree to loan him if you will sign on a note with him, which I did. And we became partners."[99] Doty bought Smith out when Lextron secured contracts with AT&T and Bell South.

Mississippi's boosters publicized the success of Lextron, a minority-owned business.[100] Starting with only ten employees, by 2003, Doty employed 185 people at Lextron's factory in Jackson and another 200 at a sister company Lextron-Visteon Automotive Systems supplying the new Nissan plant in Canton. In 2004, however, following the cancellation of a major contract, Lextron filed for bankruptcy, with debts of $50 million.[101]

Distinguishing Doty and Lextron's story from other tales of African American entrepreneurial endeavor is the close attention Doty reportedly paid to the needs of his workers. Doty chose to develop his operation within inner-city Jackson providing good health insurance and benefit packages for his workers.[102] With 90 percent of his workforce made up of women—many of them single mothers—Doty claimed to have created a "state-of-the-art" child-care center and offered tuition reimbursement for schooling.[103] The company was also a significant sponsor of Jackson's Habitat for Humanity.

The second story of Kenneth Leaks and New Deal Supermarkets is of a more dramatic commitment to urban regeneration and economic development of African American communities. In 1998, Leaks and his partner Greg Price bought the old supermarket on Monument Street right across the street from Jenkins' New Dimensions building. Leaks, who had worked for years as a manager for the supermarket chain Jitney Jungle, now wanted to develop supermarkets in neighborhoods that the large chains were abandoning.[104] With half of his customers paying for their groceries with food stamps, Leaks catered to the needs of the impoverished neighborhood. The Store's signature "Pick 5" deal (five family-sized servings of various meats) boasted you could "feed your family meat for a week for $19.99."[105]

Mission Mississippi played a role in the success of Leaks' enterprise. Leaks was a member of Word of Faith Christian Center Church, a congregation that supports Mission Mississippi; he also regularly attended the businessmen's prayer breakfast. When the New Deal store opened on Monument Avenue, the Prayer Breakfast, instead of meeting at the University Club, adjourned to the Monument Avenue store. "We went in and prayed over everything," recalls Neddie Winters. Their assistance did not stop with their intercessions; each of the businessmen present committed to spend at least $25 a week at the store. As a result, wealthy white businessmen purchased groceries alongside the poorest African American's in the Farish Street neighborhood. "I see those white guys over there shopping," Winters reported.[106] The same year the store opened, Mission Mississippi announced that Leaks would be joining their board of directors. Lee Paris, the chairman, praised Leaks for his "commitment to the inner-city."[107]

By 2002, Leaks and Price owned six stores, making New Deal among the largest black-owned grocery chains in the country and the largest in Mississippi.[108] Leaks hoped that by halting the flow of services and businesses out of the inner-city neighborhoods he could help return resources to the African American community. "The only way our neighborhoods are going to do better is the people in our neighborhoods are going to have to own businesses," explained Leaks, "[then] all of a sudden the money is coming in the neighborhood. Then all of a sudden, it's sustaining itself."[109] His faith meant Leaks refused to see these neighborhoods and their residents as hopelessly dysfunctional:

> As a Christian, I have to believe that God has placed enough of
> everything needed in a community. It's not a slight on anybody else,
> but I refuse to beg anybody else. I refuse to accept this myth that
> we as a people can't work together.... I cannot give up on us as a
> people.[110]

Leaks and Price stated their goal was to create as many minority owned businesses as they could.[111] In 2002, they turned the ownership of their stores over to their managers while retaining ownership of the in-store customer service centers.[112] This enabled the two entrepreneurs to concentrate on seeking new locations and helping other African American business owners expand their business alongside the New Deal stores.[113] However, by December 2006, five of the stores had closed, leaving only the original supermarket on Monument Street still open for business.[114]

Given the examples of Lextron and New Deal Supermarkets—and to a lesser extent, the church partnerships—Weary's insistence that Mission

Mississippi "is not [just] a place where a group of people get together and feel good," carries some weight.[115] Nevertheless, do we see the work of Mission Mississippi leading to white Christians developing what Miroslav Volf calls double vision? Do whites learn to see Mississippi from an African American perspective and decide to work to transform the systems that privilege whiteness? These are not simple questions to answer; there are, after all, forces within Mission Mississippi effectively working against systemic social transformation. Mission Mississippi's pronouncements and practices carefully seek to remain acceptable to those whites who insist that justice is not the business of the church. Those who hold this position are among the influential whites involved in the formation of the organization; and, as demonstrated in the last chapter, these whites have powerful cultural and doctrinal checks in place resisting: first, the perception of racialized systemic forces; and second, the social implications of the gospel of Jesus Christ. Is Dolphus Weary correct to trust that Mission Mississippi will lead participants deeper into reconciliation? Do the relationships formed through Mission Mississippi open whites' eyes to systemic injustice and subvert their established notions of the spirituality of the church? Simply, is there a double vision developing in which, as Volf believes, "forgiveness will name injustice as injustice and therefore demand that its causes be removed"?[116]

While spending time with participants in Mission Mississippi, it is impossible not to hear testimonies of reconciliation and tales of renegotiating racial attitudes without seeing glimmers of something that looks a lot like Volf's double vision. To try statistically to quantify double vision, even if it were possible, is beyond the scope of this project. Instead, here are two vignettes of such moments that point to the possibility of Mission Mississippi leading to action informed by a new double vision. The first example is from the vitriolic debate surrounding Mississippi's state flag; the second example is of a white couple's conscious resistance of the forces that lead to white flight and continuing residential segregation and urban decay.

The Flag

By the end of the twentieth century, Mississippi, along with other states in the Deep South, found itself examining the presence of the Confederate flag in its state flag, a symbol that many found anachronistic and inflammatory.[117] In the summer of 2000, a commission appointed by Governor Ronnie Musgrove, headed by former Governor William Winter, and including Dolphus Weary held public hearings around Mississippi to gauge opinion and garner suggestions and support for a new flag. Winter recalls that at the commission's hearings, "All of us took a lot of very harsh comments from some very irate people."[118] Following the hearings, the commission recommended a statewide election to replace the Confederate symbol in the state's flag.[119] The flag vote on April 17, 2001, resulted in a resounding victory for those who wished to keep the old flag and disappointment for those who believed that a new flag would symbolically demonstrate Mississippi's desire to move on from its troubled, racist past.

The controversy around the flag generated national media attention. The week after the state voted to keep the old flag, Lee Paris and Dolphus Weary appeared in a *Time* magazine article. Weary explained to the reporter his support for a new flag based on the Confederate symbol's connection with slavery, Jim Crow and the Ku Klux Klan, and Paris explained his sentimental attachment to the flag, "I love that flag, and I love my heritage." The article then reports a startling moment of double vision: "Weary says...that through his friendship with Paris, he has understood the history-and-heritage argument for the first time." It is not only Weary who sees the situation with new eyes. The report continues: "Because of his friendship with Weary and other African Americans, and because 'as a Christian man I cannot do that which harms my brother,' Paris voted to bring the flag down."[120]

Paris, who grew up waving the rebel flag at Ole Miss football games, explains how this was no small change for him:

> I loved that flag and I loved our state flag...but as I got to know the hearts of African American brothers and sisters in this area and when they looked at that flag they saw something completely different than I did. So a scripture came to mind—if it causes your brother to stumble then put it away. And so...I came out for changing the flag. It is painful to do so and there was much division even in my own family about the issue, but I did vote for the new flag.[121]

Here double vision, resulting from the relationship between Paris and Weary, not only enabled Weary to understand Paris's dilemma it also led Paris to question his own heritage and position as he saw it anew from another's perspective. This double vision led to a change in the way Paris voted. The fact that those desiring a new flag lost at the polls complicates the story. The result left Weary wondering if he should have involved himself in the politically divisive flag commission, whereas Paris, although he voted for the new flag, wryly acknowledges, "I guess in a way I was blessed both ways in that I got to vote my convictions and yet what I really wanted won out."[122]

The second example is of a sustained attempt by a white couple to maintain double vision and see things from the perspective of their new African American neighbors. This story did not make national news but it does demonstrate that involvement with Mission Mississippi leads some to consider the social and systemic forces at work that perpetuate racial and economic divisions in the state.

White Flight

Ben and Judy Beaird bought their modest, ranch-style house in a new white subdivision of Clinton in 1977. The neighborhood remained exclusively white until, around the turn of the twenty-first century, middle-class African Americans began moving to the neighborhood, fleeing the rising crime in South Jackson. The Beairds had been actively involved in churches promoting racial reconciliation and had been involved at various times with both Mission Mississippi and the John M. Perkins Foundation for Reconciliation and Development. Both were surprised at their own emotional reflex when, stemming from old wounds of prejudice, they found themselves in a transitioning neighborhood. Judy Beaird confesses:

> I freaked! I was so uncomfortable that I had to cry. Within the last
> year, I now have four black families adjacent to me [and] I was not
> raised to live in a black neighborhood. That just doesn't fit with my
> self image which is…antiquated but deeply ingrained…and I want
> that to change, but I was having to deal with the reality of it. It was
> just coming way up from the unconscious stuff.[123]

Such discomfort, as demonstrated by the shifting demographics of Jackson's neighborhoods, usually results in whites selling their property and moving. The Beairds actively resisted their own discomfort. When an African American family moved into the house behind their property, Judy Beaird knew what their Christian responsibility was. "I said Ben, you've got to get up and go meet these people. In order to break the barrier of hesitancy that you've got, you've got to do that."

Armed with a flyer for Mission Mississippi's Two and Two Restaurant Days, Ben Beaird introduced himself to his new neighbors and invited them out for a meal. Mission Mississippi's Two and Two Restaurant Days fit closely with Dolphus Weary's strategy of Reconciliation IOI. Offering a white couple and a black couple a 22 percent discount when they eat together at participating restaurants, the Two and Two deal aims to get African Americans and whites to sit down together at the same table and begin to talk. In the Beaird's case, this enabled them to break through their "barrier of hesitancy." Judy Beaird explains the difference these faltering steps towards relationship have made. "I used to look out of the window," she remembers, "and I would see black people going in and out and everything in me would just cringe. I look out now and I smile because I know them.... I am not proud at all of how hard it's been...[but] I am in transition just like the neighborhood."[124]

Deciding to stay and build relationships with the African Americans moving into the neighborhood came as a result of the work of Mission Mississippi. "I could not have made these kind of moves in the past without some discipling about this...[from] Mission Mississippi," explains Ben Beaird. "I've been [to Mission Mississippi events] enough to know what the issues are and I had something to draw on, and I drew on it and it worked out."[125]

Conclusion

The asymmetry between these modest tales and the reality of injustice, oppression, and continuing economic disparity between African Americans and whites in Mississippi might suggest a conclusion that dismisses Mission Mississippi as too timid. The solution of "one relationship at a time" does not appear to be a proportionate response to the problem. Certainly, the demise of Lextron and the decline of New Deal Supermarkets present a salutary reminder that changing the economic fortunes of African Americans in Mississippi is a complex and long-term undertaking. However, a critique of Mission Mississippi's simple objective—to place racial reconciliation onto churches' agendas and create opportunities for relationships to form across racial and denominational lines—can only be made after an assessment of the underlying strategy and theology articulated by Dolphus Weary as "Reconciliation 101."

Mission Mississippi has strong theological support for placing the invitation to open relationships before meeting the demands of justice. The will to embrace the other, as Miroslav Volf argues, is not conditional on both parties having atoned for past sins. At the same time, this theology of embrace reminds Mission Mississippi not to slip into cheap reconciliation. They must not forget that they are merely the ushers for the big reconciliation picture starring truth and justice. The temptation is for Mission Mississippi to be content simply playing host to the comfortable crowd in the foyer, rather than ushering them toward the discomfort of reconciliation that will change Mississippi.

Judging its approach simply as a strategy, Mission Mississippi only succeeds as far as it attracts Christians from African American and white churches and enables them to form sustained relationships that challenge and start to change the racialized structures of the state. Two factors combine in Mission Mississippi to hamper this transition from reconciliation as social interaction to reconciliation as social reconstruction. The first is Mission Mississippi's desire to involve as many churches in their activities as possible, achieved by keeping barriers to participation as low as possible. The second is that some of the key leaders and policy makers of Mission Mississippi come from white churches that balk at the faintest whiff of ecumenism or the social gospel. The result of this combination is an inertia resisting the idea that reconciliation will require examining questions of systemic economic injustice and social segregation of churches and schools. This inertia fits Volf's description of a theology of reconciliation *outside* justice. Countering this inertia is the energy and conviction of experienced and successful African American pioneers of community development in Jackson who see Mission Mississippi's strategy as essentially right and important for the future of the state.

Volf's theology of embrace affirms the importance of Mission Mississippi's project and, at the same time, exposes some of its pitfalls. Revealed are the forces working against the trajectory of the will to embrace from within the church in the name of justice, on the one hand, and forgiveness, on the other. Perhaps most important, Volf's attention to the importance of double vision justifies and enriches Mission Mississippi's insistence on the primacy of relationship in the embrace of reconciliation. The development of this double vision gives Mission Mississippi a clear theological model for understanding how, starting with individual relationships, Christians can move deeper into a reconciliation of forgiveness, truth, and justice, which could change Mississippi.

6

A Practice of Open Friendship

Prayer Breakfasts

Contemporary American theologian L. Gregory Jones wrote,
"Christian forgiveness aims at reconciliation and involves the task of
responding to God's forgiving love by crafting communities of forgiven
and forgiving people."[1] For these communities, Jones argued, "the
capacity to discover what it means to be forgiven and to forgive depends
on the richness of [their] communal habits, practices, and disciplines."[2]
If Jones is correct, then for Mission Mississippi to be about the work of
Christian reconciliation, of being the community of open friendship,
we would expect to find "communal habits, practices, and disciplines"
leading to a deepening level of forgiveness and reconciliation among
the participants. This chapter contends that Mission Mississippi's
twice-weekly prayer breakfasts are a practice of open friendship.[3]

Considering the experiences and testimonies of the participants,
those who gather regularly for the Mission Mississippi prayer
breakfasts engage in a communal habit, practice, and discipline
of a Christian open friendship. Regular participants of the prayer
meetings testify to their experience of forgiveness and the forging
of relationships across racial and denominational lines. Many of the
white participants express a new understanding and appreciation for
the lives and opinions of African Americans in Mississippi.

Mission Mississippi frequently proclaims the prayer meetings to
be the essential core of its activities. In 1996, Mission Mississippi

published a glossy eight-page booklet telling their story and presenting their ongoing work. In the booklet, Mission Mississippi described the prayer breakfasts as "the backbone" and "the heart" of the organization's work of reconciliation. The booklet continued to explain that the prayer breakfasts had produced "two striking results. First God has answered prayer.... Second, real friendships have been forged in the furnace of regular, weekly fellowship around prayer."[4] In 1997, Mission Mississippi's board reiterated the centrality of the prayer meetings in their Vision Statement: Unity in the body of Christ, they wrote, "is most effectively achieved as we pray together. The chief activity of Mission Mississippi is sponsoring regular times of prayer, including weekly morning prayer breakfasts."[5] As Mission Mississippi struggled to transition from large events to a more relationship-orientated program, John Geary, Mission Mississippi's Director of Development, wrote in a confidential memo to the chairman Lee Paris, "everything but Thursday morning prayer breakfasts should be open for change."[6]

In Jackson, Mission Mississippi holds other regular prayer meetings; every third Wednesday of the month, the Businessmen's Prayer Breakfast meets at the University Club in Jackson, and the Women's Prayer Luncheon convenes on the third Friday of the month at Galloway United Methodist Church. However, the real heart of Mission Mississippi's program of intercessory prayer is the prayer breakfasts it holds in different locations around the city from 6:45 to 7:45 every Tuesday and Thursday morning.

In order to explore the lived theology of reconciliation located in the practice of Mission Mississippi's morning prayer meetings, it is important to have an understanding of what actually happens at these breakfasts. With the venue for the prayer breakfasts changing every time, it is difficult to talk of a typical meeting. The members of the prayer committee, who manage the prayer meetings, spend a great deal of their energy contacting churches and institutions to arrange venues. A glance down a list of locations hosting the meetings reveals not only churches but also private and public schools, hospitals and medical facilities, universities and colleges, police and fire stations, the offices of the *Clarion-Ledger* newspaper, and even the Governor's Mansion.[7] The two prayer meetings described here took place in the same week in the fall of 2004; the first at a private school, the second at a Missionary Baptist church. Neither space was racially neutral. One venue (the school) was a culturally white space; the other (the church) was culturally African American.

Jackson Academy, Tuesday, October 5, 2004

Jackson Academy is located in Northeast Jackson on Ridgewood Road in an established white suburb. It is still dark as those attending the Mission Mississippi prayer breakfast arrive, and there is some confusion as to where the library—the location of the prayer breakfast—actually is. The school, established in 1959, fills a city block with its red brick facilities and sports fields. One of the largest private schools in the city, Jackson Academy provides a high standard of education from prekindergarten through twelfth grade for its almost all-white student body.[8]

As people straggle into the second floor library, they write their names on labels that they stick to their chests and make their way over to the librarian's desk where teachers from Jackson Academy have laid out the breakfast (the hosting church or organization supplies the breakfast for the prayer meetings). This morning, next to two flasks of coffee and containers of orange juice sits a mound of rapidly cooling foil-wrapped Chik-fil-A chicken biscuits. People take their food over to the worktables in the center of the library, engage the biscuits, and make polite conversation.

Janet Thomas, a staff person from Mission Mississippi, comes around the tables passing out small bulletins for today's meeting (she spends the rest of the meeting taking photographs for Mission Mississippi's website). The four pages contain a list of statewide and local prayer requests as well as three bulleted prayer requests for Jackson Academy. On the cover of the bulletin is a picture of the "Jackson Raider," a mounted Civil War–era soldier brandishing a sword.

By the time James Turner calls the prayer meeting to order, there are seventeen people present. The group is racially balanced; eight are African American and nine are white. Discounting the three teachers, everyone sitting in the library is a regular attendee of Mission Mississippi's prayer breakfasts: three are staff members and five are members of the prayer committee. With only two ministers present, one black and one white, laity outnumber clergy.[9] There are two Roman Catholic nuns participating this morning and three teachers from the Jackson Academy, including Peter Jernberg the headmaster. With a couple of exceptions, everyone is either middle-aged or past retirement.

At the end of the room, Virginia Chase, Mission Mississippi's events and activities coordinator, draws attention to the notices in the bulletin. She particularly asks for prayer for the Weary family and for Dolphus as he goes to Wheaton College, Illinois, for a meeting of the college's board of visitors. Finally, Chase gives directions to the next prayer meeting that will be held in her own church, First Hyde Park Missionary Baptist Church. Sheree Tynes, the chair of the prayer committee, briefly requests that everyone attending the prayer breakfast at the Governor's Mansion the following week put their names on the guest list. Tynes then invites Jernberg, the headmaster, to say a few words.

"What a privilege it is for us to have Mission Mississippi back on our campus," exclaims Jernberg. He goes on to explain, in good Mississippi fashion, how he is connected by geography, church, and school to Mission Mississippi. Jernberg, it turns out, attended Lee Paris's childhood church in Indianola and was one of his schoolteachers. Following his welcome, Jernberg introduces the morning's speaker: Lester Walls of the Fellowship of Christian Athletes. When the prayer meetings take place at a church, it is customary for the pastor or priest to present a short meditation from scripture; this morning Walls, whose ministry is mostly to high school students, takes this job. Walls, an African American built like a linebacker, appears the epitome of muscular Christianity.

Before he starts preaching, Walls invites Daryl Smith to share his testimony. Smith is as slight and short as Walls is stocky and tall. Standing between the library tables, Smith talks of God's support in his life before breaking into a very accomplished black gospel rendition of the old hymn "Great is thy faithfulness." Smith's voice soars, his ornamentation breaking down the strictures of meter and measure. The small congregation gathered in the library greets his final phrase, floated on an effortless falsetto, with a chorus of Amens.

Walls then delivers his message; it is a reflection on Psalm 101. Employing the style he uses when addressing high school athletes, Walls pulls out a remote control. A remote control is only useful, he explains, when we are in the presence of a television. Similarly, we need to be in God's presence if we are to be any use. The remote control is only a trifling visual aid compared to what Walls produces next. "God is tired with us playing church!" Walls declares as from behind a chair he pulls a huge two-handed sword that would make a Highland warrior wish to trade in his Claymore (see figure 6.1). Challenging

FIGURE 6.1. Lester Walls delivers the message with a very large sword, Jackson Academy, October 5, 2004. (Courtesy of Mission Mississippi)

people to lift the sword with one hand, he demonstrates to everyone's satisfaction that two hands are required. In the same way, Walls explains, "We need to be reliant on God's power that comes from his presence."

At 7:25, Walls finishes speaking and the meeting breaks into small groups of three or four to pray. Although not explicit, the expectation is clearly that these groups should be interracial. Seated at the tables with the prayer bulletins open in front of them, each person in the small group has the chance briefly to share their own personal needs and concerns. The regulars are attentive to ongoing family concerns of other participants. Often, before a participant can share their needs, another group member anticipates their request: someone asks how their sick mother is doing or if a relative has been able to find employment. The groups then bow their heads and the room fills with the earnest murmur of prayer (see figure 6.2).

With only a couple of minutes left before the scheduled end of the meeting, Sheree Tynes calls the groups to stop praying. The three teachers from the academy stand in an open space and everyone gathers around them in a scrimmage. Those closest to the teachers reach out one or both hands and touch them; those toward the edge touch the person in front (see figure 6.3). Lester Walls raises his voice and leads a prayer for the teachers and the school—his

FIGURE 6.2. Small group prayer, Jackson Academy, October 5, 2004. (Courtesy of Mission Mississippi)

FIGURE 6.3. Group prays for teachers, Jackson Academy, October 5, 2004. (Courtesy of Mission Mississippi)

tone is fervent and the African Americans in the group interject his words with "Amen" and "Yes Lord." The prayer ends and participants make their way back to their cars in the parking lot and the day's work that awaits them. White teenagers on their way to their first class of the morning cast disinterested glances toward the African Americans.

First Hyde Park Missionary Baptist Church, Thursday, October 7, 2004

Two days after the prayer meeting in Jackson's white suburbs, those attending the Thursday morning breakfast were driving in the dark trying to find a church in a very different neighborhood. Following the directions given by Virginia Chase, the participants drive down Medgar Evers Boulevard—named for Jackson's own slain civil rights leader—looking for Coleman Avenue. They recognize the intersection from the presence of Volcano. Volcano is a club, a windowless blue box sporting little more than its name, a door, and old air conditioning units jutting straight out of the walls. First Hyde Park MB Church lies a short way down Coleman Avenue in a rundown neighborhood of small houses. Once a good place to raise a family, now, according to a member of the church, it is "drug infested."[10] The church is a low brick building with narrow slits for windows and a small ornamental steeple perched over the entrance. In the corner of the parking lot, the church's minivan sits inside its own barbed

FIGURE 6.4. First Hyde Park MB Church, Jackson, Mississippi.
(Photo by author)

wire topped stockade; at 6:30 in the morning, this is the only indication this is a high crime neighborhood (see figure 6.4).

The prayer meeting is in the hall at the back of the church. It is a long room with white cinder block walls, fluorescent strip lighting and a linoleum floor. Two rows of tables with plastic floral tablecloths and metal folding chairs run the length of the room. As at Jackson Academy, people fill in nametags as they walk in. At the far end of the room, behind a heated trolley, stands R. L. Horton Sr., a deacon of the church (see figure 6.5). The trolley would put Shoney's to shame. It is loaded with food: grits, scrambled eggs, beef sausage, pork sausage patties, pork sausage links, bacon, turkey bacon, and hot biscuits. Alongside on a table with the jelly and syrup are bagels, fruit, orange juice, and coffee. This morning there are twenty people in attendance. Fifteen are African American, eight of whom are members of the Hyde Park congregation. Again, there is the core group of Mission Mississippi staff and members of the prayer committee.

Virginia Chase calls people from their plates and introduces her pastor and the minister of Hyde Park, Terry L. Davis. He brings a message of encouragement to Mission Mississippi from the story of the ten lepers found in the gospel of Luke (see figure 6.6). In the same way that the lepers cried out for Jesus attention (17:13), preaches Davis, "There [are] a lot of folks around, but

FIGURE 6.5. Deacon R. L. Horton Sr. serves breakfast, First Hyde Park
Missionary Baptist Church, October 7, 2004. (Photo by author)

there's only a few folks making a noise!" At this, the room explodes with guf-
faws and cries of "Well!" and "Amen."

"There are a lot of organizations in the city of Jackson," Davis continues, "but a lot of organizations aren't making the same noise that Mission
Mississippi is making." Davis continues to draw out the analogy: It is crucial
for Mission Mississippi, as for the lepers in the story, to see from where their
healing comes. Finally, he offers encouragement, "We never find out too much
about the nine [lepers], but [we do about the] one. And so it is alright to just be
the one."

When Davis finishes his ten-minute address, the meeting breaks into
small groups for prayer. With fewer whites to go round, the small groups are
not as racially balanced as they had been at Jackson Academy. However, in all
other aspects, this portion of the meeting consists of the same elements. The

FIGURE 6.6. Pastor Terry L. Davis preaching at the Prayer Breakfast, First Hyde Park Missionary Baptist Church, October 7, 2004. (Photo by author)

members of each group take it in turns to share prayer requests and then the members of the group close their eyes, bow their heads, and take it in turns to pray for the needs shared and for those written up in the bulletin.

The small groups are brought to a halt as the time nears 7:45. Then everyone gathers in the middle of the hall for the final prayer. This morning, the prayer meeting departs from the standard format of laying hands on the pastor and praying for his ministry and the mission of the church. Instead of gathering around the pastor, this morning people lay hands on one of their number, an African American woman called Jackie Pate. Pate is a faithful member of the prayer committee and a volunteer in the Mission Mississippi office. With her left arm paralyzed after a stroke following the birth of her sixth child, Jackie is searching for a job while struggling to raise three school-age children. Many in the room have heard Jackie's story shared through her prayer requests in small groups. "I have been going through hell for the last three and a half years," she tells people.[11]

This morning, following the small group prayer time, Pate is deeply distressed and the group gathers around. Virginia Chase holds Pate to her as

FIGURE 6.7. Virginia Chase holds Jackie Pate as Terry L. Davis leads the group in prayer, First Hyde Park Missionary Baptist Church, October 7, 2004. (Photo by author)

Pastor Davis prays for Pate to experience "God's Victory" in her situation. The emotional intensity and passionate focus of those surrounding Pate in prayer is far higher than anything experienced at Jackson Academy (see figure 6.7).

A Lived Theology of Prayer and Reconciliation

Both leaders and participants in Mission Mississippi claim that the prayer meetings are the heart of the movement and essential to their efforts at relationship-driven reconciliation. Phil Reed, a longtime supporter of Mission Mississippi, makes just such an assertion: "What makes Mission Mississippi work is people praying together." He does not want the claim dismissed as evangelical piety, "I know it sounds like a Sunday school answer, but that really is the key."[12] Lee Paris, the chairman for fifteen years and one of the founders, agrees that praying together "is the strongest and quickest way to bind with our brothers and sisters that we have traditionally not been able to dwell with."[13] This is the lived theology of the community of believers in Mission Mississippi and it deserves serious consideration. What is it about interracial intercessory prayer that, in the experience of Mississippi Christians, proves crucial for their desire to see unity between races and denominations?

In interviews with participants in Mission Mississippi, I asked the questions: "Why is prayer important for racial reconciliation?" and "What has been your experience of praying with people of a different race?" After a few interviews, I realized my questions only elicited brief formulaic answers. I switched my questions to one that tapped into the narrative convention of the evangelical culture: "What is your testimony of praying at Mission Mississippi prayer meetings?" The resulting stories gave a rich insight into the experiences of interracial intercessory prayer that help illumine the importance of this practice for Mission Mississippi.

What follows is an exploration of the major themes emerging from these testimonies of interracial intercessory prayer and observations from the particular form and practices of the prayer breakfasts in conversation with theology, biblical scholarship, and sociology. This conversation, to use Dolphus Weary's favored phrase, takes us deeper into an understanding of the relationship between intercessory prayer, open friendship, forgiveness, reconciliation, and justice. The result supports the thesis that Mission Mississippi's prayer breakfasts are indeed a rich communal practice of open friendship.

Intercessory Prayer Is the Language of Friendship

Just as Mission Mississippi links prayer to the formation of intentional relationships across the traditional boundaries of the Closed Society, Moltmann, in his "brief but seminal passage" on open friendship, locates prayer as the foremost expression of this friendship.[14] "Friendship with God comes preeminently to expression through the prayer of a free man."[15] Moltmann roots his theology of open friendship in his reading of John's gospel and Jesus telling his disciples, "I do not call you servants any longer...but I have called you friends" (15:15). Moltmann notes that Jesus follows this revelation with teaching on prayer: "the Father will give you whatever you ask him in my name" (15:16b). Moltmann succinctly summarizes this connection between friendship and prayer: "God can be talked to. He listens to his friends."[16] Understood this way, the act of gathering for corporate prayer is the principal practice of the community of the friends of God.

Following Moltmann's definition of "the friend [as] the person who 'loves in freedom,'" Christian prayer is essentially the expression of a relationship of "mutual freedom and respect."[17] If prayer is the free conversation between friends then "prayer is not a servant's desperate begging, nor is it the insistence of a demanding child. Prayer in Christ's name is the language of friendship."[18] As Mission Mississippi gathers early on a weekday morning for interracial intercessory prayer, the participants build their relationships in the context of an activity constituted by the friendship of God and the language of Jesus' open friendship.

Before the hyperbole of theological language sweeps us away, it is important to realize that small group prayer meetings in Mississippi are not an unusual occurrence. The high number of professing Christians in Mississippi means that prayer meetings occur not just in churches but also in homes, schools and places of work.[19] In fact, it is not only in the Bible Belt that prayer meetings are commonplace. The Princeton sociologist Robert Wuthnow, in a national study of support groups, estimated that four out of every ten Americans belong to a small group. Of these participants, 69 percent say they pray together in their groups.[20] That means that almost three out of every ten Americans participate in a group that involves some kind of corporate prayer. Although Wuthnow's study considered secular as well as religious small groups, his survey showed that 57 percent of those participating in small groups said their group was part of the regular activities of a church or synagogue. Of these, 94 percent of the participants reported their groups were composed mostly of members of their church or synagogue.[21] Wuthnow noted that as "virtually all" members of church-sponsored small groups (Bible studies, prayer groups, etc.) attend the same congregation, the churches or synagogues effectively "provide a screening function...ensur[ing]...they have something in common with other members and can feel safe and secure."[22] It is reasonable to conclude from Wuthnow's study that although a huge number of Americans participate in small groups that pray, the vast majority of them are praying with people who are like themselves. Indeed, the involvement of churches in these prayer groups tends to safeguard their members from praying with anyone whose racial, economic, or ideological otherness might cause them discomfort.

Wuthnow notes uneasily that the burgeoning small group movement in the United States caters to the "religion of one's choice."[23] Small groups are most often concerned with the "emotional support" of their members. This emotional support, Wuthnow finds, "is defined to mean encouragement rather than criticism or guidance."[24]

Mission Mississippi's prayer meetings are significantly different from the majority of the small groups in Wuthnow's study: a participant in a Mission Mississippi prayer breakfast is intentionally praying with people who may be racially, socially, economically, educationally, or politically different than themselves. Rather than finding comfort in a homogenous closed prayer circle, the participant engages in the often uncomfortable task of meeting people with whom they have little in common and who challenge their preconceptions.

Intercessory Prayer Challenges the Closed Society

Mission Mississippi's prayer breakfasts challenge the boundaries of social conformity that define a closed society. Meeting to pray with Christians of a different race, denomination, and culture causes levels of discomfort in the participants at the most basic level. Participants find that, although they may pray to the same God, they do not pray in the same ways. Sheree Tynes, the chair of the prayer committee and a member of First Baptist Church, sees this variety at work: "I hear so much differentness in prayer because I think Baptists pray kind of alike and Catholics...do their rosary and don't always pray out loud....And then Presbyterians have their way of praying, and Methodists."[25]

One of the most significant differences in prayer and worship styles is between African Americans and whites. Virginia Chase, Mission Mississippi's event coordinator and frequent attendee at the prayer breakfasts, finds herself moderating her usually exuberant manner of prayer and worship to minimize the discomfort for white participants. While attending a Mission Mississippi meeting in a white church, Chase recalls a white friend noting her change in behavior, "One of my friends is a member of Christ United [Methodist]. And when I was sitting beside her she said, "I know it is killing you because you are from a Missionary Baptist church and you are used to saying: Amen....But you are sitting there as quiet as we [whites] are." Chase explained to her friend, "Well I don't want to be out of line; I don't want to be insulting; I want to be able to worship and praise with you in whatever way you worship and praise." For Chase, this is a small price to pay to experience prayer and worship across racial and denominational lines. "I think that sacrifice I can withstand," she says with a smile, "I can go to my church and whoop and holler any day."[26]

Many whites reported the expressive character of the African American prayer traditions compared to their own more staid prayers. Rather than a sacrifice, they tended to consider this evidence of the enrichment that racial diversity brings to the Church. Ralph Maisel, a white Episcopalian in his sixties, referring to the difference in style of prayer between African Americans and whites, said, "One thing—at least in my private life—that I have experienced that I didn't have before was their prayers." Maisel values this difference, even considering the prayers of African Americans more efficacious than his own, stating, "These people are anointed with the ability to pray."[27]

Attending interracial and interdenominational prayer meetings involves more for the participants than simply overcoming the discomforting barriers of different styles of prayer. Participants intentionally cross the high barriers of history and tradition. Whites come from churches that, during the civil rights movement, passed resolutions excluding African Americans from their services, fearful of the changes the movement represented.[28] Sheree Tynes recalls the fear that the integration of church services generated then and that still lingers in some quarters:

> I remember when I was pretty young at my home church there was talk, just sort of under currents, that there might be some black people who'll try to break into church on Sunday morning. I remember some of the men of the church being posted at strategic locations in the church in case some blacks wanted to come in and bust up the service.[29]

Although whites deal with a history of segregation and the notional fears that interracial worship generated, for African Americans, the historic barriers to interracial prayer were far more substantial and the consequences for crossing them tangible.

Joel Weathersby, a retired nurse's assistant and deacon at Cherry Grove Missionary Baptist Church, grew up with the psychological shackles of Jim Crow. "In a sense," he explained, "we thought that white was better than black." His parents, farmers in Simpson County, warned their children to respect whites whatever their age. They told him of African Americans lynched for disregarding the mores of segregation. "You stay in your place," they told their son, "just do what you're supposed to do and respect them... and keep going." The civil rights movement changed Weathersby's view of his own worth relative to whites. "As things began to move on and change," he recounted, "I could see different and actually I thought different."[30] When he started attending Mission Mississippi's prayer breakfasts, the world was very different from the one his parents trained him to negotiate. "If it had been years previous before that I might've would've been afraid," Weathersby said, "[But] the fearfulness at that time had mostly passed over to an extent." Now a member of the prayer committee, Weathersby remembered going to his first prayer breakfasts, "I wasn't nervous, I wasn't afraid. It was more of a challenge just to be part of it, to see what it's like [to] communicate with the white person."[31]

The fear of white people may have dissipated since the days of Jim Crow and the rule of lynch law; however, for African Americans, anger at and distrust of whites is a historic barrier that they have to cross when they attend a Mission Mississippi prayer meeting. Jackie Pate, the women prayed for with such fervor at the Hyde Park prayer meeting, never imagined she would sit down twice a week with whites for morning prayer. Growing up in Mississippi and Chicago in the 1960s and 1970s, she has vivid memories of segregation and racial tension. Before going to her first Mission Mississippi prayer meeting

Pate said, "I would never intentionally try to get to be in a relationship with a white person...because of all the anger and hatred and hurt that I had experienced from white people in my past."[32] However, as a member of Ronnie Crudup's New Horizons, she went to a prayer breakfast hosted by the church. "When I went to the first prayer breakfast it was like a light bulb went off in my head and said: this is where I want you to be. And I said, "Oh yes Lord!" And so I joined the prayer committee the next committee meeting and I have been here ever since."[33] What biblical and theological resources are at hand to help interpret these deliberate crossings of fearsome cultural boundaries to pray?

The Roman Catholic scholar Luke Timothy Johnson, in his work on the Letter of James, offers a theological way of framing this act of intercessory prayer as a discipline of open friendship and a challenge to the Closed Society. Johnson shows how understanding James' use of the terms *"friendship with the world"* (4:4) and *"friendship with God"* (2:23) is key to appreciating the epistle. James writes, "Adulterers! Do you not know that friendship with the world is enmity with God? Therefore whoever wishes to be a friend of the world becomes an enemy of God" (4:4).[34] This verse would seem to encourage the church to withdraw from society—to concern itself solely with spiritual matters—and become the very closed church in a closed society that Jürgen Moltmann warns against.[35] Not so, argues Johnson. He shows how, in the Hellenistic world of James' epistle, a friend was "another self;" friends saw things the same way and were equal.[36] James uses the term friendship to indicate complete agreement with a system of values. In addition, when James uses the term "world," he means "a measure of reality, or a system of meaning, which can be contrasted to that of God."[37] Thus, Johnson states, friendship with the world means "profound agreement with a measure opposed to God's."[38] A church embracing the logic of a closed society—modeling its structures on closed friendships where like seeks after like—is friends with the world. Such friendship with the world (closed friendship) is in stark contrast to friendship with God. James describes Abraham as a friend of God: "Abraham believed God and it was reckoned to him as righteousness, and he was called the friend of God" (2:23). Friendship with God, Johnson explains, is recognizing God's claim on one's life and acknowledging that "claim in faith and action."[39] Friendship with God is to have, what Jürgen Moltmann calls, a different horizon than those who live without the hope of Christ.[40]

In light of this understanding of friendship, Johnson's commentary on the passage on prayer (5:13–18) is particularly relevant to an understanding of Mission Mississippi's prayer breakfasts. In his epistle, James instructs the church to summon the elders to pray for those who are sick. Then in a fascinating couple of verses, James links prayer, the confession of sins, forgiveness and healing: "The prayer of faith will save the sick, and the Lord will raise them up; and anyone who has committed sins will be forgiven. Therefore confess your sins to one another, and pray for one another, so that you may be healed" (5:15–16a). Johnson comments, "A community is healed as *ekklesia* when, in trust and vulnerability, it is able to pray and confess sins together."[41] Immediately following the injunction to pray for the sick and confess sins one to another, James gives the example of Elijah as a righteous man whose prayer was "powerful and effective" (5:16b). Only ten verses earlier, James uses the same word "righteous" (*dikaios*) referring to the poor and oppressed murdered by the rich. Johnson writes, "Elijah, in other words, was situated over against the powers of his world, as the oppressed poor are situated over against the rich. Yet Elijah's prayer was more powerful than them."[42] Then follows Johnson's summary of James' teaching on prayer. It is worth quoting at length because it makes explicit the connection between prayer, open friendship, and resistance to a closed society:

> This is the lesson to James' readers: the prayer that can raise the sick person and heal the community can also prove triumphant over the powers of evil in the world, for prayer is the openness of the human spirit to the powerful word of God that enables it to work. Indeed, the prayer of the community gathered in solidarity is already a victory over the world that defines itself by envy and competition. For prayer refuses that definition of reality. Prayer resists idolatry by insisting on the greater power of what is not seen than that which is seen. The prayer of the community gathered in solidarity triumphs over those forces that seek to divide and conquer, to isolate and eliminate, by insisting together on being "other" than that world, as being defined by what is totally "other" than that world, by seeking friendship with God rather than with that world (4:4).[43]

We have seen the ways in which participants in the prayer breakfasts have an awareness of how the intentional practice of praying together challenges the historic social barriers of the closed society and refuses "that definition of reality." But is there also present Johnson's understanding that in the act of praying the participants insist "on the greater power of what is not seen than that which is seen"? Asked in an interview to explain how prayer is so vital to Mission Mississippi, Lee Paris eloquently made a case for the way the practice of prayer presupposes and creates a solidarity based on a faith in things not seen:

> We serve a God who parted the Red Sea, and rescued Daniel from the lions' den, and raised his Son from the tomb.... And so, we go to

him in prayer asking what the world would deem impossible, what in my culture half a generation ago would have seemed impossible, but in Christ all things are possible. And so we go to him and say: Lord make this happen.[44]

Paris articulated Johnson's understanding that "the prayer of the community gathered in solidarity is already a victory over the world that defines itself by envy and competition."[45]

Viewed in this way, overcoming historical and cultural barriers to form communities around interracial intercessory prayer prophetically challenges the idolatry of the Closed Society and its closed churches. Participants in Mission Mississippi, however, claim far more than this for their prayer meetings. They believe that praying together actually enables or facilitates their journeys to move deeper into forgiveness and reconciliation one relationship at a time.

Intercessory Prayer, Storytelling, and Christian Friendship

As shown in the last chapter, Mission Mississippi and the theologian Miroslav Volf agree that the creation of a safe space in which participants can tell the truth and graciously hear the stories of others is crucial to the process of reconciliation. For reconciliation to be a possibility, the participants must be willing to hear and understand the other's truth and then seek to see themselves and their claims to justice and truth from this new perspective. Volf calls this new perspective "double vision."[46] The South African theologian John De Gruchy, reflecting on the lessons learned from the Truth and Reconciliation Commission, draws the same conclusion. "The process of reconciliation," De Gruchy writes, "begins through the taking of what might appear to be small and often tentative steps." The first step is "meeting and listening to the estranged 'other.'" The second is "the willingness to listen to the other side of the story even if we remain unconvinced."[47] This leads to the crucial business "of learning to put ourselves in the place of the 'other' who addresses us."[48]

In Robert Wuthnow's study of small groups, he and his team of sociologists noted the importance of storytelling to the life and continued health of the groups. Discussing these findings, Wuthnow includes an observation that has great significance for our understanding of Mission Mississippi's insistence on the importance of prayer meetings. "In many of the groups we studied," Wuthnow states, "stories came up most frequently and with the greatest candor as part of the time the group devoted to prayer."[49] Wuthnow's finding concerning truth-telling and prayer in small groups is incredibly significant for this study. Prayer meetings are the place where the claims of Mission Mississippi and the findings of sociologists converge, because a small group prayer meeting is the space in modern American culture where people tell their stories to others with candor and frequency. In Mission Mississippi's prayer breakfasts, time is formally set aside for individuals to share their prayer requests—to tell their stories—as is common practice in the participant's own congregation's Bible study groups and prayer meetings. The only difference, as we have noted, is that these prayer meetings intentionally gather people across racial and denominational lines. Here the conditions exist for people to meet and listen to the narratives of the estranged other. The candor that marks these stories is a highly unusual feature of relationships between African Americans and whites in Mississippi; but the convention of the prayer meeting fosters, even requires, this candor. As a participant in the prayer breakfasts explained, "When you say: what's going on with you? What can I pray about for you? That's when you really get the layers peeled off and you find out what a person's heart is all about and what matters to them."[50]

When a participant shares a prayer request at the prayer breakfast, often in the form of a story, they tell the story, and the other participants hear it, in a particular way. Wuthnow says of narratives told in the context of prayer meetings that they require the narrator to give "a reinterpretation of what happened."[51] They reinterpret the story to fit both their activity of prayer and the involvement of God. In other words, the participant's beliefs about what they should pray for, how God answers prayer, and even what God is telling them in this situation shape what they tell the group. For those hearing the story, their own theological convictions shape their listening: How is God at work in this situation and how does God wish us to pray for this person? It is a way of telling and hearing stories like no other.

The religious reinterpretive storytelling that Wuthnow finds prevalent in prayer meetings is an example of what the New Testament scholar Stephen Fowl considers a foundational practice of Christian friendship. In his study of Paul's letter to the Philippians, Fowl recognizes "several elements of the epistle [that] are directly designed to address and direct" the friendship Paul and the Philippians share "in Christ."[52] A central concern for Paul is that the Christians in Philippi understand their Christian friendship in the context of the life, death, and resurrection of Jesus (2:6–11). In his letter, Paul narrates (or reinterprets) his life and the lives of the Philippians in this context. "In Philippians," Fowl concludes, "Paul takes this ability of properly situating both oneself and one's friends within the drama of God's saving purposes to be foundational for all the other practices of Christian friendship."[53] In a quiet and unspectacular fashion, what Fowl calls the "practice of being able to narrate the story of one's own life into the ongoing story of God's economy of salvation" happens at every Mission Mississippi prayer breakfast.[54] Every Tuesday and Thursday morning somewhere in Jackson, through the prayer points printed in the bulletin, in the needs told to the groups, and by the intercessions, participants situate themselves and their stories within the drama of salvation.

Christians turn to the Bible as the source for their understanding of the "drama of God's saving purposes." This means that the reading and interpretation of biblical texts plays a fundamental part in the practice of Christian friendship. Fowl asserts, "Christian friends read Scripture so that they can engage each other about how to fit their stories into the economy of salvation."[55] Moreover, as already established, these narratives most often find expression in the practice of small group intercessory prayer. These elements—scripture and narrative—are always present in Mission Mississippi's prayer meetings; scripture is read and interpreted in the short message brought to the group, and participants share their narratives in the form of prayer requests.

Intercessory Prayer, Double Vision, and Networks

What of the claim that this interracial intercessory prayer plays a key part in Mission Mississippi's changing Mississippi one relationship at a time? The sociologists Michael O. Emerson and Christian Smith conclude from their study that white evangelicals' solutions to the race problem in America are "profoundly individualistic."[56] They characterize this approach as, "become a Christian, love your individual neighbors, establish a cross-race friendship, give individuals the right to pursue jobs and individual justice without discrimination by other individuals, and ask forgiveness of individuals one has wronged."[57] This approach simply does not address, what Smith and Emerson call, "major issues of racialization."[58]

The first step for white evangelicals to address the problems of racialized America, Smith and Emerson argue, is to "modify their cultural toolkit" so they recognize there is a systemic dimension to the problem. In a remarkable agreement between sociology and theology, Smith and Emerson's conclusions, as to how such a change might occur, converge with Miroslav Volf's theory of double vision. For white evangelicals to extend their individualistic cultural toolkit to include an understanding of racialized structural issues, their perceptions of society, Emerson and Smith argue, must start "to resemble those of African Americans."[59]

Smith and Emerson discovered, rather unsurprisingly, that this change in perceptual toolkit among white evangelicals occurs in direct relation to their contact with black Americans.[60] Interestingly, however, they found that individual friendships seem to have little effect on this perceptual change; instead, "changes in racial perspectives occur mainly in the contexts of inter-racial networks."[61] These include networks of family, neighborhood, work, and church. The two sociologists noted that in white evangelical culture, outside of family, church provides the most significant and time-consuming social network. Because most of these churches are racially homogenous, Smith and Emerson concluded that churches tend to function as monochromatic net-working machines that perpetuate and reinforce a racialized society.[62]

If immersing whites in interracial networks is the key to changing their racial perceptions and the most significant network in white evangelicals' lives are their monoracial churches, what hope is there for racial reconciliation in this part of the Body of Christ? Smith and Emerson's *Divided by Faith,* with its self-confessed "dismal portrait of the realities of and prospects for posi-tive race relations among American Christians in the United States," brought together a group of sociologists determined to produce a more constructive piece of work.[63] Three years after the publication of *Divided by Faith,* Oxford University Press published a companion volume with a colorful dust jacket and an optimistic title: *United by Faith: The Multiracial Congregation as an Answer to the Problem of Race.*[64] Emerson, joined by the sociologists George Yancey and Karen Chai Kim, in collaboration with Curtis DeYoung, a minister and professor of Reconciliation Studies at Bethel University in Minnesota, argued the case that "Christian congregations, when possible, should be multiracial." While presenting a compelling case for their ideal—the integrated multicul-tural congregation—the authors had to acknowledge, "We are hard pressed to cite definitive examples of such congregations from our study."[65] In 2005, with a newly assembled team of sociologists, Emerson published a book with the more chastened title: *Against All Odds: The Struggle for Racial Integration in Religious Organizations.* Their study of six different religious organizations led them to conclude, "Interracial organizations are inherently unstable."[66] It seems that multiracial churches, despite their best intentions, are more likely to be in a state of transition than sustainable integration.[67]

Undeterred by the reality they encounter as sociologists, Emerson and his colleagues continue to crusade for multiracial congregations calling them "harbingers of a new stage of U.S. race relations."[68] Multiracial congregations, however, are—by their own findings—not a realistic starting point for trans-forming the Church in America today. If evangelicals' emphasis on individual friendship as a solution to the problem of race is as ineffective as rearranging the deckchairs on the *Titanic,* then those sociologists proposing the solution of multiracial congregations are drawing up blueprints for a better liner as the ship sinks. Designing a better vessel will not help the passengers and crew in their current predicament. To change the metaphor, Emerson and his colleagues seem intent on trying to pour the new wine of multiracial congregations into the old wineskins of America's churches that, by their own findings, are very poor at containing such a brew. The problem, of course, is that when it comes to racial reconciliation in the Church, old wineskins—the existing collection of monoracial congregations and denominations—is where the work has to start.

Mission Mississippi's prayer breakfasts and other events are creating new multiracial church networks without expending energy on trying directly to change the racial makeup of preexisting congregations. Mission Mississippi carefully avoids the suggestion that member congregations should integrate or become multiracial. This avoidance draws criticism, but the strategy makes sense in light of the sociologists' findings.[69] Just considering the prayer breakfasts, we find people in networks of open friendship constituted by the Christian practice of narrating their life stories as part of the drama of salvation.[70] Maintaining these delicate cross-racial, cross-cultural, and cross-denominational networks is difficult enough without saddling the project with the insistence on achieving this in the statistically near-impossible environment of a single congregation.

Meeting the Other, and Bearing Burdens

Interracial intercessory prayer meetings establish favorable conditions for the development of double vision by establishing networks and creating the space for participants to hear and tell their stories with grace. From a theological perspective, this is a network of the friends of God challenging the idolatry of the Closed Society. The participants also contend there is more going on when people pray together than simply developing an understanding of the other's point of view. In the interviews, participants struggled to express the deeply moving spiritual reality they experienced when praying with others—a sense of profound unity with the person praying for them. The discomfiting challenge of crossing racial lines in prayer intensified this spiritual experience and participants talked of this unity in terms of reconciliation. Some believed that this reconciliation made the prayers more effective.[71]

Ralph Maisel, the white Episcopalian who grew to appreciate the African American prayer tradition, talked eloquently of the way he believed participation in the prayer meetings contributed to his experience of racial reconciliation. Maisel had never prayed with an African American before his involvement with Mission Mississippi. "Well, for me it is foreign," he explained. "Because

I am sixty-five, the generation [I] came up from, you didn't ask black people for anything much less to pray for you. And we were accustomed to giving [African American sharecroppers] things like a little bag of food or some hand-me-down clothes...to take care of them." Through the work of Mission Mississippi, Maisel now approached an African American for the first time saying, "I am in need and I am asking you to come to my need and help me."[72] What happened next proved life changing:

> I was with a couple of black men and maybe a white man. And we
> all shared something we would like the group to pray about. And
> the black man next to me, the way he prayed—it was about my
> daughter—was so powerful and so endearing. To have someone like
> that just pray like they really cared, just intensely. Like praying the
> wallpaper off the walls for someone they didn't know, my daughter.
> For me it was just...you can't help but when you have had someone
> pray for you like that, there is a bond.[73]

Asked to describe his understanding of this bond, Maisel struggled to articulate his thoughts:

> [When] someone is on your behalf praying to the Lord, and you are
> praying to the Lord, there is a meet[ing] there—just the commonal-
> ity right there and you are bonded in Christ. I don't know how to
> describe that but that is where the reconciliation is. That moment
> you are one in Christ. You are of one mind, one heart, and one soul.[74]

James Baird, one of the founders of Mission Mississippi and former minister of First Presbyterian Church, described a similar bond forming between participants of different races: "I think God is joining us together through his Spirit and the prayer is evidence of it." Baird finds that after praying together in small groups he "come[s] away from that with a sense of solidarity, not only with the Lord but with this fellow who is praying to your Lord, to your God."[75]

Dietrich Bonhoeffer, the German theologian and martyr, offers a way of understanding this relationship between prayer and reconciliation. In his book *Life Together,* Bonhoeffer concluded, "A Christian community either lives by the intercessory prayers of its members for one another, or the community will be destroyed," and recommended "a regular time during the day for them."[76] Drawing on his experiences at Finkenwalde, an underground seminary of the German Confessing Church, in this short work Bonhoeffer set out a rule of life for a Christian community. In engaging in the discipline of intercessory prayer for others, Bonhoeffer made a "blessed discovery," similar to that claimed by participants in Mission Mississippi. "I can no longer condemn or hate other

Christians for whom I pray," wrote Bonhoeffer, "no matter how much trouble they cause me. In intercessory prayer the face that may have been strange and intolerable to me is transformed into the face of one for whom Christ died, the face of a pardoned sinner."[77]

In intercessory prayer, Bonhoeffer also experienced something akin to Ralph Maisel's "bond" in Christ. Bonhoeffer believed sin locked humans in isolation, disunited from God and from their neighbor.[78] The only possibility of escape from the boundaries of the "I" comes from the one who is outside the "I": Christ, "the absolute outside of my existence."[79] Thus, Bonhoeffer argues, meeting with another is only possible through the mediation of Christ, and "only through Christ does my neighbour meet me as one who claims me in an absolute way from a position outside my existence."[80] According to Bonhoeffer's theology, when Maisel says in the prayer meetings he feels "bonded in Christ" with his African American neighbor, he is in fact meeting his neighbor in the only way he truly can.

In *Life Together,* Bonhoeffer insists that interceding for others is a duty of service for Christians. Based on the Pauline injunction "Bear one another's burdens, and in this way fulfill the law of Christ" (Gal 6:2), Bonhoeffer calls this service of intercession, "the Ministry of Bearing."[81] In Mission Mississippi, Scripture informs and shapes the common language; participants, like Bonhoeffer, often talk of prayer using the New Testament metaphor of bearing one another's burdens. For example, Sheree Tynes, now the chair of the prayer committee, attended the prayer meetings while caring for her invalid mother. "Before my mom died," Tynes recalled, "it mattered that I could be prayed for...at these prayer breakfasts. It sustained me....It was nice having some- one who didn't know me at all take on that *burden* and share in a very deep and meaningful way."[82]

At a meeting of the prayer committee, Joel Weathersby offered up a heart- felt prayer that we would all bear each other's burdens. Asked what he meant by this, he offered a detailed response: "Years ago I didn't quite understand [but] I understand it better now when it says bear one another's burden," he explained. "I was thinking of just a physical load, [but] there is a spiritual load that they have in him or her that they are carrying." These burdens could be "financial, spiritual or social...it could be a burden with families that [they] have on their hearts and on their minds that they can't shake off." For Weathersby, the telling of how you overcame similar obstacles helps relieve these burdens of the other: "Sometimes it just takes a word of encouragement to lighten that load within that person's mind or heart....telling them I have been where you are and I know where you are coming from and I overcame that through the power of God." This burden bearing is a process marked by reciprocity. After sharing words of encouragement, Weathersby explained, "Then I can share with [them] what burden I have and they relieve [me] of what [I]'ve got. That's what I am getting to when I say bear one another's burdens because my burden is your burden. That don't mean I am not to carry my own burdens, but I will help you carry [your burden]."[83] The primary understanding of burden sharing among Mission Mississippi participants is more than simply sharing stories of common obstacles surmounted or shared trials endured. The burdens of others are born and made lighter through interceding on the other's behalf to God.

Jackie Pate considers the prayers at the meetings particularly powerful because of the demands they make of the participants. "[Other participants] are humbling themselves as you are humbling yourself," she explained.[84] Just as Maisel never dreamed of sharing his story and his need with an African American, before her involvement with Mission Mississippi, Pate had never deliberately made herself vulnerable to a white person. "It is amazing that in a group of...people you don't even know and you are trying to build a relationship [with]," observed Pate, "they can come to you and you can go to them and tell them what is something that is hurting you so bad, what's going on in your home." This discipline does not come naturally to Pate. "You don't want to open those doors because we really want to keep those doors shut," she confessed. "But if you want some change you had better try to get it prayed out, and that person you might not know might be the one who prays that stronghold down."[85] Pate expressed both the power and the reciprocal nature of these prayers: "I am praying that I can tear a wall down for someone when I am in those circles of prayer: Lord just use me and anoint me that I can pray some down for them as well as myself."[86]

Bonhoeffer described this intense desire to take on the burdens of the other in intercessory prayer in spatial terms. Released from the isolation of the self, the intercessor is able to take the place of the other in prayer before God. In one of his doctoral theses, Bonhoeffer wrote, "In intercession I step into the other's place and my prayer, even though it remains my own, is nonetheless prayed out of the other's affliction and need."[87]

When participants in Mission Mississippi's prayer meetings talk about bearing the burdens of others, they usually refer to the adversities and worries placed on an individual by circumstance. They also use the term when talking of more general concerns for society: "I have a burden for the young people of Jackson," for example. In the context of the prayer meetings, participants rarely mention the burden that Bonhoeffer considered the primary responsibility for Christians to bear for one another: the burden of sin. Bonhoeffer believed it is human sin that locks the "I" within itself, and it is the in-breaking of gracious forgiveness in the person of Christ that opens up the possibility of encounter with God and neighbor. The Church as the body of Christ extends to the disciple the possibility of forgiveness for, wrote Bonhoeffer, "the community of faith bears my sin and death with me, and I no longer see sin and death in the community of faith...in Christ, but only forgiveness and life."[88]

In *Life Together*, the Protestant Bonhoeffer advocates a rediscovery of the practice of confession.[89] Drawing on the verse in the Letter of James, "Therefore confess your sins to one another, and pray for one another, so that you may be healed" (5:16a), Bonhoeffer believed confession one-to-another marked the "final breakthrough to community": the fellowship not of "pious believers" but of forgiven sinners.[90] Bonhoeffer outlines a practice of confession of sin to a fellow Christian, who themselves practice confession. The confessor represents the whole Church to the one confessing. As such, the confessor has the authority not only to hear the confession but also to forgive sin in the name of Jesus.[91]

Bonhoeffer's insight that "the community of faith bears my sin and death with me" offers Mission Mississippi a way to understand and develop its practices of prayer for reconciliation.[92] Implementing Bonhoeffer's particular discipline of confession and absolution would be foreign to all but the Roman Catholic participants in the prayer breakfasts. The evangelical culture in which Mission Mississippi operates sees confession as a personal act between the repentant sinner and God. For evangelicals, the moment of repentance may be public—walking the aisle following the gospel appeal—but the content of the confession remains a private affair.[93] While not offering a blueprint for how Mission Mississippi could develop the prayer meetings, the understanding of intercessory prayer as bearing the other's burden of sin takes on a powerful dimension in the context of churches weighed down by the legacies of the Closed Society and racism.

Reading the following passage from a lecture delivered by Bonhoeffer in 1932, in to the context of contemporary Mississippi, demonstrates the power and potential of Bonhoeffer's theology of confession and the Ministry of Bearing for Mission Mississippi's struggle for church unity across racial and denominational lines:

> The kingdom of God assumes form in the church insofar as here the
> loneliness of man is overcome through the miracle of confession and
> forgiveness. This is because in the church, which is the communion
> of saints created by the resurrection, one person can and should bear
> the guilt of another, and for this reason the last shackle of loneli-
> ness, hatred of others, is removed, and community is established

and created anew. It is through the miracle of confession, which is beyond all our understanding, that all hitherto existing community is shown to have been an illusion and is abolished, destroyed, and broken asunder, and that here and now the new congregation of the resurrection world is created.[94]

In Mississippi, closed friendships that perpetuate "loneliness" and "hatred of others" distinguish the "hitherto existing community" of the Closed Society. Mission Mississippi proclaims these barriers of race and denomination running through the Church are illusory in light of the resurrection, and, as we have seen, the act of meeting together for interracial intercessory prayer challenges the idolatry of the Closed Society. For Mission Mississippi to move people into a more profound reconciliation and unity, they would do well to explore this Ministry of Bearing. What would it mean for a white person not only to confess their sins of racism to an African American brother or sister in Christ but for the African American to share that burden of guilt and intercede for forgiveness? Conversely, what would it mean for a white Christian to hear the confession of hatred harbored by an African American against fellow white Christians and then to take it on himself and pray for forgiveness?

Intercessory Prayer: The Ground for Social Action

Mission Mississippi's prayer meetings place the participants in networks of people of different races. In these networks, participants engage their theological imaginations in the telling and hearing of life narratives. Through a particular Christian understanding of intercessory prayer, participants meet the other in the profoundest way: as a fellow sinner forgiven in Christ. John DeGruchy wrote, "Reconciliation begins to become a reality when, without surrendering our identity... but opening ourselves up to the 'other,' we enter into the space between, exchanging places with the other in a conversation that takes us beyond ourselves."[95] It is hard to imagine any process looking more like this than the discipline of regular, intentional, interracial intercessory prayer found at Mission Mississippi's prayer meetings. Although this offers grounds to endorse the significance of the prayer meetings for Mission Mississippi's project, do these prayer meetings lead participants to address systemic issues of injustice in the society outside the community of the Church?

There is an intrinsic logic to intercessory prayer that subverts attempts to limit the Church's sphere of concern. To pray for the needs of the world is to acknowledge God's sovereignty over the whole of creation; and interceding for the other in the world, is to bring them into the Church. We can see this logic at work within Mission Mississippi. The official position of Mission Mississippi's board is that questions of justice and systemic inequality are political issues and not the business of the church. Mission Mississippi, which for theological and strategic reasons only works with churches, avoids any statements or positions that its supporters might construe as political.[96] The prayer meetings, however, do not observe this logic of separation between church and politics, praying in schools, hospitals, businesses, as well as the Governor's Mansion and the steps of the State Capitol. Sheree Tynes explained how the prayer committee approached potential host organizations:

> As we contact churches and organizations, fire departments, police
> departments [we say]: We are coming to pray for you. If you fix
> us breakfast, that's fine. But the main reason we are coming is to
> develop a relationship with you and to pray for whatever needs you
> have: to bless your place of business; to bless your church.[97]

Here Tynes exhibits exactly the way that, according to Bonhoeffer, intercessory prayer reorients the church toward the world.

Just as it is in intercessory prayer that Bonhoeffer finds the highest expression of the community of Christ's body, it is also in intercessory prayer that he glimpses the possibility of "calling the world into the community of the body of Christ."[98] For Bonhoeffer, intercessory prayer demonstrates the absurdity of insisting on two separate spheres of church and politics because intercessory prayer simultaneously draws the disciples out of themselves and in a vicarious way draws the subject of the prayer into the church.[99] Put simply, as already outlined, intercessory prayer is a ministry of bearing, and in following Christ's injunction to pray for our enemies, it becomes impossible to see them as wholly other. Bonhoeffer explained, "If we pray for [our enemies], we are taking their distress and poverty, their guilt and perdition upon ourselves, and pleading to God for them."[100] "To cherish no contempt for the sinner but rather prize the privilege of bearing him means," expounded Bonhoeffer, "not to have to give him up as lost, to be able to accept him, to preserve the fellowship with him through forgiveness."[101] Jürgen Moltmann similarly understands prayer as preserving fellowship with the world. Taking the other's distress, poverty, guilt, and perdition on oneself in prayer is an act of open friendship for the isolated and estranged world. "By bringing the sighs and groans of the world's misery to God," Moltmann wrote, "[the one who prays] claims God's friendship for those who sigh and groan."[102]

Bonhoeffer goes further than simply saying that interceding on another's behalf makes it difficult for us to see them as wholly other: to realize that God's open friendship extends to them as much as to oneself. Bonhoeffer claims that intercessory prayer is a theological reality that creates its own peculiar conditions. In the act of praying for another, "a third person is drawn into my solitary relation with God."[103] As the intercessor is a member of the community of Christ which bears each other in prayer and forgiveness, this third person is not simply brought into relation with the individual but also with the Church. Bonhoeffer draws the bold conclusion that "each intercession potentially draws the one for whom it is offered into the church-community."[104] Thus, when Mission Mississippi's prayer committee says to a school principle, a state governor, or an employee at the hospital, "We are coming to develop a relationship with you and to pray for whatever needs you have," these two possibilities for intercessory prayer—claiming the open friendship of God for the other and drawing the other into the church—are present. Narrating the practice of intercessory prayer through Bonhoeffer's theology in this way, Mission Mississippi's emphasis on relationships established through prayer contains the theological resources to break down the rigid doctrinal barriers separating the Church from the world. This offer, "to develop a relationship with you and to pray for whatever needs you have," dares to draw the Closed Society into the fellowship of open friendship.

The testimony of those who regularly attend the prayer breakfasts points toward the cosmic power of prayer and the hope in friendship for reconciliation, at the same time as dealing with the mundane details of shared human friendship. "[Prayer] is relationship building," explained Sheree Tynes. "When we pray together everything else falls into place. It is foundational. It is our life. Prayer is our life and [we] begin the day in praying for one another and knowing that James Turner has stuff to do at the neighborhood Christian center and he's got a tough day."[105]

Four months after Tynes gave this interview, tragedy tested the strength of this small community of African American and white friends in Christ and their resolve and ability to bear one another's burdens.

Holy Family Church (RC), Thursday, June 24, 2004

Holy Family Church in North Jackson, the host of Mission Mississippi's prayer breakfast on June 24, 2004, has changed like the neighborhood in which it sits from a white to an African American congregation. Rain had been falling heavily all night; when Virginia Chase arrived that stormy morning, she found only a couple of people had arrived before her.[106] As the priest opened up the hall for the prayer breakfast, Chase made a call on her cell phone to Dolphus

Weary to remind him of a 7:30 appointment and not to come to the meeting. Chase remembered: "I called him and said, 'Dolphus where are you?' And he said, 'No, where are you?' And I said, 'Well I am at the church'...And he said 'who is there with you? I just need you to...stand with someone.' "[107]

Chase walked into the hall and sat down on a folding metal chair. "I don't see anyone Dolphus, you just need to tell me."

Then Weary told her, "Reggie's Dead."

Twenty-seven year old Reginald Demond Weary, Dolphus's son, had died the previous night when his car smashed through a fence and into a tree on Northside Drive, just two miles from Holy Family Church. Doctors pronounced Reggie dead at the University Medical Center, the place he came into the world and where, as a seven-year-old, he had recovered from chemotherapy and radiation treatment for non-Hodgkin's lymphoma. The crash made the nighttime television news. Virginia Chase had seen the report of a high-speed police pursuit that ended with the death of the fleeing driver, but she had not recognized the television pictures of Reggie's wrecked Chevrolet Lumina.

Weary had been drinking that Wednesday evening. With his blood alcohol level over the legal limit, he was speeding on Highway 49 in Pearl when a police car flipped on its lights. Rather than pull over, Reggie made the fateful decision to run. At times swerving onto the shoulder to avoid other motorists, he took Interstate 55 North before exiting onto Northside Drive. There he stopped at an intersection. The pursuing officer left his cruiser and ran up to the car, but Weary wagged his finger at him and sped off. Moments later Reggie crashed, sustaining his fatal head injuries.

The tragic death of his son threatened to polarize the people Dolphus Weary had dedicated his life to reconciling. The white and African American communities in Jackson held very different preconceptions of both the police and young black men. In the days that followed Reggie's death, before the toxicology lab's report revealed he had been drinking, fingers in the two communities pointed in very different directions. Reggie Weary's death was racially and politically charged. Governor Haley Barbour had, only the month before, signed a bill requiring law enforcement agencies to develop pursuit policies and training procedures for high-speed chases and instructing judges to hand out harsher penalties to those who fled.[108] An Op-Ed piece in the *Clarion-Ledger* by the African American journalist and Mission Mississippi board member Eric Stringfellow asked if the Pearl police officer had followed pursuit guidelines. Under the provocative title, "Breaking Speed Limit Should Not Merit Death," Stringfellow acknowledged Weary's "poor judgment," while voicing his concern that the police department had not suspended the pursuing police officer pending the results of the enquiry. He concluded, "The law also should make officers accountable. The idea is not to punish hardworking police officers but rather to help make sure no one receives a death sentence for breaking the speed limit."[109]

Stringfellow's piece unleashed a flurry of outraged letters to the editor defending the actions of the police. "We have charged our sworn police officers to protect us from this type of behavior," stated one letter writer.[110] White supremacist Web sites also picked up the story, weighing in on the side of the police.[111] On the other side, the liberal *Jackson Free Press* asked, "Why is it that almost every young African American we know...say[s] that they cannot afford to get stopped by police in Rankin County?" The paper called for an enquiry because "we can't afford to lose more scared young people like Reggie Weary without figuring out why they're running from Rankin County."[112]

That morning, all Dolphus Weary told Virginia Chase on her cell phone was "Reggie's dead."

While Chase was on the phone, Lee Paris walked up from the parking lot. As the chair of Mission Mississippi's board, for years Paris had faithfully attended the breakfasts, although recently his work and family commitments meant now he only came occasionally. This morning, when he saw the church had made little preparation to host Mission Mississippi, he was wondering why he had dragged himself out of bed in this wet weather. "When I saw Lee," Chase recalled, "I just lost it, I truly lost it."[113] By the time he reached her, she was hysterical and unable to tell him what was wrong and unable to speak with Dolphus on the phone.

Paris sat with Chase and tried to calm her down. She remembers him saying, "Virginia, if I could take it away I would, whatever it is."[114] While Paris tried to piece together what was troubling Chase, the regular prayer breakfast participants straggled in out of the rain and started to pray for her. Paris was able to tell the group that Reggie Weary had died and the priest said, "In light of what has happened we will just go straight to prayer."[115] Soon after the group started to pray, Neddie Winters came and told everyone how Reggie Weary had died. Then the group went back to praying. By the accounts of those who were there, something remarkable happened that morning. Brenda Donnell described feeling in a powerful way what she believed was the presence of God:

> There was a silence and it was like the Spirit was there because
> everybody was just praying and asking God for his help for that
> day because that was devastating. And that was one time that just

seemed like you could just feel the presence of the Lord. And you could feel how compassionate all the people that were there felt.[116]

Virginia Chase recalled, "It was powerful. It was really powerful...it rained harder and people kept coming, and I just remember them praying and praying and praying and just holding on to each other."[117]

Speaking to newspaper reporters later that day, Paris talked about his sense of the solidarity the group had experienced while praying together. "[This] morning's Mission Mississippi prayer time was one of the strongest I have experienced in 11 years," Paris told the reporter. "We suffered there together, black and white, backgrounds made very little difference as we came together and prayed together."[118] In an interview over three months later, Paris showed how he made sense of what happened after the group learned that Reggie Weary was dead:

> Immediately there was a spirit of unity as if everybody felt it was their own son that had gotten killed. It wasn't some distant name that we might have read about just as a matter of fact in the newspaper. It was a personal loss to every one of us and we all felt the pain simultaneously. And together [we] just started giving that pain to God. And [we experienced] an incredible spirit of oneness that we as fallen people don't get to experience very often on this side of the Jordan River.

> It was a taste of the fruit that we have been praying for [for] ten years. *Lord, make us one.* And we felt it in that hour—that we were one. In the midst of adversity, in the midst of incredible pain and loss, we knew in that room that we were one and that we were all about one heart and one mind and one subject doing one thing at that moment; and that is rare in life.[119]

Paris had interpreted the story as part of the drama of God's reconciliation and a testimony of God's involvement in Mission Mississippi. Dolphus Weary also came to intertwine the narrative of his son's death with the work of Mission Mississippi. "There was a sense this is a Mission Mississippi moment," Weary said, reflecting on the outpouring of support for his family from African Americans and whites. "It's a sad moment, but it's a moment that God is at work. It's another opportunity to live out that which we are talking about."[120]

FIGURE 6.8. Neddie Winters, Lee Paris, and John Perkins (standing left to right) lead prayers for Dolphus and Rosie Weary (seated left to right) following the death of their son. Mission Mississippi Businessmen's Prayer Breakfast, University Club, Jackson, Mississippi, November 17, 2004. (Courtesy of Mission Mississippi)

Conclusions

Mission Mississippi's morning prayer breakfasts are a practice of open friendship. This practice is rich in theological significance: prayer is the language of friendship; participants narrate each other's lives as part of the unfolding drama of God's salvation, an activity that Stephen Fowl considers the foundational practice of Christian friendship; and intercessory prayer opens the possibility of truly encountering the other in Christ and drawing the world into God's fellowship of open friendship.

Particular elements of the prayer breakfasts embody these theological truths and point beyond themselves to the road Mission Mississippi must travel if it is to lead its participants deeper into reconciliation and truly to have a hope of changing Mississippi one relationship at a time. First, just as participants in the prayer breakfasts pray for each other's physical and emotional needs, Mission Mississippi must encourage them to move beyond civility toward bearing one another's burdens of sin through hearing confessions of racism, hatred, prejudice, and injustice. Second, Mission Mississippi as an organization must relax its dogmatic insistence on the separation between spiritual and social spheres. The executive board should embrace the logic inherent in the prayer breakfast's practice of meeting in the secular space of schools, government offices, newspapers, and hospitals. The location of these prayer breakfasts declares that the open friendship of Jesus embraces not only Christians of different races and denominations but also the whole community: in intercession, the church takes on and bears the sins of the sacred *and* secular world.

The lived theology of reconciliation, present in the practice of the prayer breakfasts, points to the cost that such a discipline demands of the participants. The "taste of the fruit" of unity experienced in the prayer meeting at Holy Family Church following Reggie Weary's death came at a terrible price. That morning, the open friendship of Jesus meant that those present experienced the power of God in their willingness "to mourn with those who mourn" (Rom 12:15). The reconciliation glimpsed at these prayer breakfasts is not some cheap reconciliation. Entering into this network of intentional interracial intercessory prayer, one is mindful of the proximity of hope and grief, of solidarity and sacrifice.

7

Conclusion

The problem and the promise found in Mission Mississippi lies neatly summarized in two different understandings of their slogan: "Changing Mississippi one relationship at a time." The distinction between these two understandings is one of emphasis. The problematic interpretation is that the goal of Mission Mississippi is simply to establish individual relationships and, if successful in this, the task of changing Mississippi will take care of itself. As Michael O. Emerson and Christian Smith argued, such a "profoundly individualistic" approach typical of evangelical racial reconciliation initiatives fails to address, let alone change, the "major issues of racialization" faced by Mississippi and the United States.[1] The promise of Mission Mississippi lies in a second construal of the same slogan. If the goal moves from establishing "one relationship at a time" and shifts to "Changing Mississippi," then building individual relationships across racial and denominational lines becomes the strategic, as well as theologically coherent, starting point for this transformation.

Both of these understandings currently coexist within Mission Mississippi. To risk a gross generalization, African Americans take little convincing that Mississippi needs to change and they stand to gain the most from such a change. Conversely, the *status quo* works well for many whites, and it is harder for them to focus on the need for systemic change. Emerson and Smith point out that the white evangelical's cultural toolkit comes with a self-serving emphasis on freewill individualism.[2] As Mission Mississippi found in the 1990s, it is relatively easy to convince white churchgoers that they need to improve relationships with individual African American Christians; however, it is much harder to move them to address some of the massive disparities that exist between the African American and white communities.

There is active resistance to focusing on the goal of "Changing Mississippi" from within the leadership of Mission Mississippi for two interrelated reasons. First, concerned to keep as many people at the table as possible, some justifiably fear that talking about these hard issues will cause churches to withdraw their support for Mission Mississippi. Second, Southern Presbyterians cleverly codified their opposition to imposed change of the racist white hegemony in the doctrine of the spirituality of the church. Conservative Presbyterians, who form an influential part of the leadership of Mission Mississippi, adhere to this doctrine and strongly resist any proposal that they deem moves Mission Mississippi from the spiritual purview of the church into the realm of politics and the unconscionable social gospel.

Mission Mississippi's commitment to reach all churches causes this apparent impasse. How challenging can Mission Mississippi make the demands of racial reconciliation while maintaining the participation of a large number of conservative white churches? Multiracial congregations such as Voice of Calvary, although inspirational, fail to move significant numbers of people to leave or change their large monoracial churches. Perhaps those who seek the new wine of racial reconciliation and justice should abandon hope in reforming the old ecclesiastical wineskins, but this is not the position taken by those in Mission Mississippi. Their commitment to move the mainstream church culture toward "unity," and the care with which they proceed, opens them to the charge of accommodating themselves to the very attitudes that they are trying to reform.

Those within Mission Mississippi striving to change the state for the better believe that intentional interracial relationships constituted by participants' unity in Christ is the fulcrum about which they can leverage this change in the mainstream of Mississippi's church life. This is the logic behind Dolphus Weary calling Mission Mississippi, "Reconciliation 101." It is insufficient to call this a strategy; it is a hope placed in a theology of Christian friendship.

The point at which the lever of Christian friendship has greatest purchase—the fulcrum's locus—is not found in Mission Mississippi's church partnerships, its impressive statewide distribution of participating congregations, nor in its sponsorship of civic functions with their attendant dignitaries and politicians. The fruits of these efforts seem paltry compared to the publicity surrounding them, and on investigation, the much-vaunted church partnerships have produced little in the way of sustained activity. The fulcrum's locus, as participants will tell you, is in the prayer breakfasts. Here a small community gathers and creates a network of open friendship between people from different racial, denominational, and socioeconomic groups. Through intentional interracial intercessory prayer, the participants display Miroslav Volf's will to embrace. They open themselves to hear the needs of the other and bear their burdens. Through activities such as this, participants take the first step, and only the first step, on the road to reconciliation.

Is there evidence that the lever of open friendship has enough mechanical advantage to move the closed churches of the Closed Society toward a desire to change Mississippi, and how is one to make such an assessment? Certainly any assessment of the success of Mission Mississippi must take into account the incredible resistance to change built into the very fabric of the powerful white churches and recognize the significance of even incremental change. The history of First Presbyterian Church, Jackson and its response to Mission Mississippi demonstrates this militant inertia.

Any assessment must also recognize the scale of the task facing those who want to transform Mississippi into a more equitable society. If there had been any doubt as to the disparity of opportunity between African American and white communities in Mississippi, Hurricane Katrina lifted the veil from the region's struggle to overcome the effects of racism and injustice. At the end of the summer in 2005, the world watched in shock as its greatest superpower seemed unable or unwilling to rush to the aid of tens of thousands of their poor, mostly African American, citizens stranded in the wake of the storm.

Two weeks after Katrina hit the Louisiana and Mississippi Gulf coasts, President George W. Bush, in his speech from a devastated and deserted New Orleans, acknowledged the ongoing systemic injustice of America's racialized society. "As all of us saw on television, there's . . . some deep, persistent poverty in this region," the president told the nation. "That poverty has roots in a history of racial discrimination, which cut off generations from the opportunity of America. We have a duty to confront this poverty with bold action."[3]

Before Hurricane Katrina, one had to look closely to find any evidence that Mission Mississippi's reconciliation efforts contributed to a significant material change for the victims of the "racial discrimination, which cut off generations from the opportunity of America." Although Mission Mississippi pointed to a handful of black entrepreneurs establishing white business contacts at prayer breakfasts and community development projects in African American neighborhoods receiving support from white churches, these examples seemed insignificant given the scale of the problem. Concerned not to alienate its conservative white base, Mission Mississippi did not publicly challenge its rich and powerful participant churches to "confront this poverty with bold action." Instead, the leaders hoped that in establishing networks of relationships that subverted the boundary walls of the closed society, they were doing the preliminary work necessary for a more lasting change. In some measure, the hurricane of 2005 vindicated their belief.

Following Katrina, as federal and state agencies floundered, nongovernmental organizations stepped into the gap.[4] Mission Mississippi, with its unique links to African American and white congregations in the affected region, its support network of churches and Christian organizations across the country, and its connections with local community development organizations, played a significant role in coordinating faith-based aid to the Mississippi Gulf Coast. Collaborating with World Vision, Mission Mississippi helped the large Christian charity with "logistical and advisory services" in its twelve million dollar relief operation.[5] Mission Mississippi also helped set up a weekly teleconference call between local churches and governmental and nongovernmental relief agencies.[6] In 2006, Mission Mississippi hired an extra staff person to work with a placement program for Hurricane Katrina evacuees.[7] This activity did not go unrecognized; within a month of the disaster, the Federal Emergency Management Agency (FEMA) listed Mission Mississippi as a key organization in the coordination of relief.[8]

Mission Mississippi's response to Katrina drew attention to, and strengthened its links with, organizations with an explicitly "social" emphasis. This resulted, in part, from the number of Mission Mississippi's leading figures who were also leaders in organizations that collaborated in the relief effort. These organizations included: Ronnie Crudup's Mississippi Faith-Based Coalition for Community Renewal; Dolphus Weary's Rural Education and Leadership Christian Foundation (REAL); The Hope Credit Union with Neddie Winters on the board; and, of course, Voice of Calvary Ministries and Mendenhall Ministries. It is too early to see how the experience of Katrina will affect the prejudice found in some powerful quarters of Mission Mississippi against any form of social gospel and the accompanying resistance to naming systemic injustice.

White churches in Mississippi have a long history of patronage and philanthropy toward the African American community. The energy expended in these charitable endeavors has often reinforced the racialized perceptions and prejudices for all the parties involved: whites can grow more convinced of their superiority through shouldering their "burden" to assist, as they understand them, the less able African Americans, who in turn risk internalizing a sense of inferiority. Will Mission Mississippi effectively harness the unprecedented attention and compassion in the state's churches generated by Katrina to bring about lasting changes in their perceptions and practices? Will the networks of intentional interracial and interdenominational friendships that Mission Mississippi has spent over a decade building enable Katrina's victims and volunteers to move beyond mere philanthropy and paternalism and towards reconciliation and justice? This challenge will test the strength of the fulcrum of open friendship.

South African theologian John De Gruchy wrote, "A challenge facing the Christian Church as God's agents of reconciliation is, the erecting of signposts of reconciliation in the world that signify the reality of God's gift."[9] This book suggests there are good practical and theological reasons to support Mission Mississippi's insistence that reconciliation starts with relationships. Churches and theologians need to take notice of this story unfolding in Mississippi because these unlikely friendships between African American and white Christians are signposts of reconciliation signifying the reality of God's gift.

Reflecting on the practical application of Moltmann's theology of open friendship, British theologian Liz Carmichael wrote, "Where walls of division have been put up, we should ask ourselves and the others: what do friends do together? And start doing these things at every level."[10] Neddie Winters, the executive director of Mission Mississippi, talks about the criticism he receives from skeptics who refuse to come to any Mission Mississippi events. When he asks them why, some respond, "Well, all y'all do is talk. Y'all ain't doing [nothing] but talking." Winters' reply to this challenge echoes Carmichael's understanding of open friendship and demonstrates the singular logic at the heart of Mission Mississippi. "Well, when it really boils down to it, what do you and your friends do?"[11]

The friendship of Mission Mississippi is, in one critical regard, different from the closed friendship of what "you and your friends do." In obedience to Christ's call to open friendship, Mission Mississippi directs people to develop friendships that cross the boundaries of race, class, and denomination. The challenge facing Mission Mississippi, if this open friendship is to bring significant change to the state, is to do what friends do at all levels of the Closed Society, not just in the private spheres of family and church but also at every level of education, business, and politics in Mississippi.

Notes

ABBREVIATIONS

LPP   Private papers of LeRoy H. Paris II, Jackson, Mississippi.
MMP   Private papers of Mission Mississippi, Jackson, Mississippi.
MSSC   Mississippi State Sovereignty Commission Files, Mississippi
        Department of Archives and History, Jackson, Mississippi.

PREFACE

1. Robert Wuthnow, *After the Baby Boomers: How Twenty- and Thirty-somethings are Shaping the Future of American Religion* (Princeton: Princeton University Press, 2007), xiii.

2. Eric Stringfellow, interview by the author, October 7, 2004, Jackson, MS.

CHAPTER 1

1. Joseph H. Crespino, *In Search of Another Country: Mississippi and the Conservative Counterrevolution* (Princeton, NJ: Princeton University Press, 2007), 5–6.

2. Louis R. Harlan, "Review of Mississippi: The Closed Society," *The Journal of American History* 54 (Dec, 1967), 724.

3. William Winter, "Freedom for All" (speech given at Mission Mississippi's 10th Anniversary Conference, Clarion Hotel, Jackson, MS, May 2, 2003, transcribed from recording).

4. Michael O. Emerson and Christian Smith, *Divided by Faith: Evangelical Religion and the Problem of Race in America* (New York: Oxford University Press, 2000).

5. James W. Silver, *Mississippi: The Closed Society* (New York: Harcourt, Brace & World, 1964).

6. David L. Chappell, *A Stone of Hope: Prophetic Religion and the Death of Jim Crow* (Chapel Hill: University of North Carolina Press, 2004), 107.

7. Miroslav Volf, Exclusion and Embrace: A Theological Exploration of Identity, Otherness, and Reconciliation (Nashville: Abingdon Press, 1996).

8. Mary R. Jackman and Marie Crane, "'Some of My Best Friends Are Black': Interracial Friendship and Whites' Racial Attitudes," *Public Opinion Quarterly* 50 (1986); Emerson and Smith, Divided by Faith.

CHAPTER 2

1. Martin Luther King Jr., "The Ethical Demands for Integration" (speech delivered before a church conference, Nashville, Tennessee, December 27, 1962) in Martin Luther King and James Melvin Washington, *A Testament of Hope: The Essential Writings of Martin Luther King, Jr.* (San Francisco: Harper & Row, 1986), 124.

2. Jürgen Moltmann, *How I Have Changed: Reflections on Thirty Years of Theology* (London: SCM Press, 1997), 13; Jürgen Moltmann, *A Broad Place: An Autobiography* (Minneapolis: Fortress Press, 2008), 9.

3. Jürgen Moltmann, "Reborn to a Living Hope," (paper presented at the Spring Institute for Lived Theology, University of Virginia, April 26, 2005).

4. Moltmann, *How I Have Changed*, 13.

5. Jürgen Moltmann, *Experiences of God* (Philadelphia: Fortress Press, 1980), 6.

6. Moltmann, "Reborn to a Living Hope."

7. Jürgen Moltmann, interview by the author, April 29, 2005, Charlottesville, VA.

8. Ibid.

9. Ibid.

10. Ibid; Moltmann, *A Broad Place: An Autobiography*, 9.

11. Jürgen Moltmann, *The Source of Life: The Holy Spirit and the Theology of Life* (Minneapolis: Fortress Press, 1997), 44.

12. Moltmann, April 29, 2005.

13. Ibid; Moltmann, *Experiences of God*, 3–4.

14. Moltmann, *A Broad Place: An Autobiography*, 15.

15. Moltmann, April 29, 2005.

16. Ibid; Martin Middlebrook, *The Battle of Hamburg: Allied Bomber Forces against a German City in 1943* (London: Allen Lane, 1980), 91.

17. Middlebrook, *The Battle of Hamburg*, 142.

18. Ibid., 95–97.

19. The recollections of Flight Lieutenant A. Fosdike, 78 Squadron. This second RAF raid took place on the night of 27/28 July. Ibid., 244.

20. Moltmann, *A Broad Place: An Autobiography*, 16.

21. Middlebrook, *The Battle of Hamburg*, 261.

22. Ibid., 266.

23. Moltmann, April 29, 2005.

24. Jürgen Moltmann, *Experiences in Theology: Ways and Forms of Christian Theology* (Minneapolis: Fortress Press, 2000), 3. This raid took place on July 29/30, 1943. Middlebrook, *The Battle of Hamburg*, 292.

25. Moltmann, *The Source of Life*, 2.

26. Moltmann, *How I Have Changed*, 13.

27. Jürgen Moltmann and G. McLeod Bryan, *Communities of Faith and Radical Discipleship*, Luce Program on Religion and the Social Crisis, no. 2 (Macon, GA: Mercer University Press, 1986), 5.

28. Middlebrook, *The Battle of Hamburg*, 328.

29. Moltmann, *Experiences of God*, 7.

30. Moltmann, April 29, 2005.

31. Moltmann, "Reborn to a Living Hope."

32. Ibid.

33. Moltmann, *A Broad Place: An Autobiography*, 26.

34. Moltmann, *The Source of Life*, 3.

35. Moltmann, *Experiences of God*, 6; Jürgen Moltmann, *The Crucified God: The Cross of Christ as the Foundation and Criticism of Christian Theology* (New York: Harper & Row, 1974), 1.

36. Moltmann, *Experiences of God*, 6.

37. Ibid.

38. Ibid., 8.

39. Ibid., 7.

40. Moltmann, *How I Have Changed*, 13.

41. Moltmann, "Reborn to a Living Hope."

42. Richard Bauckham, *The Theology of Jürgen Moltmann* (Edinburgh: T&T Clark, 1995), 4.

43. Moltmann, *The Source of Life*, 7.

44. Moltmann, "Reborn to a Living Hope."

45. Moltmann, *The Source of Life*, 8.

46. Elisabeth Moltmann-Wendel, *Autobiography* (London: SCM Press, 1997), 22.

47. Otto Dibelius, *In the Service of the Lord* (New York: Holt, 1964), 140.

48. Victoria Barnett, *For the Soul of the People: Protestant Protest against Hitler* (New York: Oxford University Press, 1992), 33.

49. Ibid., 35.

50. *The Barmen Confession*, in Robert McAfee Brown, *Kairos: Three Prophetic Challenges to the Church* (Grand Rapids, MI: Eerdmans, 1990), 156–58.

51. James Bentley, *Martin Niemöller* (London: Hodder and Stoughton, 1986), 169.

52. Dibelius, *In the Service of the Lord*, 171–73; Bentley, *Martin Niemöller*, 170.

53. Moltmann, *Experiences of God*, 10.

54. Moltmann, *How I Have Changed*, 14.

55. Moltmann, *Experiences of God*, 10.

56. The Confessing Church, during the years of the *Kirchenkampf* (church struggle), organized themselves in nonhierarchical regional governing boards called Councils of Brethren. Following the war, the Confessing Church's National Council of Brethren continued within the EKD until the mid-1960s. Moltmann, *How I Have Changed*, 14; Barnett, *For the Soul of the People*, 249, 274.

57. Barnett, *For the Soul of the People*, 248.

58. Moltmann-Wendel, *Autobiography*, xi.

59. Ibid., 35.

60. Dietrich Bonhoeffer, *Widerstand Und Ergebung; Briefe Und Aufzeichnungen Aus Der Haft* (Mèunchen: C. Kaiser, 1951), first English translation Dietrich Bonhoeffer, *Letters and Papers from Prison,* ed. Eberhard Bethge, trans. Reginald H. Fuller (London: SCM Press, 1953).

61. Dietrich Bonhoeffer, *Letters and Papers from Prison,* ed. Eberhard Bethge, Reginald H. Fuller and John Bowden trans., enl. ed. (London: SCM Press, 1971), 280–81.

62. Moltmann, *How I Have Changed*, 15.

63. Barnett, *For the Soul of the People*, 289–90.

64. Moltmann and Bryan, *Communities of Faith and Radical Discipleship*, 6.

65. Moltmann-Wendel, *Autobiography*, 40.

66. Ernst Bloch, *Das Prinzip Hoffnung*, vol. 1 (Frankfurt am Main: Suhrkamp, 1959), 242, quoted in Jürgen Moltmann, *Theology of Hope: On the Ground and the Implications of a Christian Eschatology* (New York, Harper & Row: 1967), 79.

67. Moltmann, *How I Have Changed*, 16.

68. Moltmann, *Experiences of God*, 11.

69. Moltmann, *How I Have Changed*, 16.

70. Moltmann, *Experiences of God*, 12. Moltmann's eschatology differs from Barth's at this point. Moltmann's restlessness comes from an insistence that everything has not already come to completion in Christ and his resurrection. Jürgen Moltmann, *Theology of Hope*, 163; Timothy Gorringe, "Eschatology and Political Radicalism: The Example of Karl Barth and Jürgen Moltmann," in *God Will Be All in All: The Eschatology of Jürgen Moltmann,* ed. Richard Bauckham (Minneapolis: Fortress Press, 2001), 105.

71. Jürgen Moltmann, *Theologie Der Hoffnung: Untersuchungen Zu Begründung Und Zu Den Konsequenzen Einer Christlichen Eschatologie* (Munich: Chr. Kaiser Verlag, 1964).

72. Moltmann and Bryan, *Communities of Faith and Radical Discipleship*, 6.

73. Prissy Tate, "Task of Theology Discussed," *The Duke Chronicle*, April 5, 1968, 1.

74. Moltmann, April 29, 2005.

75. Moltmann, *Experiences in Theology*, 189.

76. Moltmann, April 29, 2005.

77. Moltmann-Wendel, *Autobiography*, 43.

78. Moltmann and Bryan, *Communities of Faith and Radical Discipleship*, 6.

79. Moltmann, *The Crucified God*, 4.

80. Ibid., 201.

81. Moltmann, *How I Have Changed*, 17.

82. Moltmann, *The Crucified God*, 37.

83. On November 16, 1989, at the University of San Salvador, government soldiers murdered six Jesuits and two women. In the blood of Brother Ramon Moreno was found a copy of *El Dios Crucificado*. It is now kept as a relic in the "Martyr's Room." Moltmann, *How I Have Changed*, 19.

84. Moltmann, *The Crucified God*, 37.

85. Phillip Berryman, *Liberation Theology: Essential Facts About the Revolutionary Movement in Latin America—and Beyond* (Philadelphia: Temple University Press, 1987), 24–28.

86. Jürgen Moltmann, *The Church in the Power of the Spirit: A Contribution of Messianic Ecclesiology* (London: SCM Press, 1977), xiii.

87. Ibid., xvii.

88. Ibid., xvi.

89. The section is found in ibid., 114–21. It also appeared in English the following year in slightly revised and expanded form under the title "Open Friendship" in Jürgen Moltmann and M. Douglas Meeks, *The Passion for Life: A Messianic Lifestyle* (Philadelphia: Fortress Press, 1978), 50–63. The same book was published in Britain as Jürgen Moltmann and M. Douglas Meeks, *The Open Church: Invitation to a Messianic Lifestyle* (London: SCM Press, 1978). With slight revision, the piece appeared as an article in Jürgen Moltmann, "Open Friendship: Aristotelian and Christian Concepts of Friendship," in *The Changing Face of Friendship*, ed. Leroy S. Rouner, Boston University Studies in Philosophy and Religion (Notre Dame, IN: University of Notre Dame Press, 1994). Liz Carmichael describes this short work on friendship as a "brief but seminal passage" Elizabeth D. H. Carmichael, *Friendship: Interpreting Christian Love* (London: T & T Clark International, 2004), 178.

90. Moltmann, *Experiences of God*, 7.

91. Literally translated as, "man bent in upon himself."

92. Moltmann, *The Church in the Power of the Spirit*, 194.

93. Moltmann, *Experiences of God*, 8.

94. Moltmann, *How I Have Changed*, 16.

95. Moltmann, *The Church in the Power of the Spirit*, 194. The Spirit of Hope captures the imagination thus transforming the present. Trevor Hart, "Imagination for the Kingdom of God? Hope, Promise and the Transformative Power of an Imagined Future," in *God Will Be All in All: The Eschatology of Jürgen Moltmann*, ed. Richard Bauckham (Minneapolis: Fortress Press, 2001), 75–76.

96. Moltmann uses the Latin, "*societas incurvatus in se.*" Moltmann, *The Church in the Power of the Spirit*, 194.

97. Ibid.

98. Moltmann, *Theology of Hope*, 328.

99. J Stephen Rhodes, "The Comfort and Challenge of Open Friendship," *The Asbury Theological Journal* 49 (Spring 1994): 67.

100. Moltmann, *The Crucified God*, 27.

101. Ibid., 28.

102. Moltmann, "Open Friendship: Aristotelian and Christian Concepts of Friendship," 33.; Moltmann, *The Church in the Power of the Spirit*, 315. Feminist theologians have taken up Moltmann's Christology of friendship. Elisabeth Moltmann-Wendel, theologian and Moltmann's wife, traces this development in Elisabeth Moltmann-Wendel, *Rediscovering Friendship: Awakening to the Power and Promise of Women's Friendships* (Minneapolis: Fortress Press, 2001), 17–30.

103. A similar account is found in Matthew 11:19 "...the Son of man came eating and drinking, and they say, 'Look, a glutton and a drunkard, a friend of tax collectors and sinners!'"

104. Moltmann, "Open Friendship: Aristotelian and Christian Concepts of Friendship," 35.

105. Moltmann, *The Church in the Power of the Spirit*, 316.

106. Ibid., 115.

107. Ibid., 316.

108. Jürgen Moltmann, *The Trinity and the Kingdom: The Doctrine of God* (San Francisco: Harper & Row, 1981), 172; Bauckham, *The Theology of Jürgen Moltmann*, 164; J Stephen Rhodes, "The Church as the Community of Open Friendship," *The Asbury Theological Journal* 55 (Spring 2000): 41–42.

109. Moltmann, *The Church in the Power of the Spirit*, 115.

110. Aristotle, Ethics, Book VIII, cited in Moltmann, *The Crucified God*, 28.

111. Moltmann, *The Church in the Power of the Spirit*, 120.

112. Moltmann, "Open Friendship," 39.

113. Ibid., 35.

114. Moltmann, *The Crucified God*, 20–21.

115. Ibid., 19.

116. Ibid. Moltmann bemoans the increase in sectarian conflict between those who claim to be the "'Church of Mary' which alone hears the word of the Lord, and the 'Church of Martha' preoccupied with useless social activity'" Moltmann, *The Crucified God*, 20–21.

117. Moltmann, *The Crucified God*, 22.

118. Moltmann, *Theology of Hope*, 327.

119. Ibid.

120. Sally O'Quin, "Campus Scourge at Ole Miss," *Life*, July 17, 1964, 74.

121. James W. Silver, *Running Scared: Silver in Mississippi* (Jackson: University Press of Mississippi, 1984), 102.

122. Claude Sitton, "Southern Dissenter," *New York Times*, November 8, 1963, 19.

123. Silver, *Running Scared*, 86.

124. Ibid., 6.

125. Ibid., 9.

126. James W. Silver, *Edmund Pendleton Gaines and Frontier Problems, 1801–1849* (PhD diss., Vanderbilt University, 1935).

127. Silver, *Running Scared*, 38.

128. Ibid., x.

129. Ibid., 21.

130. Ibid., 20.

131. William Winter, interview by the author, October 13, 2004, Jackson, MS.

132. Ibid.

133. Silver, *Running Scared*, 35.

134. William F. Winter and Andrew P. Mullins, *The Measure of Our Days: Writings of William F. Winter* (Jackson: William Winter Institute for Racial Reconciliation: Distributed by University Press of Mississippi, 2006), xviii.

135. Winter, Oct. 13, 2004; Silver, *Running Scared*, 33.

136. Winter, Oct. 13, 2004.

137. Ibid.

138. ODK Mortar Board Presentation flyers, William Winter's private papers.

139. Conservatives as well as Liberals spoke at the forum. Winter remembers Dr. George Stuart Benson of Harding College "was about the most conservative you ever saw." Winter, Oct. 13, 2004. Other speakers at the forum over the years included Emil Ludwig, Edward Weeks, Virginius Dabney, Clement Atlee, Jacob Potofsky, Eric Sevareid, Gus Dyer, and Sir Oliver Franks. Silver, *Running Scared*, 35.

140. "Solons in Secret Session Here to Hear 'Red' Names Name Ole Miss Profs," *Jackson Daily News*, February 2, 1950, 1.

141. Winter and Mullins, *The Measure of Our Days: Writings of William F. Winter*, xviii.

142. Nadine Cohodas, *The Band Played Dixie: Race and the Liberal Conscience at Ole Miss* (New York: Free Press, 1997), 44.

143. Will D. Campbell, *Brother to a Dragonfly* (New York: Seabury Press, 1977), 108.

144. Ibid., 109.

145. Ibid., 111; Neil R. McMillen, *The Citizens' Council: Organized Resistance to the Second Reconstruction, 1954–64* (Urbana: University of Illinois Press, 1971), 17; Yasuhiro Katagiri, *The Mississippi State Sovereignty Commission: Civil Rights and States' Rights* (Jackson: University Press of Mississippi, 2001), xxx.

146. Tom P. Brady, *Black Monday* (Winona, MS: Association of Citizens' Councils, 1955), iii.

147. McMillen, *The Citizens' Council*, 16.

148. Hodding Carter III, "Citadel of the Citizens' Council," *New York Times Magazine*, November 12 1961, 23.

149. Will D. Campbell, interview by the author, October 19, 2004, Mt. Juliet, TN.

150. Silver, *Running Scared*, 64.

151. Campbell, Oct. 19, 2004.

152. Silver, *Running Scared*, 65; Cohodas, *The Band Played Dixie*, 42.

153. Cohodas, *The Band Played Dixie*, 43.

154. Katagiri, *The Mississippi State Sovereignty Commission*, 5.

155. Ibid., 5.

156. Ibid., 6.

157. Ibid., 7.

158. Campbell, Oct. 19, 2004.

159. Campbell, *Brother to a Dragonfly*, 113.

160. Campbell, Oct. 19, 2004.

161. Campbell, *Brother to a Dragonfly,* 113; David G. Sansing, *The University of Mississippi: A Sesquicentennial History* (Jackson: University Press of Mississippi, 1999), 278.

162. Campbell, *Brother to a Dragonfly,* 119.

163. Ibid., 121.

164. "Reply to Allegations Concerning Certain Members of the Faculty and Staff of the University of Mississippi," 1959, SCRID# 3-9-1-8-1-1-1 to 3-9-1-8-34-1-1, MSSC.

165. Silver, *Running Scared,* 64; Campbell, *Brother to a Dragonfly,* 126.

166. Cohodas, *The Band Played Dixie,* 47.

167. Campbell, October 19, 2004.

168. Ibid.

169. Katagiri, *The Mississippi State Sovereignty Commission,* 67; Zack J. Van Landingham, "Memo to Director, State Sovereignty Commission: N.A.A.C.P., Lexington, Mississippi," January 23, 1959, SCRID# 2-54-1-5-1-1-1, MSSC; Cohodas, *The Band Played Dixie,* 49.

170. Silver, *Running Scared,* 66.

171. Sansing, *The University of Mississippi,* 278.

172. "Alumni Repeating Criticisms against Dr. Lyon," *Clarion-Ledger,* July 15, 1959.

173. Charles M. Hills, "Affairs of State," *Clarion-Ledger,* July 17, 1959.

174. Ibid.

175. "Reply to Allegations," 18.

176. Ibid., 20; Silver, *Running Scared,* 67.

177. "Reply to Allegations," 25.

178. Bob Gordon, "University Prof Hits Red Hunter," *State Times,* March 4, 1961.

179. Silver, *Running Scared,* xi.

180. James Meredith, *Three Years in Mississippi* (Bloomington: Indiana University Press, 1966), 243.

181. Ibid., 55.

182. Sansing, *The University of Mississippi,* 299–301; Henry Hampton, Steve Fayer, and Sarah Flynn, *Voices of Freedom: An Oral History of the Civil Rights Movement from the 1950s through the 1980s* (London: Vintage 1995, 1990), 116.

183. James W. Silver, *Mississippi: The Closed Society* (New York: Harcourt, Brace & World, 1964), 164.

184. Evans Harrington, interview by William Thomas, February 9, 1996 in William Thomas, "The Meredith Event at the University of Mississippi: The Creaking of Modern America under Post-Modern Stress" (MA Thesis, University of Mississippi, 1998). 95.

185. Silver, *Mississippi: The Closed Society,* 166; Numan V. Bartley, *The New South, 1945–1980,* A History of the South; vol. 11 (Baton Rouge: Louisiana State University Press, 1995), 253; David G. Sansing, *Making Haste Slowly: The Troubled History of*

Higher Education in Mississippi (Jackson: University Press of Mississippi, 1990),
193. Russell H. Barrett, *Integration at Ole Miss* (Chicago: Quadrangle Books, 1965),
161. William Doyle, *An American Insurrection: The Battle of Oxford, Mississippi, 1962*
(New York: Doubleday, 2001), 23.

186. Silver, *Mississippi: The Closed Society*, 167.

187. Hampton, Fayer, and Flynn, *Voices of Freedom*, 116; Barrett, *Integration at Ole Miss*, 167.

188. William Simmons, "Victory at Oxford," *The Citizen*, September 1962, 2.

189. Silver, *Mississippi: The Closed Society*, 168.

190. Silver, *Running Scared*, 138.

191. Ibid.

192. Ibid., x–xi.

193. Ibid., 139.

194. Silver to Leslie Dunbar, Oct.25, 1963, in Carol Polsgrove, *Divided Minds: Intellectuals and the Civil Rights Movement* (New York: Norton, 2001), 215.

195. Silver, *Running Scared*, 76; Polsgrove, *Divided Minds*, 212.

196. Silver, *Running Scared*, xi.

197. Claude Sitton, "Mississippi Professor Declares That His State Is 'Totalitarian,'" *New York Times*, November 8, 1963.

198. Polsgrove, *Divided Minds*, 217.

199. Silver, *Mississippi: The Closed Society*, 6.

200. Ibid.

201. Moltmann, *The Church in the Power of the Spirit*, 194.

202. Moltmann, *The Crucified God*, 19.

203. Silver, *Mississippi: The Closed Society*, 22.

204. "Ole Miss Professor Lectures in Atlanta," September 1963, SCRID# 99-137-0-9-1-1-1 to 99-137-0-9-5-1-1, MSSC.

205. Erle Johnston, Jr. to Honorable Tom Tubbs, n.d., SCRID# 99-137-0-8-2-1-1, MSSC.

206. Erle Johnston, Jr., "Memo to File Dr. James Silver," December 9, 1963, SCRID# 99-137-0-4-1-1-1, MSSC.

207. "Field-Notes to File," SCRID# 3-9-2-3-1-1-1 and 3-9-2-3-2-1-1, MSSC.

208. Silver, *Running Scared*, 97.

209. Ibid., 103.

210. Silver, *Mississippi: The Closed Society*, 104.

211. Ibid., 136.

212. Ibid., 155.

213. Silver, *Running Scared*, 136.

214. Sitton, "Southern Dissenter."

215. Silver, *Mississippi: The Closed Society*, 53–54.

216. Cohodas, *The Band Played Dixie*, 75.

217. Will D. Campbell, *And Also with You: Duncan Gray and the American Dilemma* (Franklin, TN: Providence House, 1997), 25–34.

218. Moltmann, *The Crucified God*, 19.

219. Will D. Campbell, *Race and the Renewal of the Church* (Philadelphia: Westminster Press, 1962), 4.

220. Ibid., 5.

221. Ibid., 53.

222. Ibid., 85–86.

CHAPTER 3

1. LeRoy H. Paris to Jarvis Ward, October 15, 1997, MMP.

2. Charlotte Graham, "Mission Mississippi Takes Religious Tack toward Racial Harmony," *Clarion-Ledger*, January 16, 1993.

3. Ibid.

4. Ibid.

5. Michael O. Emerson and Christian Smith, *Divided by Faith: Evangelical Religion and the Problem of Race in America* (New York: Oxford University Press, 2000), 63–66. Promise Keepers published a two-hundred-page set of Bible studies on racial reconciliation. Raleigh Washington, Glen Kehrein, and Claude V. King, *Break Down the Walls: Experiencing Biblical Reconciliation and Unity in the Body of Christ* (Chicago: Moody Press, 1997). The theologian Charles Marsh considers Mission Mississippi part of the "quiet revolution" of evangelical Christians in the United States baring "the same spiritual vision that animated the Civil Rights Movement." Charles Marsh, *The Beloved Community: How Faith Shapes Social Justice, from the Civil Rights Movement to Today* (New York: Basic Books, 2005), 7, 203–06.

6. Charles L. Dunn, Director of Marketing, Mission Mississippi, e-mail to author, March 2, 2006.

7. "Our Vision: Ministry of Reconciliation," Mission Mississippi, 2005. Available: http://www.missionmississippi.org/VISION.dsp (accessed March 3, 2006).

8. Even in Methodist and Episcopal churches, the congregation's wield significant power. See, for example, W. J. Cunningham, *Agony at Galloway: One Church's Struggle with Social Change* (Jackson: University Press of Mississippi, 1980).

9. Perkins founded the Christian Community Development Association in 1989. For more on Perkins and the significance of his work, see Marsh, *The Beloved Community*, 153–88; Emerson and Smith, *Divided by Faith*, 51–68. Perkins wrote his own biography and manifesto. John Perkins, *A Quiet Revolution: The Christian Response to Human Need, a Strategy for Today* (Waco, TX: Word Books, 1976). There are also extensive holdings in the Billy Graham Archive at Wheaton College pertaining to John Perkins and Voice of Calvary.

10. Victor Smith, interview by the author, October 12, 2004, Pearl, MS.

11. "NAACP vs. Angelo Primos, Mrs Angelo Primos, Gus Primos, Kenneth Primos, Alice Primos, Alec Primos and Mrs Victor Smith, Randolph Boehm et al.," *Papers of the NAACP* (Frederick, MD, 1982). Microfilm, part 23, series A.

12. Smith, October 12, 2004.

13. "1963–1964 Board of Directors Jackson Citizens' Council Elected at Annual Meeting, May 17, 1963, Olympic Room, Heidelberg Hotel," SCRID# 99-30-0-74-1-1-1,

MSSC; A.L. Hopkins, "Meeting with Committee of Citizens' Council, Plaza Building, Jackson, Mississippi, on Night of November 9, 1962," November 13, 1962, SCRID# 2-55-10-20-1-1-1, MSSC.

14. "NAACP vs. Angelo Primos."

15. In 1970, following the federal court's decision forcing Mississippi to desegregate public high schools, St. Andrews Episcopal school was flooded with applicants for admission. Dean Jenkins refused to increase the number of admissions and to add a high school. Sherwood Willing Wise, *The Cathedral Church of St. Andrew: A Sesquicentennial History, 1839–1989* (Jackson, MS: The Cathedral Church of St. Andrew, 1989), 202.

16. Smith, Oct. 12, 2004. Evangelism Explosion was a program developed in Coral Ridge Presbyterian Church. Fort Lauderdale, Florida, in the 1960s. Harriet A. Harris, *Fundamentalism and Evangelicals*, Oxford Theological Monographs (Oxford, New York: Clarendon Press; Oxford University Press, 1998), 195.

17. Smith, October 12, 2004.

18. Perkins, *A Quiet Revolution*, 207.

19. Smith, October 12, 2004. Mission Mississippi honored Smith by holding a banquet for his sixty-fifth birthday. John Perkins was one of the presenters and VOC was a co-sponsor of the event. "Reward of Reconciliation Banquet," event program, May 11, 1995, MMP.

20. Patrick M. Morley, *The Man in the Mirror: Solving the 24 Problems Men Face* (Brentwood, TN: Wolgemuth & Hyatt, 1989).

21. *Unifying the Body of Christ: And the Walls Come Tumbling Down,* (Jackson: Mission Mississippi, 1996), 2.

22. Lee Paris, interview by the author, May 19, 2003, Jackson, MS.

23. James Baird, interview by the author, February 9, 2004, Flowood, MS.

24. Paris, May 19, 2003.

25. Tom Skinner, interview by Robert Shuster, June 13, 1990, Collection 430—Tom Skinner. T2 Transcript, Billy Graham Center Archives, Wheaton College. Available: http://www.wheaton.edu/bgc/archives/GUIDES/430.htm#3 (accessed April 13, 2005).

26. Paris, May 19, 2003; Joe Maxwell, "Beating Racism, One Friendship at a Time," *Chicago Tribune*, November 3, 1993; *Unifying the Body of Christ*, 2. Mission Mississippi did not formally adopt its name until December 7, 1992. "Agenda Mission Mississippi Steering Committee Meeting," December 7, 1992, MMP.

27. Dan Hall to Pat Morley and Tom Skinner, January 21, 1993, MMP; Maxwell, "Beating Racism"; *Unifying the Body of Christ*, 2.

28. John Hugh Tate, "Mission Mississippi Salutes Its Pioneers," *The Messenger* 12 (Winter 2003), 1; "Top Ten Milestones!" *The Messenger* 15 (January 2004), 1; Dan Hall to the author, May 23, 2005.

29. James Washington, interview by the author, October 13, 2004, Jackson, MS.

30. Baird, February 9, 2004.

31. Washington, October 13, 2004.

32. For an account of the movement in Jackson, read John R. Salter, *Jackson, Mississippi: An American Chronicle of Struggle and Schism* (Malabar, FL: R.E. Krieger, 1987).

33. Washington, Oct. 13, 2004. For an account of these arrests and the "concentration camp" at the fairground, see Salter, *Jackson, Mississippi*, 148–155.

34. Cade Chapel, founded in 1880 on land donated by Isham Cade, an ex-slave, is the second oldest African American congregation in Jackson. Washington served as assistant pastor under Rev. J. D. Hayden who was minister at Cade for an astonishing forty-one years from 1927 to 1968. Jimmie Ann Hampton Hartfield, ed., *100th Anniversary of Baptist Church. 1880–1980 Jackson, Mississippi* (Jackson, MS: Cade Chapel, 1980).

35. Washington, October 13, 2004. For an account of the killings and subsequent protests see: Tim Spofford, *Lynch Street: The May 1970 Slayings at Jackson State College* (Kent, OH: Kent State University Press, 1988).

36. The most complete accounts of the clergy participation in the movement in Selma are in David J. Garrow, *Protest at Selma: Martin Luther King, Jr., and the Voting Rights Act of 1965* (New Haven, CT: Yale University Press, 1978); Charles Fager, *Selma, 1965: The March That Changed the South*, 2nd ed. (Boston: Beacon Press, 1985).

37. Baird, February 9, 2004. Paul Harvey, *Freedom's Coming: Religious Culture and the Shaping of the South from the Civil War through the Civil Rights Era* (Chapel Hill: University of North Carolina Press, 2005), 212; Joseph H. Crespino, *In Search of Another Country: Mississippi and the Conservative Counterrevolution* (Princeton, NJ: Princeton University Press, 2007), 64.

38. Baird, February 9, 2004.

39. Ibid.; Ronnie Crudup, interview by the author, February 5, 2004, Jackson, MS.

40. Crudup, February 5, 2004.

41. Washington, October 13, 2004.

42. Ibid.

43. Ronnie Crudup recalls that the prayer meetings "had probably gone on at least a good year or more before any thought ever came about in terms of Pat Morley and Tom Skinner." This probably places the first prayer meeting in early 1990. Crudup, February 5, 2004.

44. Ibid.

45. Smith, Oct. 12, 2004.

46. "Agenda Mission Mississippi Steering Committee Meeting, December 7, 1992."

47. The first executive board consisted of Lee Paris (Chair), Dr. James Baird, Alvin Benson, Gwen Cannon, Dr. John Case, Rev. Michael Culbreth, Rev. Dan Hall, Rev. Hosea Hines, Beth Holmes, O. Kendall Moore, Victor Smith, Father Richard Somers, and Dorothy Stewart. *Mission Mississippi Memos* 1 (August 1993): 3.

48. Gwen Ann Mills, "A Social History of Jackson, Mississippi, 1920–1929" (MA thesis, University of Mississippi, 1966). 87.

49. *Jackson Daily News*, May 3, 8, 14, 1922 in ibid., 83–94.

50. E.L. Stanford, *The History of Calvary Baptist Church, Jackson, Mississippi* (Jackson, MS: Hederman Brothers, 1980), 184–85.

51. Ibid.

52. William Martin, "Billy Graham," in *Varieties of Southern Evangelicalism*, ed. David Edwin Harrell (Macon, GA: Mercer University Press, 1981), 84; Emerson and Smith, *Divided by Faith*, 47.

53. Cunningham, *Agony at Galloway*, 28.

54. Stanford, *The History of Calvary Baptist Church, Jackson, Mississippi*, 247.

55. Ibid., 257–58. John Perkins noted the interracial cooperation of ministers at the Billy Graham Crusade as a "hopeful sign" Perkins, *A Quiet Revolution*, 207.

56. Art Toalston, "Diverse Group of Churches Active in Robison's Crusade," *Clarion-Ledger*, March 21, 1981.

57. Washington, October 13, 2004.

58. "Attention Members," *Mission Mississippi Memos* I (Spring 1993): 2.

59. LeRoy H Paris, "Message from the Chairman," *Bringing Down the Walls that Divide Us*, promotional newspaper, 1993, MMP.

60. Paris, May 19, 2003.

61. Martin, "Billy Graham," 79.

62. "Mission Mississippi Committees," *Mission Mississippi Memos* I (Spring 1993): 1.

63. The retreat took place at the Southwest Holiday Inn on Highway 80, June 15–16.Dan Hall and Melvin Anderson to Jackson area pastors, May 26, 1993, MMP.

64. LeRoy H. Paris to Jackson area pastors, January 12, 1993, MMP.

65. "Mayor's Annual Leadership Prayer Breakfast," *Mission Mississippi Memos* I (June 1993), 2.

66. LeRoy H. Paris to Tom Skinner, April 22, 1993, MMP.

67. LeRoy H. Paris, "From the Chair," *Mission Mississippi Memos* I (June 1993), 1.

68. LeRoy H. Paris to the Friends of Mission Mississippi, July 12, 1993, MMP; LeRoy H. Paris to the Friends of Mission Mississippi, August 24, 1993, MMP.

69. "Mission Mississippi October Events Speaking Engagements for Tom Skinner and Pat Morley," 1993, MMP.

70. The fascinating story of the media's role in Jackson during the civil rights era is told in Steven D. Classen, *Watching Jim Crow: The Struggles over Mississippi TV, 1955–1969* (Durham, NC: Duke University Press, 2004).

71. Maxwell, "Beating Racism."

72. "Who's Involved?" *Bringing Down the Walls that Divide Us*. Noticeably absent are Jackson's historic African American churches: Cade Chapel and Central Methodist Church.

73. *Jackson Daily News*, May 3, 8, 14, 1922 in Mills, "A Social History of Jackson, Mississippi, 1920–1929," 83–94.

74. Charlotte Graham, "Mission: Reconciliation," *Clarion-Ledger*, October 16, 1993.

75. "Mission Mississippi Meeting with Jitney Jungle Ad Group, September 14, 1993," 1993, MMP. Emphasis added.

76. "Return of Organization Exempt from Income Tax for 1/15/93 to 12/31/93," 1994, MMP.

77. Mission Mississippi's tax return for 1993 shows they spent $244,056 on the stadium rallies and accompanying publicity. Ibid.

78. Hue Ha, "Quiet Faith Undergirds Main Street Commerce," *Clarion-Ledger*, October 16, 1996.

79. Robert McFarland, "Henry Paris of Planters Bank: Banker, Entrepreneur and Community Leader," *Delta Business Journal* (January 1999).

80. LeRoy H. Paris to Jack Garner, Union Planters Bank, August 1, 1995, MMP.

81. "Mission Mississippi Rally Flyer," 1993, MMP.

82. *Unifying the Body of Christ*, 2.

83. "Music/Speakers/Worship," *Bringing Down the Walls that Divide Us*.

84. Youth Musical Extravaganza, October 25, 1993. Transcribed by author from VHS tape from WAPT-TV, LPP.

85. Ibid.

86. "Agenda Mission Mississippi Steering Committee Meeting, December 7, 1992."

87. Youth Musical Extravaganza, October 25, 1993.

88. *Unifying the Body of Christ*, 3.

89. Ibid.

90. William Doyle, *An American Insurrection: The Battle of Oxford, Mississippi, 1962* (New York: Doubleday, 2001), 112–13.

91. Joe Maxwell, "Racial Healing in the Land of Lynching," *Christianity Today*, January 10, 1994.

92. Patrick M. Morley, "Mission Mississippi Highlights," *Patrick Morley Ministries Newsletter* (December 1993).

93. "Committed Churches," *Mission Mississippi Memos* 1 (November/December 1993): 4.

94. Maxwell, "Beating Racism."

95. "Mission Missisippi De-Briefing, Notes," October 27, 1993, MMP.

96. Morley, "Mission Mississippi Highlights."

97. "Mission Misisippi De-Briefing, Notes."

98. Phil Reed to LeRoy H. Paris, November 1, 1993, MMP.

99. Dan Hall to Pat Morley and Tom Skinner, January 21, 1993, MMP.

100. Ibid.

101. Patrick M. Morley, "Patrick Morley Ministries Inc. Purpose," January 29, 1993, MMP. Mission Mississippi organizers looked to the success of the new evangelical men's movement Promise Keepers who that year gathered fifty thousand men in University of Colorado's Folsom Field. In 1994, 278,000 men attended Promise Keeper Conferences. In 1995, it was 738,000; in 1996, the attendance at twenty-two stadium conferences was 1.1 million men. "The History of Promise Keepers" Promise Keepers, 2001. Available: http://www.promisekeepers.org/genr12 (accessed May 16, 2005). Large events in the 1990s were not the exclusive domain of evangelical Christians. In 1995, the Nation of Islam's Louis Farrakhan organized the Million Man March.

102. Jarvis Ward, interview by the author, February 9, 2004, Jackson, MS; Lee Paris, "From the Chairman," *Mission Mississippi Memos* 2 (August 1994), 1.

103. "Tom Skinner's Homegoing—June 17, 1994," *Mission Mississippi Memos* 1 (August 1994), 1.

104. Evans, an African American, was senior pastor of the twenty-five hundred member Oak Cliff Bible Fellowship in Dallas, Texas, and founder of *The Urban Alternative* which has its own radio ministry. "1994 Celebration of Reconciliation in Christ," 1995, MMP.

105. Charlotte Graham, " 'God Is Doing a Remarkable Work in Our City,' " *Clarion-Ledger*, October 19, 1994.

106. Ibid.

107. "Press Release," 1994, MMP. Numbers are a slippery thing. By the time Mission Mississippi wrote its own official account just over a year later the number had risen to 12,000. *Unifying the Body of Christ*, 4.

108. Charlotte Graham, "Brothers in Faith," *Clarion-Ledger*, October 14, 1995.

109. *Unifying the Body of Christ*, 4.

110. Jarvis C Ward, "Executive Director Activities Status Report," April 1997, MMP.

111. "Mission Mississippi Hosts Dinner Event," *The Northside Sun*, October 13, 1994.

112. "Minutes of the Meeting of the Executive Board of Mission Mississippi, January 16, 1996," MMP. The paid staff at this time was Ward as Executive Director, John Geary, the pastor of North Jackson Vineyard Christian Fellowship, as the Director of Development. There was also a part-time assistant to the Director of Development, a full-time secretary and a part-time secretary.

113. Ibid.

114. Ward, February 9, 2004.

115. John Geary, "Mission Mississippi: Evaluation and Direction—Memo to Lee Paris," 1997, MMP.

116. Jarvis C. Ward, "Mission Mississippi Vision 1997 and Beyond, Jarvis Ward's Proposed Revisions (2/13/97)," MMP. Members of the Administrative Committee were Ronnie Crudup, Lee Paris, Victor Smith, and Ebbie Spivey.

117. LeRoy H. Paris to Jarvis Ward, October 15, 1997, MMP.

118. Jarvis C Ward to Lee Paris, October 1, 1997, MMP.

119. Perkins, *A Quiet Revolution*, 41–47.

120. John Perkins, interview by the author, October 12, 2004, Jackson, MS.

121. Dolphus Weary and William Hendricks, *I Ain't Comin' Back* (Wheaton, IL: Tyndale House Publishers, 1990), 43.

122. Ibid; Interviews with Dolphus Douglas Weary, Collection 373, Billy Graham Center Archives, Wheaton College. Available: http://www.wheaton.edu/bgc/archives/GUIDES/373.htm (accessed May 17, 2005).

123. Charlotte Graham, "Building Bridges 2 by 2," *Clarion-Ledger*, September 7, 1996.

124. Charlotte Graham, "Same Mission: Reconciliation," *Clarion-Ledger*, January 4, 1998.

125. Dolphus Weary, interview by the author, February 25, 2000, Jackson, MS.

126. Charlotte Graham, "Mission Mississippi Exec Leaving Office in November," *Clarion-Ledger*, October 8, 1997.

127. Weary, February 25, 2000.

128. "Mission Mississippi Board Planning Retreat Minutes," November 17, 1998, MMP.

129. Grace Murrey, "Reconciliation Weekend," *Mission Mississippi Insights* (Summer, 1998): 4.

130. Ibid.

131. Dolphus Weary, "A Word from the Executive Director," *Mission Mississippi Insights* (Winter–Spring 1999), 1.

132. LeRoy H Paris, "From the Board of Directors," *Mission Mississippi Insights* (Winter-Spring 1999), 2.

133. "Grace Is Greater Than Race," *Mission Mississippi Messenger* 5 (Fall 2000), 5. The cities were Hattiesburg, Biloxi, Meridian, Columbus, Tupelo, Oxford, Grenada, Greenville, Vicksburg, and Jackson.

134. Dolphus Weary, "Grace Is Greater Than Race Tour Challenges Mississippi Christians to Break Dividing Walls," *Mission Mississippi Messenger* 6 (Winter 2000), 1.

135. Counting and freezing conducted by the author.

136. Jon Elder, "Assistant Director's 2001 Report," MMP. By 2005, Mission Mississippi listed seven chapters and five affiliates on their Web site. "Statewide," Mission Mississippi. Available: http://www.missionmississippi.org/STATEWIDE/ (accessed May 17, 2005).

137. Dolphus Weary, "Going Deeper!" *The Messenger* 14 (September 2003), 1.

138. Dolphus Weary, *Grace Is Greater Than Race* (sermon, Smith-Wills Memorial Stadium, Jackson, MS, November 19, 2000).

139. Francis J Cosgrove to Jackson area priests, April 29, 1993, MMP.

140. Wayne Rogers to Mission Mississippi, copied to Jackson Area PCA pastors, May 18, 1993, MMP.

141. Ibid.

142. Jerry Clark et al. to LeRoy H. Paris, March 1, 1993, MMP.

143. Mission Mississippi created the position of president for Weary in 2005 to allow him to concentrate on his preaching and public speaking. Neddie Winters became the Executive Director responsible for the day-to-day running of the organization.

144. Dolphus Weary, "Annual Executive Director's Report," November 27, 2001, MMP.

145. Hall led the workshops in Mission Mississippi's 2004 and 2005 Statewide Unity Conferences and facilitated the board's retreat in 2004. Alongside Weary and Winters, in 2007, Hall was listed as part of Mission Mississippi's Preaching Team. "Meet the Preaching Team." Available: http://www.missionmississippi.org/MEETTHEPREACHINGTEAM/ (accessed July 25, 2008).

146. *2007 Highlights*, Mission Mississippi, 2008, MMP.

147. Barry A. Kosmin, Egon Mayer, and Ariela Keysar, *American Religious Identification Survey 2001* (New York: The Graduate Center of the City University of New York, 2001), 43.

148. Here the term evangelical is used to include the broad sweep of Protestant churches that are part of a modern movement within Protestantism dating from the 1940s that rejected liberal theology, but wished to avoid the controversies and mud slinging associated with fundamentalism. This movement, championed by Billy Graham, was embodied in the National Association of Evangelicals founded in 1942, in Fuller Theological Seminary, Wheaton College; and in the pages of *Christianity Today*. D. G. Hart, *Deconstructing Evangelicalism: Conservative Protestantism in the Age of Billy Graham* (Grand Rapids, MI: Baker Academic, 2004), 23–26, 111; George M. Marsden, *Understanding Fundamentalism and Evangelicalism* (Grand Rapids, MI: W.B. Eerdmans, 1991), 62–82. The term evangelical as used here includes Southern Baptists. Despite the recent fundamentalist "takeover" of the Southern Baptist Convention, the term evangelical still best describes their defense of evangelical orthodoxy and cultural engagement. Barry Hankins, *Uneasy in Babylon: Southern Baptist Conservatives and American Culture* (Tuscaloosa: University of Alabama Press, 2002), 12–40. There was a vigorous internal debate within the SBC over whether they were in fact evangelicals. See James Leo Garrett, E. Glenn Hinson, and James E. Tull, *Are Southern Baptists "Evangelicals"?* (Macon, GA: Mercer University Press, 1983), and David S. Dockery, *Southern Baptists & American Evangelicals: The Conversation Continues* (Nashville, TN: Broadman & Holman, 1993).

149. Randy J. Sparks, *Religion in Mississippi* (Jackson: University Press of Mississippi for the Mississippi Historical Society, 2001), 201.

150. Ted Ownby, "Evangelical but Differentiated: Religion by the Numbers," in *Religion and Public Life in the South: In the Evangelical Mode*, ed. Charles Reagan Wilson and Mark Silk (Walnut Creek, CA: AltaMira Press, 2005), 40–44., Kosmin, Mayer, and Keysar, *American Religious Identification Survey 2001*, 43. *Churches and Church Membership in the United States, 1990*, (Glenmary Research Center: Mars Hill, NC) in *Largest Religious Groups in the United States of America*, Adherents.com, December 7, 2005. Available: http://www.adherents.com/rel_USA.html#ubiquitous (accessed May 19, 2005).

151. The strong Southern Baptist influence on the state and Mission Mississippi comes with a conservative social agenda and support of the Republican Party. For a detailed analysis of the relationship between Southern Baptists and politics, see Oran P. Smith, *The Rise of Baptist Republicanism* (New York: New York University Press, 1997).

152. Charles W. Colson and Ellen Santilli Vaughn, *The Body* (Dallas: Word Pub., 1992).

153. *About Us*, Mission Mississippi. Available: http://www.missionmississippi.org/ABOUT/ (accessed May 19, 2005).

154. Lee Paris, interview by the author, May 19, 2003, Jackson, MS.

155. "Mission Misisippi De-Briefing, Notes."

156. Andrew Michael Manis, *Southern Civil Religions in Conflict: Civil Rights and the Culture Wars* (Macon, GA: Mercer University Press, 2002), 119; John Shelton Reed, *Southerners, the Social Psychology of Sectionalism*, Institute for Research in Social Science Monograph Series (Chapel Hill: University of North Carolina Press, 1983), 70.

157. Baird, February 9, 2004.

158. Harris, *Fundamentalism and Evangelicals*, 39. For Southern Baptist reaction against NCC, see Manis, *Southern Civil Religions in Conflict*, 118. For an account of the NCC's work in Mississippi during the Civil Rights Movement, read Mark Newman, *Divine Agitators: The Delta Ministry and Civil Rights in Mississippi* (Athens: University of Georgia Press, 2004).

159. *Mission Mississippi Memos*, 1 (Spring 1993): 1. The word Unity is found in Psalm 133:1, "How good and pleasant it is when brothers live together in unity!" It was already in use by evangelicals to link ecumenism and race: "Together, the entire evangelical community must and can reaffirm the wonderful ethnic diversity among the body of Christ, while at the same time strengthening its unity." *Consultation on Racism Jointly Sponsored by the Social Action Commission of the National Association of Evangelicals and the National Black Evangelical Association's Statement on Prejudice and Racism* (January 26–27, 1990), 3. Promise Keepers adopted a similarly heavy emphasis on the term Unity, rendering it ubiquitous. In 1997, Promise Keepers had Raleigh Washington and Glen Kehrein turn their 1993 book *Breaking Down the Walls: A Model of Reconciliation in an Age of Racial Strife*, into a set of Bible studies; the sub-title changed to: *Experiencing Biblical Reconciliation and Unity in the Body of Christ*. The word "Unity" appears in the title of six of these Bible studies.

160. LeRoy H. Paris to Charles W. Colson, June 6, 1994, MMP; Steve Johnson Manager, Focus on the Family to Lee Paris, April 6, 1994, MMP. Pat Fordice, wife of Governor Kirk Fordice, unsuccessfully lobbied Dobson's wife. Pat Fordice to Shirley Dobson, October 24, 1995, MMP.

161. Evangelicals are very concerned with family life believing it is "their primary, positive means of contributing to social change." Christian Smith, *Christian America? What Evangelicals Really Want* (Berkeley: University of California Press, 2000), 167. According to sociologist James Hunter, "the family is the most conspicuous field of conflict in the culture war." James Davison Hunter, *Culture Wars: The Struggle to Define America* (New York: Basic Books, 1991), 176. The Southern Baptist Convention is at the vanguard of this culture war. Hankins, *Uneasy in Babylon*, 41–73.

162. Charlotte Graham, "Jackson-Area Clergy Launch Effort to Reduce Mississippi Divorce Rate," *Clarion-Ledger*, September 27, 1996; Randall Nulton to LeRoy Paris, August 19, 1996, MMP.

163. "Upcoming Events 1997," MMP.

164. In the 2004 elections (in which 59.64 percent of Mississippians voted to reelect George W. Bush), on the ballot paper was the question of an amendment to define marriage as being between a man and a women; 86.05 percent voted for the amendment. "Mississippi 2004–11–09 15:13:54 GMT" *Clarion-Ledger* [online]. Available: http://network.ap.org/dynamic/files/elections/2004/general/by_state/

ballot_other/MS.html?SITE=MSJAD&SECTION=POLITICS (accessed May 20, 2005).

165. "Grace Is Greater Than Race." American Family Radio (AFA) is the broadcasting arm of the conservative Christian family values organization American Family Association. American Family Association, "General Information" [Web page]. Available: http://www.afa.net/about.asp (accessed May 18, 2005).

166. "Mission Mississippi De-Briefing, Notes."

167. Lee Paris, interview by the author, October 14, 2004, Jackson, MS.

168. Ibid.

169. Lee Paris, interview by the author, October 10, 2004, Jackson, MS.

170. Marsden, *Understanding Fundamentalism and Evangelicalism*, 5.

171. "About Us."

172. Neddie Winters, interview by the author, October 18, 2004, Jackson, MS.

173. Ibid.

174. Ward, "Mission Mississippi Vision 1997 and Beyond, Jarvis Ward's Proposed Revisions (2/13/97)."

175. "Mission Mississippi De-Briefing, Notes."

176. "Minutes of the Meeting of the Executive Board, February 9, 1994," MMP. Moltmann draws the connection between a church that extends open friendship to the other and its outreach. "It is only as a unity in diversity that the Christian community will become an inviting community." Jürgen Moltmann, *The Source of Life: The Holy Spirit and the Theology of Life* (Minneapolis: Fortress Press, 1997), 60.

177. Dan Hall, untitled seminar address, (presented at Mission Mississippi Unity Conference, Mikhail's, Jackson, MS, February 6, 2004).

178. Ibid.

179. Spencer Perkins and Chris Rice, *More Than Equals: Racial Healing for the Sake of the Gospel,* revised and expanded. (Downers Grove, IL: InterVarsity Press, 2000), 48.

180. Hall, untitled seminar address.

181. Jürgen Moltmann, *How I Have Changed: Reflections on Thirty Years of Theology* (London: SCM Press, 1997), 16. and Moltmann, *The Source of Life: The Holy Spirit and the Theology of Life,* 40.

182. Jürgen Moltmann, *The Church in the Power of the Spirit: A Contribution of Messianic Ecclesiology* (London: SCM Press, 1977), 194.

183. Hall, untitled seminar address.

184. This emphasis on "heart religion" has a noble evangelical pedigree in the English-speaking world stretching back to John Wesley and the Methodist revivals of the Eighteenth Century. For influence of Methodism on the development of American evangelicalism, see John H. Wigger, *Taking Heaven by Storm: Methodism and the Rise of Popular Christianity in America* (New York: Oxford University Press, 1998).

185. Dolphus Weary, "Mission Mississippi: Movement of the Heart," *Mission Mississippi Messenger* (Fall 2000).

186. Weary, *Grace Is Greater Than Race.*

187. Ibid.

188. Ibid.

189. For a detailed description of the "color-blind" tendencies in evangelical churches see the chapter "Jesus is Color-Blind" in Brad Christerson, Korie L. Edwards, and Michael O. Emerson, *Against All Odds: The Struggle for Racial Integration in Religious Organizations* (New York: New York University Press, 2005), 126–150. Bonilla-Silva launches a devastating critique of how whites insistence they are "color-blind" simply masks racism in Eduardo Bonilla-Silva, *Racism without Racists: Color-Blind Racism and the Persistence of Racial Inequality in the United States* (Lanham, MD: Rowman & Littlefield, 2003). Howard Winant identifies color blindness in political policy as a "neo-conservative project." Howard Winant, *The New Politics of Race: Globalism, Difference, Justice* (Minneapolis: University of Minnesota Press, 2004), 43.

190. Morley, "Mission Mississippi Highlights."

191. Morley, "Patrick Morley Ministries Inc. Purpose."

192. Maxwell, "Beating Racism."

193. "Relationships Make a Difference," *Bringing Down the Walls that Divide Us,* (October 1993). Featured friendships included Dan Hall and Melvin Anderson; Victor Smith and Charles Doty; and Janice Smith and Mary Stitt.

194. Dolphus Weary named "intentionality" one of Mission Mississippi's key principles. Dolphus Weary, "Get Set," Presentation at the Inter-Varsity Conference, "Jubilee VI: The Grace Race," October 2, 2004, Voice of Calvary Ministries, Jackson, MS. The word "intentionality" features prominently in evangelical's literature on racial reconciliation. Washington and Kehrein name "intentionality" as "the locomotive that drives racial reconciliation." Washington, Kehrein, and King, *Break Down the Walls: Experiencing Biblical Reconciliation and Unity in the Body of Christ,* 127.

195. Hall, untitled seminar address.

196. I polled participants of Mission Mississippi as to the difference between friendship and relationship and there was no consensus. Some felt that relationships were more profound than friendships, whereas an equal number thought the exact opposite.

197. Jürgen Moltmann, "Open Friendship: Aristotelian and Christian Concepts of Friendship," in *The Changing Face of Friendship,* ed. Leroy S. Rouner, Boston University Studies in Philosophy and Religion (Notre Dame, IN: University of Notre Dame Press, 1994), 40.

198. Spencer Perkins and Chris Rice, *More Than Equals: Racial Healing for the Sake of the Gospel* (Downers Grove, IL: InterVarsity Press, 1993).

199. Perkins and Rice, *More Than Equals,* 229.

200. Ibid., 227.

201. Ibid., 230.

202. Mission Mississippi co-sponsored the Jackson book signing of *More than Equals.* Chris Rice and Spencer Perkins to Lee Paris and Jim Hitt, June 29, 1993, MMP. Rice and Perkins in turn saw the potential in Mission Mississippi and

"determined to join the budding network and labor behind the scenes to see the truth-telling element didn't get lost." Chris Rice, *Grace Matters: A True Story of Race, Friendship, and Faith in the Heart of the South* (San Francisco, CA: Jossey-Bass, 2002), 181. In 1996, Mission Mississippi invited Rice and Perkins to open the "Celebration of Reconciliation in Christ Seminar" by speaking on the biblical mandate for the ministry of reconciliation. "Mission Mississippi Reconciliation in Christ Seminar, October 22, 1996, 1:30–4:00pm," program, MMP.

203. "Book Review: More Than Equals," *Mission Mississippi Messenger* 5 (Fall 2000): 7.

204. Moltmann, "Open Friendship," 39.

205. Dolphus Weary, Presentation to the Theology and Race Work Group, Project on Lived Theology, February 24, 2001, Oxford, MS.

206. Will D. Campbell, *Race and the Renewal of the Church* (Philadelphia: Westminster Press, 1962), 85.

207. Jürgen Moltmann, *Experiences of God* (Philadelphia: Fortress Press, 1980), 12–13.

CHAPTER 4

1. Michael O. Emerson and Christian Smith, *Divided by Faith: Evangelical Religion and the Problem of Race in America* (New York: Oxford University Press, 2000), 170.

2. Ibid., ix.

3. Ibid., 74. Other sociologists support their findings. Kinder and Sanders talk about symbolic racism—a racism obsessed with moral character informed by traditions of American individualism. Donald R. Kinder and Lynn M. Sanders, *Divided by Color: Racial Politics and Democratic Ideals, American Politics and Political Economy* (Chicago: University of Chicago Press, 1996) 291–294.

4. Emerson and Smith, *Divided by Faith*, 78.

5. Ibid.

6. Ibid., 67.

7. Ibid.

8. Ibid., 77.

9. Ibid., 168.

10. Emerson and Smith found "Other than an occasional acquaintance, they had few interracial contacts...none lived in worlds that were not at least 90 percent white in their daily experience." Ibid., 80. Evangelicals also spent more time than other Christians in congregational activities and so are more likely to form friendships from within their own congregation and denomination Emerson and Smith, *Divided by Faith*, 133.

11. Emerson and Smith, *Divided by Faith*, 83.

12. Ibid., 131. They corroborate their findings with those of sociologists Mary Jackman and Marie Crane. Mary R. Jackman and Marie Crane, "'Some of My Best Friends Are Black': Interracial Friendship and Whites' Racial Attitudes," *Public Opinion Quarterly*, Vol. 50, No. 4 (1986), 459–86.

13. Emerson and Smith, *Divided by Faith*, 130.

14. *Jackson, the City Beautiful* (Jackson, MS: Chamber of Commerce, 1927), 1.

15. Both buildings are finally being renovated. VOC and Galloway United Methodist Church are restoring Capitol Street Methodist Church as a center for the arts by. Laura Hipp, "Ministry to Take Root with Some Aid," *Clarion-Ledger*, November 30, 2003. After being empty for thirty-eight years, the King Edward is to be renovated by HRI Inc. of New Orleans. Arnold Lindsay, "King Edward Renovation Ok'd," *Clarion-Ledger*, October 20, 2004.

16. Census data in Laura Hipp, "Historical Perspective," *Clarion-Ledger*, October 5, 2003.

17. Clay Harden, "The Question: Where Are We Today?" *Clarion-Ledger*, October 5, 2003.

18. Census data in Hipp, "Historical Perspective." One interesting effect of the white flight is that a new generation of whites is unaware of large sections of their own city. Jane Ross was surprised by her son's reaction after he was taken to West Jackson:

> He said, "Mama, I didn't even know west Jackson existed out there." He said, "I have never been out there." Because, see they stay in their own little worlds and I never thought just to take my children out there to look at it. He said, "My friends don't know that exists." He said "my friends"—I mean their parents are lawyers, surely their parents know this exists in Jackson. I am having a hard time justifying in my heart. How do their parents know that that exists and they have so much wealth and they are not doing any- thing to help those people over there? He said, "There are kids who are my age, we just never go out there. We don't even know that exists."

After a pause, Ross added in a quiet and determined voice, "I wanted to flee that. I wanted to go off and just go and live and do my own thing and get away from it. But that wasn't the Lord's plan." Jane Virden Ross, interview by the author, February 9, 2004, Jackson, MS.

19. Laura Hipp, Pamela Berry, and Gregg Mayer, "Jackson Struggles to Find Its Identity," *Clarion-Ledger*, October 5, 2003.

20. Jeremy Hudson, "City's Murder Rate 5 Times U.S. Average," *Clarion-Ledger*, January 30, 2005.

21. Cheryl Phillips' decision to send her son to Callaway High School mak- ing him one of two whites in the school was worthy of a human-interest piece in the newspaper. Laura Hipp, "They Assume Public Can't Be Good," *Clarion-Ledger*, October 19, 2003.

22. Ibid. James Baird summarized the dilemma facing white parents: "Public schools are black, private schools are white. What would you do if you had a child? Would you put your child into public school for the sake of a witness? I admire some who do. But, I have grandchildren. I want them to have an education. I want them to have the education that is as good as can be afforded and so they go into First

Presbyterian Day School." James Baird, interview by the author, February 9, 2004, Flowood, MS.

23. Hipp, "They Assume Public Can't Be Good." Jane Ross, a white math tutor at the black Lanier High School, had this assessment of her students: "When I got to Lanier they had nothing. I mean, they live in homes that are boarded up and basically, a lot of those kids are rearing themselves because their mothers are on drugs. Some of them, even their grand moms are on drugs. Very few households have a father figure." Ross, February 9, 2004.

24. Craig E Van Gelder, "Growth Patterns of Mainline Denominations and Their Churches: A Case Study of Jackson, Mississippi 1900–1980" (PhD diss. Southwestern Baptist Theological Seminary, 1982). 157; E.L. Stanford, *The History of Calvary Baptist Church, Jackson, Mississippi* (Jackson, MS: Hederman Brothers, 1980), 27. Central Presbyterian Church was organized on Sept. 25, 1894 as West Side Presbyterian Church. The name was changed to Central Presbyterian Church in 1909. William David McCain, ed., *The Story of Jackson: A History of the Capital of Mississippi, 1821–1951.*, vol. 1 (Jackson, MS: J.F. Hyer, 1953), 276–277.

25. Census figures in Harden, "The Question: Where Are We Today?"

26. Van Gelder, "Growth Patterns," 160; Charlotte Graham, "Churches Redefining, Thriving," *Clarion-Ledger*, October 19, 2003. Graham lists nine other white churches that have closed or moved because of the city's demographic shift.

27. Charlotte Graham, "As Communities Change, Ministries Decide to Stay," *Clarion-Ledger*, October 19, 2003.

28. In 2000, First Baptist Church opened *Mission First:* a community center with a dental clinic and after school clubs in West Jackson. First Baptist Church added $4 million to their building fund to renovate a section of project housing and build a huge sports hall (completed in 2004). Lee Thigpen a white member of First Baptist Church and Mission Mississippi board member, inspired by John Perkins, spearheaded the project. Frank Pollard, interview by the author, October 5, 2000, Jackson, MS (telephone). Lee Thigpen, interview by the author, November 19, 2000, Jackson, MS. *Mission First*, is one of a multiplicity of mission projects undertaken by First Baptist Church and does not challenge the majority of the congregation with Perkins' "R" of relocating back to Jackson, supporting public schools and local businesses, and paying city taxes.

29. W. J. Cunningham, *Agony at Galloway: One Church's Struggle with Social Change* (Jackson: University Press of Mississippi, 1980), 5. Cunningham's book is a classic history of and reflection on his time as minister at Galloway from 1963 to 1966. He arrived at a church that was "cultured, comfortable, and contented" and left with the observation, "In the church are some of the most vicious, vindictive people I have ever known." Cunningham, *Agony at Galloway*, x, 137. Galloway became the center of the "church visits" by students from Tougaloo and Methodists, black and white, challenging the church's closed door policy. For more on this see Charles Marsh, *God's Long Summer: Stories of Faith and Civil Rights* (Princeton, N.J., Chichester: Princeton University Press, 1997), 116–51.

30. "Galloway Staff—Ross Olivier," Galloway Memorial Methodist Church, Jackson, MS. Available: http://www.gallowayumc.org/staff/ross.shtml (accessed May 27 2005).

31. Ross Oliver, interview by the author, October 14, 2004, Jackson, MS.

32. Ibid.

33. Ross Oliver, "The Persistent Widow," (sermon preached at Galloway United Methodist Church, Jackson, MS, October 17, 2004).

34. Oliver, October 14, 2004.

35. John Perkins, interview by the author, October 12, 2004, Jackson, MS.

36. Phil Reed, interview by the author, October 7, 2004, Jackson, MS.

37. Ibid.

38. Perkins, October 12, 2004.

39. Dolphus Weary to Lee Paris, September 24, 1997, MMP. Weary adopted the "economic bridge" from his mentor John Perkins. An economic critique is key to Perkins' theology/strategy of the three Rs. In a chapter entitled "The Economics of Equality," Perkins called for talented African Americans to relocate to the black community and to help develop an economic base. For this to be successful, Perkins challenges the white community that "equality must be economic to have an impact on the poor community." Whites must help African Americans develop their own "indigenous financial support systems." This will require a redistribution of economic resources unfairly and disproportionately located in the white community. John Perkins, *A Quiet Revolution: The Christian Response to Human Need, a Strategy for Today* (Waco, TX: Word Books, 1976), 144–153. Perkins brought the message of the three "Rs" to Mission Mississippi when Weary placed his mentor as the main speaker at Mission Mississippi's Celebration Rallies in 1998 and 1999. Grace Murrey, "Reconciliation Weekend," *Mission Mississippi Insights* (Summer, 1998): 3; "Rev. John Perkins Speaks at Reconciliation Celebration," *Mission Mississippi Messenger* 2 (Fall 1999): 5.

40. Dolphus Weary, interview by the author, February 25, 2000, Jackson, MS.

41. John W. De Gruchy, *Reconciliation: Restoring Justice* (Minneapolis: Fortress Press, 2002), 45.

42. Ibid., 54.

43. Desmond Tutu, *No Future without Forgiveness* (New York: Doubleday, 1999), 179.

44. Eric Stringfellow, interview by the author, October 7, 2004, Jackson, MS.

45. Reed, October 7, 2004.

46. Emerson and Smith, *Divided by Faith*, 164.

47. Lee Paris, interview by the author, October 10, 2004, Jackson, MS.

48. Lee Paris, interview by the author, October 14, 2004, Jackson, MS.

49. Pat Morley, "Changing Mississippi One Relationship at a Time," (speech given at the Governor's Prayer Breakfast, Clarion Hotel , Jackson, Mississippi, May 2, 2002 (transcribed from recording)).

50. James C. Cobb, *The Most Southern Place on Earth: The Mississippi Delta and the Roots of Regional Identity* (New York: Oxford University Press, 1992), 99.

51. Robert McFarland, "Henry Paris of Planters Bank: Banker, Entrepreneur and Community Leader," *Delta Business Journal* (January 1999): 1.

52. Morris Lewis, *Wholesaler-Retailer: The Story of the Lewis Grocer Company and Sunflower Food Stores,* Newcomen Publication; No. 1021 (New York: The Newcomen Society in North America, 1975), 12. For a detailed analysis of the sharecropper system, commissary stores, and the exploitative nature of credit extended to share-croppers, see Cobb, *The Most Southern Place on Earth,* 102–13; Neil R. McMillen, *Dark Journey: Black Mississippians in the Age of Jim Crow* (Urbana: University of Illinois Press, 1989), 127–34. Dolphus Weary gives a personal account of growing up in a family caught in the sharecropping system. Dolphus Weary and William Hendricks, *I Ain't Comin' Back* (Wheaton, IL: Tyndale House Publishers, 1990), 30–32.

53. Lewis, *Wholesaler-Retailer: The Story of the Lewis Grocer Company and Sunflower Food Stores,* 9.

54. Lee Paris, interview by the author, May 19, 2003, Jackson, MS.

55. Lee Paris, Oct. 10, 2004.

56. The anthropologist Hortense Powdermaker called the town "Cottonville." Hortense Powdermaker, *After Freedom: A Cultural Study in the Deep South* (New York: Viking Press, 1939). The sociologist John Dollard kept the identity of Indianola secret, giving it the name "Southerntown." John Dollard and Institute of Human Relations, Yale University, *Caste and Class in a Southern Town* (New Haven: Yale University Press, 1937); William Ferris, "John Dollard: Caste and Class Revisited," *Southern Cultures* 10 (Summer 2004): 7–18. Historian Jennifer Ritterhouse revisits these stud-ies in her excellent work on the way children learned the society's racial etiquette. Jennifer Lynn Ritterhouse, *Growing up Jim Crow: How Black and White Southern Children Learned Race* (Chapel Hill: University of North Carolina, 2006), 52–54.

57. Lee Paris, October 10, 2004.

58. Ibid.

59. Paris, October 10, 2004.

60. Ibid.

61. Ibid. The Mississippi Historic Preservation Inventory dates Temple Beth El from 1905. Mississippi Historic Preservation Inventory, Buildings Report: Temple Beth El, Lexington, Mississippi. Available: http://isjm.best.vwh.net/Buildings/records/BR238.htm (accessed June 24, 2005).

62. Paris, October 10, 2004.

63. Ibid.

64. James Peter Jernberg, "Biographical Résumé of James Peter Jernberg, Jr." Available: http://www.jacksonacademy.org/jernberg.html (accessed June 24, 2005).

65. Paris, October 10, 2004.

66. Nadine Cohodas, *The Band Played Dixie: Race and the Liberal Conscience at Ole Miss* (New York: Free Press, 1997), 188.

67. Paris, October 10, 2004.

68. Paris, May 19, 2003.

69. Paris, October 10, 2004.

70. Paris, May 19, 2003.

71. Ibid.

72. Ibid.

73. Jeff Robinson, "Gender Roles and Pastoral Ministry: Q&A with J. Ligon Duncan, Part II," in *Gender-News.com* (October 25, 2004) Available: http://www.gender-news.com/article.php?id=42 (accessed June 21, 2005); George R. Fair to Calvin L. Wells, March 1, 1994, MMP; Other significant contributions from congregations came from Christ United Methodist, and Cornerstone Church. "Mission Mississippi Contribution List," March 16, 1993, MMP.

74. By comparison, First Baptist Church with almost three times the membership had seven members serving on committees; five came from Galloway, eighteen from Dan Hall's Cornerstone Church, sixteen from College Hill MB, twenty-three from Community Christian Church, three from St. Richard Catholic Church, six from Anderson United Methodist, four from New Hope Baptist Church, two from St. Andrews Episcopal Cathedral, and six from St. Peter MB, nine from VOC and Mendenhall Bible Church. George R. Fair to Calvin L. Wells, March 1, 1994, MMP.

75. James Baird, interview by the author, February 9, 2004, Flowood, MS.

76. Ibid.

77. Dolphus Weary, Presentation to the Theology and Race Work Group, Project on Lived Theology, February 24, 2001, Oxford, MS.

78. Ibid.

79. William Faulkner gave perhaps the most famous example of gradualism as an approach to solving the problem of race in the South when he advised those who wished to "eradicate" the "evil" of segregation "overnight" to "Go slow now. Stop now for a time, a moment," and "give [the Southerner] a space in which to get his breath." William Faulkner, "A Letter to the North," *Life*, March 5, 1956, 51–52.

80. Paris, May 19, 2003.

81. Baird, February 9, 2004.

82. "Mission Mississippi October Events Speaking Engagements for Tom Skinner and Pat Morley," 1993, MMP; Baird, February 9, 2004.

83. Anonymous letter to the Congregation First Presbyterian Church, December 29, 1993, MMP.

84. Mission Mississippi requested another contribution of $12,000 matching the church's contribution for 1993. Calvin L. Wells to Mission Mississippi, February 3, 1994, MMP.

85. Anonymous to the Congregation First Presbyterian Church, December 29, 1993.

86. Ibid.

87. Calvin L. Wells to Mission Mississippi, February 3, 1994, MMP.

88. Resolution of the session of First Presbyterian Church March 14, 1994 printed in the church's bulletin *First Epistle*, quoted in "Concerning MISSION MISSISSIPPI," anonymous letter to the Congregation First Presbyterian Church, March 28, 1994, MMP.

89. Ibid.; This change in contributions to Mission Mississippi meant that instead of $12,000, Mission Mississippi had only received $4,645 from First

Presbyterian Church by October 7, 1994. "Mission Mississippi 1994 Contributions of Affiliated Churches as of October 7, 1994," MMP.

90. The postmark reads JACKSON, MS 392 / PM / 7 APR 1994.

91. The anonymous letter writer only revealed his identity under pressure to the session whose meetings and minutes are strictly confidential.

92. "Concerning MISSION MISSISSIPPI."

93. Anonymous letter to the Congregation First Presbyterian Church, December 29, 1993.

94. Ernest Trice Thompson, *The Spirituality of the Church* (Richmond: John Knox Press, 1961), 30; Ernest Trice Thompson, *Presbyterians in the South*, vol. 3: *1890–1972* (Richmond: John Knox Press, 1973), 504–29.

95. William David McCain, ed., *The Story of Jackson: A History of the Capital of Mississippi, 1821–1951*, vol. 1 (Jackson, MS: J.F. Hyer, 1953). 152; Julie L. Kimbrough, *Jackson*, Images of America (Charleston, SC: Arcadia, 1998), 7.

96. McCain, ed., *The Story of Jackson*, 1.

97. Ibid.

98. Ibid. 22.

99. Amos R. Johnson, *Southern Sun*, Nov 17, 1838 in Alfred P. Hamilton, *Galloway Memorial Methodist Church, 1836–1956: A History Compiled from Very Scanty Records of Private Individuals, Archives from the Methodist Room, Millsaps College, General Minutes of the Church at Large and Mississippi Conference Journals, Minutes of the Woman's Society of Christian Service, and of the Official Board of Our Church* (Nashville, TN: Parthenon, 1956), 23.

100. Baptists organized a congregation in 1838, Episcopalians in 1844, and Roman Catholics in 1846. The Methodists built Jackson's first church in 1839. Ibid., 19.

101. Judge T. J. Wharton, "Reminiscences," *Clarion-Ledger*, 1895 in ibid., 23–24.

102. James C. Cobb, *The Most Southern Place on Earth: The Mississippi Delta and the Roots of Regional Identity* (New York: Oxford University Press, 1992), 8.

103. *Minutes of the General Assembly of the Presbyterian Church in the United States of America,* (Philadelphia: Presbyterian Board of Publication, 1836), 250.

104. Ibid.

105. *The Directory for the Worship of God in the Presbyterian Church in the United States of America,* adopted in 1821 VIII: IV in *The Constitution of the Presbyterian Church in the United States of America: Containing the Confession of Faith, the Catechisms, and the Directory for the Worship of God,* (Philadelphia: Presbyterian Board of Publication, 1841), 501.

106. *Minutes of the General Assembly of the Presbyterian Church in the United States of America,* 272.; Irving Stoddard Kull, "Presbyterian Attitudes toward Slavery," *Church History* 7 (June 1938): 107.

107. James Oscar Farmer, *The Metaphysical Confederacy: James Henley Thornwell and the Synthesis of Southern Values* (Macon, GA: Mercer University Press, 1986), 170.

108. C Bruce Staiger, "Abolitionism and the Presbyterian Schism of 1837–1838," *The Mississippi Historical Review* 36 (December 1949): 393.

109. Steven Mintz, *Moralists and Modernizers: America's Pre-Civil War Reformers*, The American Moment (Baltimore: Johns Hopkins University Press, 1995), 48.

110. Ernest Trice Thompson, *Presbyterians in the South*, 3 vols., vol. 1: 1607–1861 (Richmond, VA: John Knox Press, 1963), 362.

111. Mark A. Noll, *America's God: From Jonathan Edwards to Abraham Lincoln* (Oxford; New York: Oxford University Press, 2002), 308; Thompson, *Presbyterians in the South*, 363; Kull, "Presbyterian Attitudes toward Slavery," 106.

112. Kull, "Presbyterian Attitudes toward Slavery," 107.

113. Staiger, "Abolitionism and the Presbyterian Schism of 1837–1838," 409.

114. *Minutes of the General Assembly of the Presbyterian Church in the United States of America*, (Philadelphia: Presbyterian Board of Publication, 1837), 421. A number of other resolutions passed that further secured the Old School position. In each instance, the South voted as a regional block with fifty-one of the sixty-one Southern votes consistently cast for the Old School. Staiger, "Abolitionism and the Presbyterian Schism of 1837–1838," 411.

115. *Minutes of the General Assembly 1836 & 1837*, 422.

116. Noll, *America's God*, 311.

117. "Narrative of the State of Religion" in *Minutes of the General Assembly 1836 & 1837*, 509–510.

118. McCain, ed., *The Story of Jackson*, 152. There were a small number of African Americans who were not enslaved. The 1825 Hinds County census showed a population of 1536 free whites; 522 slaves were the property of 93 slaveholders. Of the 198 taxpayers, only two were "free men of color." McCain, ed., *The Story of Jackson*, 19.

119. *Southern Reformer*, February 9, 1846 in McCain, ed., *The Story of Jackson*, 154.

120. Ibid.

121. Hunter stepped down in September 14, 1895, ibid. 276.

122. Comment from a teacher at Tougaloo College, n.d., in Clarice T. Campbell and Oscar A. Rogers, *Mississippi, the View from Tougaloo* (Jackson: University Press of Mississippi, 1979), 98.

123. Hamilton, *Galloway Memorial Methodist Church*, 74.

124. Martha Boman, "A Social History of Jackson, Mississippi: 1821–1861, State Capital in the Old South" (University of Mississippi, 1952), 197.

125. In 1855, the Episcopal Church conducted 27 funerals (one for the minister), although the congregation numbered only 102. The epidemic caused the Episcopalians to close their St. Andrews College the following year. Sherwood Willing Wise, *The Cathedral Church of St. Andrew: A Sesquicentennial History, 1839–1989* (Jackson, MS: The Cathedral Church of St. Andrew, 1989), 18. The epidemic of 1878 was so bad that one person called it a calamity, "worse than war, carpetbaggers or the Negro question." Ibid., 39.

126. McCain, ed., *The Story of Jackson*, 155.

127. Hunter stepped down in September 14, 1895. Ibid., 276.

128. Randy J. Sparks, *Religion in Mississippi* (Jackson: University Press of Mississippi for the Mississippi Historical Society, 2001), 119. Misgivings about slavery led to the formation of groups dedicated to resettling slaves in Africa. The Methodist-

dominated *Mississippi Colonization Society*, founded in 1831 resettled 570 freed slaves in Liberia in a colony called Mississippi in Africa. For a remarkable account of this journey of freed slaves from a Mississippi Delta plantation to Africa, read Alan Huffman, *Mississippi in Africa* (New York: Gotham Books, 2004).

129. Thornwell is one of the most influential of the antebellum divines. Southern Presbyterians revere him as one of their foundational theologians. In the years following the Civil War, Benjamin Morgan Palmer, the minister of New Orleans' First Presbyterian Church, a student of Thornwell and his biographer—Benjamin Morgan Palmer, *The Life and Letters of James Henley Thornwell* (Richmond, VA: Whittet & Shepperson, 1875)—became "one of the South's preeminent clergymen during the second half of the nineteenth century." Stephen R. Haynes, *Noah's Curse: The Biblical Justification of American Slavery* (Oxford, New York: Oxford University Press, 2002), 13.

130. James W. Miles to David McCord, n.d., in Farmer, *The Metaphysical Confederacy*, 132.

131. James Henley Thornwell, "The Baptism of Servants," *Southern Presbyterian Review* 1 (June 1847): 77. It is important to note that making the slaveholder responsible for bringing slave children for baptism, placed the slaveholder in a difficult position with regard to the laws of South Carolina that forbade teaching slaves to read. *The Directory of Worship* stipulated that those bringing a child for baptism must promise, "That they teach the child to read the word of God; that they instruct it in the principles of our holy religion." *The Constitution of the Presbyterian Church in the United States of America*, 499.

132. James Henley Thornwell, *The Rights and Duties of Masters: A Sermon Preached at the Dedication of a Church Erected in Charleston Sc., for the Benefit and Instruction of the Coloured Population* (Charleston, SC: Walker & James, 1850).

133. Ibid., 33.

134. Ibid., 15.

135. James Henley Thornwell, *Hear the South! The State of the Country. An Article Republished from the Southern Presbyterian Review.* (New York: D. Appleton and Company, 1861), 12.

136. Ibid., 13.

137. Richard Aubrey McLemore, ed., *A History of Mississippi*, 2 vols., vol. 1 (Hattiesburg: University & College Press of Mississippi, 1973). 447; James Wilford Garner, *Reconstruction in Mississippi* (New York, London: Macmillan, 1901), 6; Wise, *The Cathedral Church of St. Andrew*, 22.

138. Wise, *The Cathedral Church of St. Andrew*, 22.

139. Ibid.

140. Quoted in Garner, *Reconstruction in Mississippi*, 12.

141. Wise, *The Cathedral Church of St. Andrew*, 22.

142. McLemore, ed., *A History of Mississippi*, 542.

143. Thompson, *Presbyterians in the South*, 13–17.

144. John Edwards Richards, *The Historical Birth of the Presbyterian Church in America*, (Liberty Hill, SC: Liberty Press, 1987), 35.

145. Ibid., 30–31.

146. Jack P. Maddex, "From Theocracy to Spirituality: The Southern Presbyterian Reversal on Church and State," *Journal of Presbyterian History* 54 (Winter 1976): 441.

147. *Minutes of the General Assembly*, PCUS, 1865, 383, Richards, *The Historical Birth of the Presbyterian Church in America*, 4.

148. Thompson, *The Spirituality of the Church*, 1.

149. Neil R. McMillen, *Dark Journey: Black Mississippians in the Age of Jim Crow* (Urbana: University of Illinois Press, 1989), 38.

150. For a detailed description of the politics of this period, read McLemore, ed., *A History of Mississippi*, 542–589.

151. Ibid. 587. W. Calvin Wells' great-grandson Calvin L. Wells, also an elder at First Presbyterian Church, was the chairman of the sub-committee formed in 1994 to look into the allegations against Mission Mississippi.

152. W. Calvin Wells, "Reconstruction and Its Destruction in Hinds County," in *Publications of the Mississippi Historical Society*, ed. Franklin L. Riley (Oxford: The Mississippi Historical Society, 1906), 104–105.

153. McLemore, ed., *A History of Mississippi*. 589.

154. Cobb, *The Most Southern Place on Earth*, 80–81.

155. Craig E Van Gelder, "Growth Patterns of Mainline Denominations and Their Churches: A Case Study of Jackson, Mississippi 1900–1980" (Southwestern Baptist Theological Seminary, 1982), 65.

156. *Clarion-Ledger*, July 23, 1891; *Clarion-Ledger*, July 9, 1891, in McCain, ed., *The Story of Jackson*, 275–276.

157. McLemore, ed., *A History of Mississippi*. 10.

158. The numbers of registered voters in 1892 demonstrates the effectiveness of these new requirements in disenfranchising African American's: there were 56,587 whites and only 6,648 blacks on the poll books. Ibid., 14–17.

159. McMillen, *Dark Journey: Black Mississippians in the Age of Jim Crow*, 4–5.

160. McLemore, ed., *A History of Mississippi*, 618.

161. Henry Billings Brown, "Majority Opinion in Plessy V. Ferguson," in *Desegregation and the Supreme Court*, ed. Benjamin Munn Ziegler (Boston: D.C. Heath and Company, 1958), 50–51.

162. Joel L. Alvis, *Religion & Race: Southern Presbyterians, 1946–1983* (Tuscaloosa: University of Alabama Press, 1994), 13.

163. Ibid., 13–15. By 1917, the synod, named after James G. Snedecor, a member of the Executive Committee on Colored Evangelization, claimed 1,492 communicants.

164. Thompson, *Presbyterians in the South*, 292.

165. Ibid.

166. Thompson, *The Spirituality of the Church*, 1.

167. Thomas Carey Johnson, "The Presbyterian Church in the United States," *Journal of the Presbyterian Historical Society* 1 (1901): 80, in Morton H. Smith, *How Is the Gold Become Dim! (Lamentations 4:1) the Decline of the Presbyterian Church in the United States as Reflected in Its Assembly Actions* (Jackson, MS: The Steering

Committee for a Continuing Presbyterian Church, Faithful to the Scriptures and the Reformed Faith, 1973), 20.

168. "In Memoriam: James Buchanan Hutton" *Mississippi Visitor,* XXVIII (October 1940): 9. In Gwen Ann Mills, "A Social History of Jackson, Mississippi, 1920–1929" (MA thesis, University of Mississippi, 1966). 78.

169. Van Gelder, "Growth Patterns," 66, 72.

170. Ibid., 74; *Jackson, the City Beautiful* (Jackson, MS: Chamber of Commerce, 1927), 2.

171. McCain, ed., *The Story of Jackson,* 276–78.

172. B. Baldwin Dansby, *A Brief History of Jackson College: A Typical Story of the Survival of Education among Negroes in the South* (Jackson, MS: Jackson College, 1953), 119.

173. Ibid., 130–31. Jackson College finally became a state institution in 1940.

174. Robert L. Zangrando, *The NAACP Crusade against Lynching, 1909–1950* (Philadelphia: Temple University Press, 1980). Before the Senate debated the Gavagan anti-lynching bill in 1937, the NAACP published a report of a double lynching in Duck Hill, Mississippi. Howard Kester, "Lynching by Blow Torch: A Report Upon the Double Lynching at Duck Hill, Miss., April 13, 1937," in *Howard A. Kester Papers, 1923–1972,* ed. Edward M. Wayland (Glen Rock, N. J.: Microfilming Corporation of America, 1973). When in 2005 the U.S. Senate formally apologized for having rejected decades of pleas to make lynching a federal crime, Mississippi Senators Trent Lott and Thad Cochran, were among the twenty senators who did not sign. Sheryl Gay Stolberg, "The Nation: The Senate Apologizes, Mostly," *New York Times,* June 19, 2005.

175. Dansby, *A Brief History of Jackson College: A Typical Story of the Survival of Education among Negroes in the South,* 91.

176. George M. Marsden, *Fundamentalism and American Culture: The Shaping of Twentieth Century Evangelicalism, 1870–1925* (New York: Oxford University Press, 1980), 4. The movement gained its name in 1920 after the publication of *The Fundamentals,* a series of twelve paperbacks published between 1910 and 1917. Marsden, *Fundamentalism and American Culture,* 118–19.

177. J. Gresham Machen, *Christianity and Liberalism* (New York: Macmillan, 1923).

178. George M. Marsden, *Understanding Fundamentalism and Evangelicalism* (Grand Rapids, MI: W.B. Eerdmans, 1991), 149; Thompson, *Presbyterians in the South,* 300.

179. R. Milton Winter, "Division & Reunion in the Presbyterian Church, U.S.: A Mississippi Retrospective," *Journal of Presbyterian History* 78 (Spring 2000): 76. Van Til went on to provide the intellectual backbone behind conservative Presbyterians' rejection of Karl Barth's neo-orthodoxy linking him to the social activism of the liberals that so disturbed Southern Presbyterians: "Barth replaces the Christ of Luther and of Calvin," Van Til wrote, "with a Christ patterned after modern activist thought." Cornelius Van Til and Karl Barth, *Christianity and Barthianism* (Philadelphia: Presbyterian and Reformed, 1962), vii.

180. Winter, "Division & Reunion," 76.

181. Van Til was a proponent of the Dutch Calvinist Abraham Kuyper's doctrine of "sphere sovereignty." This separation of the social order into separate spheres fitted neatly with, and added complexity to, the Southern Presbyterian doctrine of the spirituality of the church. For a detailed exegesis of Kuyper's doctrine as it evolved through Westminster Seminary, see Harriet A. Harris, *Fundamentalism and Evangelicals*, Oxford Theological Monographs (Oxford, New York: Clarendon Press; Oxford University Press, 1998), 233–77.

182. General Assembly Minutes of the PCUS, 1935, 160–265, quoted in Thompson, *Presbyterians in the South*, 509–10.

183. Alvis, *Religion & Race*, 48; Thompson, *Presbyterians in the South*, 530.

184. Thompson, *Presbyterians in the South*, 530.

185. Alvis, *Religion & Race*, 51; Richards, *The Historical Birth of the Presbyterian Church in America*, xiv.

186. Alvis, *Religion & Race*, 51–52; Thompson, *Presbyterians in the South*, 566.

187. W. Calvin Wells, "Church Union," *Southern Presbyterian Journal* (April 1944), 7–18. Partisan historian Frank Joseph Smith considers Well's argument based on doctrinal purity, "one of the best articles" written opposing the union. Frank Joseph Smith, *The History of the Presbyterian Church in America*, 1st ed. (Manassas, VA: Reformation Educational Foundation, 1985), 8.

188. Wells, "Church Union," 13.

189. First Presbyterian Church of Jackson, *A Brief History of the First Presbyterian Church, Jackson, Mississippi*, 2004, Available: http://www.fpcjackson.org/general/history/index.htm (accessed July 8, 2005).

190. McCain, ed., *The Story of Jackson*, 276.

191. Robert C. Cannada, interview by the author, June 21, 2005, Jackson, MS (telephone).

192. "Infiltration—to What End?" *Presbyterian Outlook* 139 (June 17, 1957): 5.

193. Ibid.

194. Ibid.; Winter, "Division & Reunion," 84.

195. Rick Nutt, "The Tie That No Longer Binds: The Origins of the Presbyterian Church in America," in *The Confessional Mosaic: Presbyterians and Twentieth-Century Theology*, ed. Milton J. Coalter, John M. Mulder, and Louis B. Weeks, The Presbyterian Presence: The Twentieth Century Experience (Louisville, KY: Westminster/John Knox Press, 1990), 252; Winter, "Division & Reunion," 76.

196. "The Christian Relations Report to the General Assembly: The Church and Segregation," *The Presbyterian Outlook* 136 (May 3, 1954): 8.

197. Thompson, *Presbyterians in the South*, 540; Alvis, *Religion & Race*, 21.

198. Neil R. McMillen, *The Citizens' Council: Organized Resistance to the Second Reconstruction, 1954–64* (Urbana: University of Illinois Press, 1971), 16; Ernest Trice Thompson, *Presbyterians in the South*, vol. 3: 1890–1972 (Richmond: John Knox Press, 1973), 540; Joel L. Alvis, *Religion & Race: Southern Presbyterians, 1946–1983* (Tuscaloosa: University of Alabama Press, 1994), 21.

199. "Concerning MISSION MISSISSIPPI."

200. "Mississippi Asks Reconsideration," *The Presbyterian Outlook* 136 (22 November 1954): 3; *Minutes of the Ninety-Fifth General Assembly of the Presbyterian Church in the United States* (1955), 38. The Synod of Mississippi voted sixty-two to forty to send the overture. In 1955, the General Assembly resoundingly defeated the overture by 287 to 93. "U.S. Assembly Sustains Emphasis of Recent Years," *The Presbyterian Outlook* 137 (June 20, 1955): 6.

201. G.T. Gillespie, "Defense of the Principle of Racial Segregation," *The Presbyterian Outlook* 137 (March 14, 1955): 5–9; Thompson, *Presbyterians in the South*, 540; Joseph Hardin Crespino, "The Christian Conscience of Jim Crow: White Protestant Ministers and the Mississippi Citizens' Councils, 1954–1964," *Mississippi Folklife* 31 (Fall 1998, 1998): 40.

202. Gillespie, "Defense of the Principle of Racial Segregation."

203. "Statement Adopted by the Session of the First Presbyterian Church of Jackson, Mississippi," *The Southern Presbyterian Journal* (June 19, 1957): 8.

204. Randall Nulton to LeRoy Paris, August 19, 1996, MMP.

205. Ibid.

206. Writing in 1961 of the PCUS, the Presbyterian historian Ernest Trice Thompson noted "the quality of Presbyterian membership [in the South] does give it an influence which is out of proportion to its numbers." With the exception of Episcopalians, Presbyterians had proportionately more wealthy, college-educated, and professional members than other denominations. "We can be proud of the fact that our church does appeal to this important group in every community, but," warned Thompson, "it does bring some dangers." Ernest Trice Thompson, *The Spirituality of the Church* (Richmond, VA: John Knox Press, 1961), 18.

207. "Statement Adopted by the Session of the First Presbyterian Church of Jackson, Mississippi," *The Southern Presbyterian Journal* (June 19, 1957): 10.

208. Cannada, June 21, 2005; "1963–1964 Board of Directors Jackson Citizens' Council Elected at Annual Meeting, May 17, 1963, Olympic Room, Heidelberg Hotel," SCRID# 99-30-0-74-1-1-1, MSSC; Erle Jr. Johnson to Charlie H. Griffin, June 14, 1965, SCRID# 99-30-0-15-1-1-1, MSSC; Winter, "Division & Reunion," 76.

209. "Mississippi Lambasted by Tougaloo Chaplain," *Jackson Daily News*, May 3, 1964. Miller, following his departure from Jackson and while the minister at Macon Presbyterian Church, was a member of a clandestine group of whites determined to break the black boycott of white businesses and schools in the town. The group met in secret with representatives of the Sovereignty Commission, "seeking advice as to what action they might take in solving the present problem.... They are not agreeable to meeting with a Negro committee or having it known that such a committee is in existence." Edgar C. Fortenberry, "Memorandum To: Director, Sovereignty Commission Subject: Negro Boycot of Public Schools—Noxubee County," May 19, 1970, SCRID# 2-113-0-29-1-1, MSSC.

210. A.P., "Calmness Is Urged on 'Mixing' Suit," *Clarion-Ledger*, March 9, 1963; Cannada, June 21, 2005.

211. Hendrick became the moderator of the PCA's General Assembly in 1975 and a Mississippi Supreme Court Justice. Frank Joseph Smith, *The History*

of the Presbyterian Church in America, (Manassas, VA: Reformation Educational Foundation, 1985), 101.

212. Bob Pittman, "Legal Circles Trap Riders," *Clarion-Ledger,* June 18, 1961.

213. W.C. Shoemaker, "Negroes Declare Aimed to Agitate," *Jackson Daily News,* 12 March 1962; Bobby DeLaughter, *Never Too Late: A Prosecutor's Story of Justice in the Medgar Evers Case* (New York: Scribner, 2001), 85.

214. A.P., "Mize Upholds Negro Rights in Mix Case," *Jackson Daily News,* May 18, 1962.

215. John R. Salter, *Jackson, Mississippi: An American Chronicle of Struggle and Schism* (Malabar, FL: R.E. Krieger, 1987), 180. For a detailed account of Ed King's involvement, see Charles Marsh, *God's Long Summer: Stories of Faith and Civil Rights* (Princeton, NJ: Princeton University Press, 1997), 116–51. This first day of church visits led to the resignation of Galloway's two ministers, W. B. Selah and Jerry Furr, when the ushers barred the students' way. W. J. Cunningham, *Agony at Galloway: One Church's Struggle with Social Change* (Jackson: University Press of Mississippi, 1980), 7.

216. Edwin King, "The White Church in Mississippi" (unpublished manuscript), 230. Anne Moody, one of the student leaders of the pray-ins, wrote her memoir of the movement. Anne Moody, *Coming of Age in Mississippi* (New York: Dial Press, 1968).

217. A.P., "Negroes Attend Jackson Church," *Jackson Daily News,* June 17, 1963, in Wise, *The Cathedral Church of St. Andrew,* 159; Moody, *Coming of Age in Mississippi,* 284.

218. United Press International, "Church Mix Groups Fail in Attempts," *Clarion-Ledger,* July 29, 1963. The Methodist Church in Jackson received the main focus of church visits because they were part of a national denomination (Baptists and Presbyterians were protected from Northern ministers of their denomination paying them a visit) and also because of their participation in the National Council of Churches (Southern Baptists escaped this connection). In addition, Ed King was a Methodist minister with a stake in the reformation of his own denomination. King saw the Methodists as a fruitful target because "there were probably more moderates here than any other white church in Mississippi King, "The White Church in Mississippi," 16. He recounts how often the destination of visits was based on the sermon title announced in the Saturday newspaper. King, "The White Church in Mississippi," 102.

219. King, "The White Church in Mississippi," 164.

220. "Concerning MISSION MISSISSIPPI."

221. Quoted from "Council Plans Fight against Church Mixing," an undated clipping in Ed King's possession quoted in King, "The White Church in Mississippi," 17.

222. James Henley Thornwell, *The Collected Writings of James Henley Thornwell,* ed. John B. Adger, vol. 4 (Richmond, VA: Whittet & Shepperson, 1871–73), 449.

223. Cannada, June 21, 2005.

224. McMillen, *The Citizens' Council,* 349; Joseph H. Crespino, *In Search of Another Country: Mississippi and the Conservative Counterrevolution* (Princeton, NJ: Princeton University Press, 2007), 118.

225. Yasuhiro Katagiri, *The Mississippi State Sovereignty Commission: Civil Rights and States' Rights* (Jackson: University Press of Mississippi, 2001), 143.

226. McMillen, *The Citizens' Council,* 303.

227. Ibid., 300.

228. Semmes Luckett to Governor Paul Johnson, October 5, 1966, SCRID# 2-62-2-48-1-1-1, MSSC.

229. Cannada, June 21, 2005. In 2005, First Presbyterian Church Day School had 740 children in grades K–6. The student body is over 99 percent white; only three students were African American. Private Schools Report, 2005, Available: http://mississippi.privateschoolsreport.com/schools/MS/Jackson.html (accessed December 21, 2005).

230. Crespino, *In Search of Another Country,* 13.

231. Thornwell, *The Collected Writings of James Henley Thornwell,* 449.

232. Winter, "Division & Reunion," 70.

233. Becky Hobbs, "Partnership Pays Off," *Reformed Quarterly* 18 (Winter 1999), Available: http://www.rts.edu/quarterly/winter99/duncan.html (accessed December 18, 2005).

234. Ibid.

235. Robert C. Cannada, Jr., Unity in the Family of God: Sermon Preached at 2nd Presbyterian Church, Memphis, TN, August 10, 2003. [Audio File] Available: http://www.2pc.org/resource_media.html (accessed November 12, 2004).

236. Winter, "Division & Reunion," 76.

237. Smith, *The History of the Presbyterian Church in America,* 52; Winter, "Division & Reunion," 74; Thompson, *Presbyterians in the South,* 492, 503.

238. Hobbs, "Partnership Pays Off."

239. "Cannada Retires," *Reformed Quarterly* 19 (Summer 2000). Available: http://www.rts.edu/quarterly/summer00/news.html (accessed March 1, 2005).

240. Rick Nutt, "The Tie That No Longer Binds: The Origins of the Presbyterian Church in America," in *The Confessional Mosaic: Presbyterians and Twentieth-Century Theology,* ed. Milton J. Coalter, John M. Mulder, and Louis B. Weeks, The Presbyterian Presence: The Twentieth Century Experience (Louisville, KY: Westminster/John Knox Press, 1990), 240.

241. William Winter is qualified to reflect on the schism: "I was the chairman of the judicial commission in the synod of Mississippi to investigate the efforts to cause a schism in the church. That was in the early sixties, last place in the world an aspiring politician should have been. I found myself right in the middle of that huge church conflagration—and it was a lose-lose for everybody. There was no way we were going to preserve the unity of the church given the mindset of the [conservatives]. And they looked at me as a heretic.... I have been in a lot of secular political battles but I have never been in a battle where there was as much real gut wrenching animosity expressed towards me.... They threatened me." [William Winter, interview by the author, October 13, 2004, Jackson, MS.]

242. For an extensive account of the Delta Ministry—the World Council of Churches' first missionary campaign to the United States—see Mark Newman,

Divine Agitators: The Delta Ministry and Civil Rights in Mississippi (Athens: University of Georgia Press, 2004).

243. "Presbytery Opposes Influx Into Delta," *Jackson Daily News*, April 18, 1964 in King, "The White Church in Mississippi," 84; Alvis, *Religion & Race*, 119.

244. Alvis, *Religion & Race*, 113.

245. Thompson, *Presbyterians in the South*, 503.

246. Nutt, "The Tie That No Longer Binds," 239.

247. Kenneth S. Keyes, "A Brief History of the Developments in the Presbyterian Church in the United States (Southern) Which Led to the Formation of the Presbyterian Church in America," Committee for Christian Education & Publications. Available: http://www.fpcjackson.org/resources/apologetics/keyes.htm (accessed March 2, 2005).

248. Winter, "Division & Reunion," 77; Keyes, "A Brief History."

249. Morton H. Smith, *How Is the Gold Become Dim! (Lamentations 4:1) the Decline of the Presbyterian Church in the United States as Reflected in Its Assembly Actions* (Jackson, MS: The Steering Committee for a Continuing Presbyterian Church, Faithful to the Scriptures and the Reformed Faith, 1973).

250. Ibid., 152.

251. Ibid., 153. The Bible says nothing about observing Christmas (98–99), but it does talk about segregation; thus, according to Smith, the PCUS is wrong in wishing to adopt the first and it is debatable whether it should abolish the latter!

252. Ibid., 61, 165–75.

253. Alvis, *Religion & Race*, 136–38; Keyes, "A Brief History."

254. Winter, "Division & Reunion," 77; Smith, *The History of the Presbyterian Church in America*, 209.

255. Smith, *The History of the Presbyterian Church in America*, 79; Winter, "Division & Reunion," 72; James Baird, interview by the author, February 9, 2004, Flowood, MS. Robert C. "Rick" Cannada, Jr. attributes the conservative trend of the church and presbytery to Miller. In a sermon, Cannada reflected: "Yet why did that church remain strong? Well it had a strong group of elders. It had a strong session, but it also had a strong preacher, Dr. John Reed Miller who preached the truth [which] kept the church strong, which kept the presbytery strong." Cannada, [Audio File].

256. John Edwards Richards, *The Historical Birth of the Presbyterian Church in America* (Liberty Hill, S.C.: Liberty Press, 1987), 354.

257. Smith, *How Is the Gold Become Dim!*, vii.

258. Alvis, *Religion & Race*, 132; Richards, *The Historical Birth of the Presbyterian Church in America*, xvi.

259. Richards, *The Historical Birth of the Presbyterian Church in America*, 407.

260. Cannada, June 21, 2005.

261. Lee Paris, May 19, 2003.

262. Ibid.

263. James M. Baird, "Concerning the Anonymous and Other Letters About the Involvement of First Presbyterian Church in Mission Mississippi," May 4, 1994, LPP.

264. Paris, May 19, 2003.

265. A. Jerry Sheldon, "Memorandum to Ad Hoc Mission Mississippi Committee," January 5, 1995, LPP.

266. "Session's Action Regarding Mission Mississippi," *The First Epistle* 25 (February 16, 1995).

267. LeRoy H. Paris to George R. Fair, November 1, 1994, LPP.

268. LeRoy H. Paris to William H. Cox Jr., February 13, 1996, LPP.

269. Lee Paris, October 10, 2004.

270. Paris, May 19, 2003.

271. Ibid.

272. Thomas Jenkins to Dr. James Dobson, November 10, 1995, MMP.

273. "Minutes of the Executive Board Meeting, October 22, 1998," MMP.

274. David L. Chappell, *A Stone of Hope: Prophetic Religion and the Death of Jim Crow* (Chapel Hill: University of North Carolina Press, 2004), 107.

275. Ibid., 111.

276. Ibid., 122.

277. Crespino makes the compelling argument that the white elites in Mississippi "rearticulated their resentment of the liberal social policies that allowed for black advancement" and "contribute[d] to a [national] broad conservative counter-movement against the liberal triumphs of the 1960s." Crespino, *In Search of Another Country: Mississippi and the Conservative Counterrevolution*, 4.

278. Chappell, *A Stone of Hope*, 107. Chappell himself acknowledges by the end of his book that "a later conservative movement...sublimated the racism of the southern white masses and built its power within the churches [forming]...a radical (and largely successful) conservative insurgency." Chappell, *A Stone of Hope*, 178. In another recent work, historian Paul Harvey, who sees the Civil Rights Movement as a kind of "regionwide revival movement," argues that the conservative white churches were, "discredited after their defeat in the freedom movement," however, now "freed from the historic burden of defending segregation" conservative churches have "roused themselves to preserve God-ordained hierarchies of gender and class." Paul Harvey, *Freedom's Coming: Religious Culture and the Shaping of the South from the Civil War through the Civil Rights Era* (Chapel Hill: University of North Carolina Press, 2005), 216–17.

279. Chappell, *A Stone of Hope*, 2.

280. Winter, Oct. 13, 2004.

281. Spencer Perkins and Chris Rice, *More Than Equals: Racial Healing for the Sake of the Gospel*, revised & expanded. (Downers Grove, IL: InterVarsity Press, 2000), 10.

282. Ligon Duncan, "What in the World Is a Worldview? Thinking Christianly About All of Life" (sermon preached at First Presbyterian Church, Jackson, MS, Summer 2004). Available: http://www.fpcjackson.org/resources/sermons/Worldviews%202004/1a_duncan.htm (accessed June 9, 2005).

283. Jürgen Moltmann, *The Crucified God: The Cross of Christ as the Foundation and Criticism of Christian Theology* (New York: Harper & Row, 1974), 19.

284. Ibid.

285. King, "The White Church in Mississippi," 159.

286. Paris, May 19, 2003.

287. Michael O. Emerson and Christian Smith, *Divided by Faith: Evangelical Religion and the Problem of Race in America* (New York: Oxford University Press, 2000), 77.

CHAPTER 5

1. Mission Mississippi set out the three key tasks for the organization: "1. To challenge the body of Christ to pray, socialize, minister and work together. 2. To serve the Church by providing specific opportunities for Christians to fellowship on neutral ground for the purpose of developing relationships. 3. To act as a catalyst for the movement of reconciliation and provide resources, perspective and experience in racial reconciliation." Mission Mississippi, Our Vision [Web Page] 2005. Available: http://www.missionmississippi.org/VISION.dsp (accessed March 9, 2006). Charles Marsh reports, based on his interview with Weary, that for Mission Mississippi, "the emotionally uplifting work of "Reconciliation 101" has come to an end" by November 2000. Charles Marsh, *The Beloved Community: How Faith Shapes Social Justice, from the Civil Rights Movement to Today* (New York: Basic Books, 2005), 205. Weary certainly talks of moving people "deeper" in reconciliation, however, six years later, there was no evidence in Mission Mississippi's literature or programs that it had relinquished its singular focus on "providing specific opportunities for Christians to fellowship on neutral ground for the purpose of developing relationships." In 2006, Weary told a reporter the Mission Mississippi wanted people, "to stay in the room long enough…to begin to get to know some people beyond their label." Jean Gordon, "Man on a Mission," *Clarion-Ledger*, March 11, 2006.

2. Dolphus Weary, interview by the author, February 25, 2000, Jackson, MS.

3. Ibid.

4. Ibid.

5. Miroslav Volf, *Exclusion and Embrace: A Theological Exploration of Identity, Otherness, and Reconciliation* (Nashville, TN: Abingdon Press, 1996). The book received wide attention from both academic theological publications and popular religious magazines. In 2002, it won the prestigious Louisville Grawemeyer Award for Religion.

6. Miroslav Volf, *After Our Likeness: The Church as the Image of the Trinity*, Sacra Doctrina (Grand Rapids, MI: William B. Eerdmans, 1998), ix; Mark Oppenheimer, "Embracing Theology," *Christian Century*, January 11, 2003, 18.

7. Miroslav Volf, *The End of Memory: Remembering Rightly in a Violent World* (Grand Rapids, MI: W.B. Eerdmans Pub. Co., 2006), 4; Miroslav Volf, *Free of Charge: Giving and Forgiving in a Culture Stripped of Grace* (Grand Rapids, MI: Zondervan, 2005), 125.

8. Tim Stafford, "Miroslav Volf: Speaking Truth to the World," *Christianity Today*, 8 Feb 1999, 30.

9. Volf, *The End of Memory: Remembering Rightly in a Violent World*, 3–6.

10. Stafford, "Miroslav Volf: Speaking Truth to the World." Volf's work at Tübingen was on a Trinitarian theology of the church under Moltmann for his *Habilitationsschrift*. The second of two required dissertations was published as Miroslav Volf, *Trinität Und Gemeinschaft: Eine Oekumenische Ekklesiologie* (Mainz: Neukirchener Verlag, 1996). Published in English translation as Volf, *After Our Likeness*.

11. Stafford, "Miroslav Volf: Speaking Truth to the World," 30.

12. Kevin D. Miller, "The Clumsy Embrace: Croatian Miroslav Volf Wanted to Love His Serbian Enemies; the Prodigal's Father Is Showing Him How," *Christianity Today*, October 26, 1998, 65.

13. Ibid.

14. Miroslav Volf, "The Social Meaning of Reconciliation," *Interpretation* 54 (April 2000): 162; Miroslav Volf, "Forgiveness, Reconciliation, & Justice: A Christian Contribution to a More Peaceful Social Environment," in *Forgiveness and Reconciliation: Religion, Public Policy & Conflict Transformation,* ed. Raymond G. Helmick and Rodney Lawrence Petersen (Philadelphia: Templeton Foundation Press, 2001), 41.

15. Volf, "Forgiveness, Reconciliation, & Justice,"), 34. Here Volf consciously echoes Dietrich Bonhoeffer's famous condemnation of "cheap grace." Dietrich Bonhoeffer, *Discipleship,* ed. Kuske Kuske, et al., Barbara Green and Reinhard Krauss trans., Dietrich Bonhoeffer Works (Minneapolis, MN: Fortress Press, 2001), 43.

16. Volf, "The Social Meaning of Reconciliation," 162.

17. Ibid; Volf, "Forgiveness, Reconciliation, & Justice," 41.

18. John W. De Gruchy, *Reconciliation: Restoring Justice* (Minneapolis: Fortress Press, 2002), 169.

19. Volf, "Forgiveness, Reconciliation, & Justice," 41.

20. Volf, *Exclusion and Embrace,* 159.

21. Ibid., 23.

22. England Church of, *Common Worship: Services and Prayers for the Church of England* (London: Church House Publishing, 2000), 265.

23. Volf, *Exclusion and Embrace,* 9.

24. Ibid.

25. Ibid., 9. Moltmann's challenge does not mean that he is at odds with his student's theology of embrace. Volf's "embrace" is clearly commensurate with, and a development of, his teacher's theology of open friendship. As with Moltmann's friendship, embrace is rooted in Volf's "narrative of the triune God" that shapes his ecclesiology. Volf, *Exclusion and Embrace,* 110. Friendship for Moltmann and Embrace for Volf both describe the desire of God to be in relationship with the other while respecting the other's integrity and freedom.

26. Volf, *Exclusion and Embrace,* 29.

27. Ibid.

28. Volf, "The Social Meaning of Reconciliation," 168.

29. Volf, "The Social Meaning of Reconciliation," 169; Volf, *Exclusion and Embrace,* 224–5.

30. Volf, *Exclusion and Embrace*, 220.

31. Ibid., 110.

32. Ibid., 226.

33. Ibid., 29.

34. Ibid., 271.

35. Ibid., 215.

36. Ibid., 213.

37. Volf finds support for double vision in the story of Jesus' encounter with the Syrophoenecian woman (Matthew 15:21–38). Ibid., 272.

38. Ibid., 272.

39. Pamela Berry, "All God's Children Really Want a Better World," *Clarion-Ledger*, 5 October 2003.

40. This direction of reconciliation from the offended to the offender is integral to the Pauline doctrine of Reconciliation. De Gruchy notes that when Paul speaks of reconciliation: "God is the subject or agent of reconciliation. In speaking of God this way, Paul becomes the first Greek author to speak of the person offended as the one who initiates the act or process of reconciliation." De Gruchy, *Reconciliation: Restoring Justice*, 52.

41. Lee Paris, interview by the author, October 10, 2004, Jackson, MS.

42. Ronnie Crudup, interview by the author, February 5, 2004, Jackson, MS.

43. Neddie Winters, interview by the author, October 18, 2004, Jackson, MS.

44. Dolphus Weary, "Get Set," presentation at the Inter-Varsity Conference, "Jubilee VI: The Grace Race," Voice of Calvary Ministries, Jackson, Mississippi, October 2, 2004.

45. Volf, *Exclusion and Embrace*, 272.

46. Weary, "Get Set."

47. Volf, in a nuanced argument moving from the call of Abraham to "Go from your country and your kindred and your father's house to the land that I will show you" (Gen 12:1b) to Paul's theology of a new covenant, argues that Christians can now distance themselves from their own culture while at the same time retaining their own cultural identity. Volf, *Exclusion and Embrace*, 50.

48. Stafford, "Miroslav Volf: Speaking Truth to the World," 30.

49. Jerry Mitchell, "Can the Dream of Racial Reconciliation Be Rekindled?" *Clarion-Ledger*, October 5, 2003.

50. Henry Wadsworth Longfellow, *Hiawatha; a Poem, by Henry Wadsworth Longfellow* (Chicago: Reilly and Britton Co., 1909), 93. Jarvis Ward, interview by the author, February 9, 2004, Jackson, MS.

51. James Turner, interview by the author, October 7, 2004, Jackson, MS.

52. Ibid.

53. Ibid.

54. Hollywood used the square as a location in the movies *A Time to Kill* (1996), *My Dog Skip* (2000), and *O Brother Where Art Thou* (2000).

55. John Dittmer, *Local People: The Struggle for Civil Rights in Mississippi*, Blacks in the New World (Urbana: University of Illinois Press, 1994), 189–191.

56. Turner, October 7, 2004.

57. Ibid.

58. Ibid.

59. Ibid.

60. Ibid.

61. De Gruchy, *Reconciliation: Restoring Justice*, 178.

62. Ibid.

63. Volf, *The End of Memory*, 16. Answering the question: will the victim ever forget? Volf argues that the wronged will forget when it is finally safe to forget—when God finally makes "all things new." For Volf, forgetting is the final (eschatological) act of reconciliation. Volf, *Exclusion and Embrace*, 132.

64. Volf, *The End of Memory*, 119.

65. Jürgen Moltmann, *Experiences in Theology: Ways and Forms of Christian Theology* (Minneapolis: Fortress Press, 2000), 215.

66. Phil Reed, interview by the author, October 7, 2004, Jackson, MS.

67. *Mission Mississippi Memos* 1 (Spring 1993): 4.

68. A photograph the two men and their wives eating together at a restaurant appeared in the *Northside Sun* in 1994 promoting Mission Mississippi's Two and Two Restaurant program. "Mission Mississippi Hosts Dinner Event," *Northside Sun*, October 13, 1994.

69. Thomas Jenkins, interview by the author, October 18, 2004, Jackson, MS.

70. In 1969, McKnight completed a two-year Ford Foundation program organizing cooperatives in four Southern states. As part of this program, McKnight created and ran the Southern Development Cooperative Fund (SDCF). Based in Lafayette, Louisiana, the SCDF is a development bank serving low-income coopera-tives, community organizations, rural enterprises, and minority businesses that are unable to obtain loans from conventional sources. In 1979, President Jimmy Carter appointed McKnight to the first board of directors of the National Cooperative Bank. Albert J. McKnight, "Why I Am Retiring to Haiti," *Mission Diary* (July–August 2005): 2. Cooperative Development Foundation, Father Albert J. Mcknight [Web page] 2003. Available: http://www.coopheroes.org/inductees/mcknight.html (accessed September 10, 2005).

71. Jenkins, October 18, 2004.

72. Winters, October 18, 2004.

73. Reed, October 7, 2004.

74. Ibid.

75. Winters, October 18, 2004.

76. Hope Community Credit Union, "all about hope," [Web page]. Available: http://www.hopecu.org/AboutHOPE/index.htm (accessed July 28, 2008); William Baue, "Community Credit Union Brings Hope to Low-Income Residents of the Mississippi Delta," *SRI-adviser.com* (March 3, 2005). Available: http://www.sri-adviser.com/article.mpl?sfArticleId=1653 (accessed July 28, 2008).

77. New Dimensions Development Foundation, Inc. [Web site]. Available: www.ndifom.org (accessed July 21, 2005).

78. Ibid.

79. Neddie Winters, "The Church of the City—Vision Statement," 2004.

80. Dolphus Weary, presentation to the Theology and Race Work Group, Project on Lived Theology, February 24, 2001, Oxford, MS.

81. "Vision in Action," *Mission Mississippi Memos* 3 (November 1995): 1.

82. Dolphus Weary, interview by the author, February 10, 2004, Jackson, MS.

83. Jean Gordon, "Mission Mississippi Working to Break Racial Barriers," *Clarion-Ledger,* January 29, 2005.

84. In each service, the congregation recites a creed written by Crudup that includes the line "I am somebody in the Lord! I am special, talented, brilliant, beautiful, courageous, competent—I am strong!" Ronnie Crudup, "The New Horizon Creed." Available: http://www.newhorizonchurchms.org/creed.html (accessed October 10, 2005).

85. In November 2004, Trinity started worshipping in their new larger building, the former Christ United Methodist Church on Old Canton Rd.

86. Ross left Trinity in 2006 and was replaced by Ken Pierce in January 2007. "Reverend Kenneth A. Pierce" [Web page] Available: http://www.trinitychurchpca.com/staff_ken_pierce.htm (accessed May 17, 2008).

87. Crudup, February 5, 2004.

88. Mike Ross, interview by the author, February 9, 2004, Jackson, MS.

89. Crudup, February 5, 2004.

90. Ross, February 9, 2004.

91. Ibid.

92. Janet Thomas, "Churches Stand Together in a Covenant," *The Messenger* 10 (Summer 2002): 4.

93. Neddie Winters, interview by the author, February 10, 2004, Jackson, MS.

94. Neddie Winters and Barry Cotter, "Covenant Relationship between Church in the City and St Peter's by the Lake Episcopal Church" (n.d.).

95. "Mission Mississippi," leaflet, 1993, MMP.

96. Lisa Maisel and Ralph Maisel, interview by the author, October 5, 2004, St. Peter's by-the-Lake, Brandon, MS.

97. Victor Smith, interview by the author, October 12, 2004, Pearl, MS.

98. "Charles Doty and Victor Smith Succcessful in Christ, in Friendship, in Business," *Proclaim* 2 (January 2002): 6. MMP.

99. Smith, October 12, 2004.

100. Mississippi Development Authority, "Case Study: Lextron Corporation" [Web page] 2003. Available: http://www.mississippi.org/press/PressKit/case_studies/case_study_four.htm (accessed September 22, 2005).

101. Arnold Lindsay, "Indebted Lextron Files for Chap. 11," *Clarion-Ledger,* March 24, 2004.

102. "Case Study: Lextron Corporation"; ICIC, "Inner City 100 Winners" [Web page] 2002. Available: http://www.innercity100.org/2002Details.asp?Rank=82 (accessed September 23, 2005).

103. ICIC, "Inner City 100 Winners." Interestingly it was Doty's skilled, loyal and un-unionized labor force which attracted the partnership with Detroit's Visteon.

Jamie Butters, "Meet Lextron Visteon Assembly Systems: Constructing a Winning Venture," *Detroit Free Press*, June 3, 2003; Lextron Corporation [Web site] Available: www.lextroncorporation.com. (accessed September 23, 2005).

104. Eric Stringfellow, "2 Entrepreneurs Reclaim Groceries Others Abandoned," *Clarion-Ledger*, June 17, 1999.

105. Arnold Lindsay, "Grocer Ponders Future of Chain," *Clarion-Ledger*, November 1, 2001; "Welcome to New Deal Supermarket" [Web site] 2004. Available: http://www.newdealsupermarket.com/ (accessed October 12, 2005).

106. Winters, Oct. 18, 2004.

107. Lee Paris, "A Note from Lee Paris," *Mission Mississippi Insights* (Summer 1998): 2.

108. Arnold Lindsay, "A Store to Call Their Own," *Clarion-Ledger*, February 19, 2003.

109. Arnold Lindsay, "Making Successful New Deals," *Clarion-Ledger*, June 5, 2003; Lindsay, "A Store to Call Their Own."

110. Lindsay, "Making Successful New Deals."

111. Lindsay, "A Store to Call Their Own."

112. Ibid.

113. Lindsay, "Making Successful New Deals."

114. Arnold Lindsay, "Just 1 New Deal Remains," *Clarion-Ledger*, January 5, 2007.

115. Dolphus Weary, *Grace Is Greater Than Race* (sermon, Smith-Wills Memorial Stadium, Jackson, MS, November 19, 2000).

116. Volf, *Exclusion and Embrace*, 224.

117. W. Fitzhugh Brundage, *The Southern Past: A Clash of Race and Memory* (Cambridge, MA: Belknap Press of Harvard University Press, 2005), 341.

118. William Winter, interview by the author, October 13, 2004, Jackson, MS.

119. Gina Holland, "Flag Commission Calls for Statewide Election on Mississippi Flag," *CNN.com*, December 12, 2000. Available: http://archives.cnn.com/2000/ALLPOLITICS/stories/12/12/mississippiflag.ap/index.html (accessed July 28, 2008).

120. Steve Lopez, "Ghosts of the South," *Time*, April 30, 2001, 66.

121. Lee Paris, interview by the author, October 14, 2004, Jackson, MS. Sociologist John Shelton Reed attributes the failure of the proponents of the new flag to win popular support to their concentration on the economic argument—the old flag discourages investment—rather than on "the argument from good manners, or from Christian charity." John Shelton Reed, "The Banner That Won't Stay Furled," *Southern Cultures* 8 (Spring 2002): 85.

122. Taken from Weary's comments about the Flag Commission at Mission Mississippi's Executive Board retreat, Entergy Conference Center, Jackson, MS, October 4, 2004; and Paris, Oct. 14, 2004.

123. Ben Beaird and Judy Beaird, interview by the author, October 6, 2004, Clinton, Mississippi.

124. Ibid.

125. Ibid.

CHAPTER 6

1. L. Gregory Jones, "Crafting Communities of Forgiveness," *Interpretation* 54 (April, April, 2000): 122.

2. Ibid.: 131.

3. The term practice is used here mindful of Alisdair MacIntyre's definition of a practice as a "coherent and complex form of socially established co-operative human activity through which goods internal to that form of activity are realised in the course of trying to achieve those standards of excellence which are appropriate to, and partially definitive of, that form of activity, with the result that human powers to achieve excellence, and human conceptions of the ends and goods involved, are systematically extended." Alasdair C. MacIntyre, *After Virtue: A Study in Moral Theory* (Notre Dame: University of Notre Dame Press, 1981), 187. "The goods internal" to the practice of the prayer meetings include learning to listen to the other's story, interpreting the stories through the lens of scripture, extending forgiveness and interceding for the other in prayer. The "ends" of this practice include the establishment of relationships that lead to reconciliation.

4. *Unifying the Body of Christ: And the Walls Come Tumbling Down* (Jackson: Mission Mississippi, 1996), 4.

5. Jarvis C. Ward, "Mission Mississippi Vision 1997 and Beyond, Jarvis Ward's Proposed Revisions (2/13/97)," 1997, MMP.

6. John Geary, "Mission Mississippi: Evaluation and Direction—Memo to Lee Paris," 1997, MMP.

7. From an Excel spreadsheet of Mission Mississippi's prayer breakfast locations from February 5, 2002, to February 5, 2004, e-mailed to the author by David Arnold, February 13, 2004.

8. In 2005, Jackson Academy had 1558 students, making it the largest private school in the Jackson Area followed by St. Andrews Episcopal School with 1,158. Jackson Prep, with 885 students between 7th and 12th grades, was the largest private high school. The schools were all overwhelmingly white with Jackson Academy— with only twelve (0.83 percent) black students—the whitest. Statistics from Private Schools Report, "Jackson, Mississippi" 2005. Available: http://mississippi. privateschoolsreport.com/schools/MS/Jackson.html (accessed December 21, 2005).

9. Clergy present: Fred Rohlfs, the pastor of Northeast Christian Church, Madison, and James Turner, Church of Christ Holiness (USA), a pastor and executive director of Jackson's Neighborhood Christian Center.

10. Virginia Chase, interview by the author, October 18, 2004, Jackson, MS.

11. Jackie Pate, interview by the author, October 14, 2004, Jackson, MS.

12. Phil Reed, panel discussion at the Inter-Varsity Conference, "Jubilee VI: The Grace Race," Voice of Calvary Ministries, Jackson, MS, October, 2, 2004.

13. Lee Paris, interview by the author, October 10, 2004, Jackson, MS.

14. Elizabeth D. H. Carmichael, *Friendship: Interpreting Christian Love* (London: T & T Clark International, 2004), 178.

15. Jürgen Moltmann, *The Church in the Power of the Spirit: A Contribution of Messianic Ecclesiology* (London: SCM Press, 1977), 118.

16. Ibid.

17. Ibid., 316.

18. Jürgen Moltmann, "Open Friendship: Aristotelian and Christian Concepts of Friendship," in *The Changing Face of Friendship*, ed. Leroy S. Rouner, Boston University Studies in Philosophy and Religion (Notre Dame, IN: University of Notre Dame Press, 1994), 38.

19. Hue Ha, "Quiet Faith Undergirds Main Street Commerce," *Clarion-Ledger*, October 16, 1996.

20. Robert Wuthnow, *Sharing the Journey: Support Groups and America's New Quest for Community* (New York: Free Press, 1994), 4, 92. Wuthnow's team conducted a sample survey of over a thousand participants and closely studied a dozen groups for three years. Robert Putnam in his book *Bowling Alone*, that traces the loss of social capital and civic involvement for most Americans, supports Wuthnow's findings, noting that the upsurge in small groups "alert us to the heartening potential of civic renewal." Robert D. Putnam, *Bowling Alone: The Collapse and Revival of American Community* (New York: Simon & Schuster, 2000), 180. Since the publication of *Sharing the Journey*, there has been no sign of an end in the growth of the small group movement. In the evangelical churches in particular, the success of Rick Warren's small group study guide, *The Purpose-Driven Life*, which sold more than 23 million copies since its publication in 2002, indicates the growth of small groups. Richard Warren, *The Purpose-Driven Life: What on Earth Am I Here For?* (Grand Rapids, MI: Zondervan, 2002). For more on Warren, see Putnam's chapter on his church in Robert D. Putnam, Lewis M. Feldstein, and Don Cohen, *Better Together: Restoring the American Community* (New York: Simon & Schuster, 2003). Also see Malcolm Gladwell's article, which includes an interview with Putnam. Malcolm Gladwell, "The Cellular Church: How Rick Warren's Church Grew," *The New Yorker*, September 12, 2005.

21. Wuthnow, *Sharing the Journey*, 92–95.

22. Ibid., 105.

23. Ibid., 8.

24. Ibid., 14.

25. Sheree Tynes, interview by the author, February 7, 2004, Jackson, MS.

26. Chase, October 18, 2004. Chase's statement, that she is making a sacrifice (albeit a small one) to attend Mission Mississippi events, fits with the sociologists Christerson, Edwards, and Emerson's findings. They hypothesize that "Numerical minority group members bear the highest relational costs of being involved in interracial organizations." The hypothesis concludes, "The costs are reduced as representation increases." Brad Christerson, Korie L. Edwards, and Michael O. Emerson, *Against All Odds: The Struggle for Racial Integration in Religious Organizations* (New York: New York University Press, 2005), 156. This was observable in the greater enthusiasm expressed physically and vocally in the prayer meeting held at Hyde Park MB Church where African Americans were numerically the majority and on the home ground of an African American church.

27. Lisa Maisel and Ralph Maisel, interview by the author, October 5, 2004, St. Peter's by-the-Lake, Brandon, MS.

28. For a vivid firsthand account of the fear that gripped white congregations in Mississippi during this period, read Charles Marsh, *The Last Days: A Son's Story of Sin and Segregation at the Dawn of a New South* (New York: Basic Books, 2001).

29. Tynes, February 7, 2004.

30. Joel Weathersby, interview by the author, October 12, 2004, Jackson, MS.

31. Ibid.

32. Pate, October 14, 2004.

33. Ibid.

34. Johnson argues that the best candidate for authorship is James of Jerusalem, called by Paul "the Brother of the Lord" (Gal 1:19). Luke Timothy Johnson, *The Letter of James: A New Translation with Introduction and Commentary* (New York: Doubleday, 1995), 93.

35. Jürgen Moltmann, *The Crucified God: The Cross of Christ as the Foundation and Criticism of Christian Theology* (New York: Harper & Row, 1974), 19.

36. For his survey of Hellenistic sources, see Johnson, *The Letter of James*, 244.; Luke Timothy Johnson, *Brother of Jesus, Friend of God: Studies in the Letter of James* (Grand Rapids, MI: W.B. Eerdmans Pub., 2004), 214.

37. Johnson, *Brother of Jesus, Friend of God*, 213.

38. Ibid., 215.

39. Ibid., 216.

40. Jürgen Moltmann, *Theology of Hope; on the Ground and the Implications of a Christian Eschatology* (New York, Harper & Row, 1967), 327.

41. Johnson, *The Letter of James*, 343. Johnson notes other examples of the physical healing of Jesus symbolizing social reconciliation (Acts 4:22, 30; 28:27). Johnson, *The Letter of James*, 335. L. Gregory Jones did not have the benefit of Johnson's work when he first wrote about this passage in his book, L. Gregory Jones, *Embodying Forgiveness: A Theological Analysis* (Grand Rapids, MI: W.B. Eerdmans, 1995). However, Jones comes to rely heavily on Johnson's commentary in the development of his own work on understanding forgiveness as a set of communal habits, practices, and disciplines. Jones, "Crafting Communities of Forgiveness."

42. Johnson, *The Letter of James*, 344–45.

43. Ibid.

44. Paris, October. 10, 2004.

45. Johnson, *The Letter of James*, 344–45.

46. Miroslav Volf, *Exclusion and Embrace: A Theological Exploration of Identity, Otherness, and Reconciliation* (Nashville: Abingdon Press, 1996), 213.

47. John W. De Gruchy, *Reconciliation: Restoring Justice* (Minneapolis: Fortress Press, 2002), 152.

48. Ibid. DeGruchy comments that this is the "regarding no one from a human point of view" that Paul talks of as the result of Christ's reconciliation (2 Cor 5:16).

49. Wuthnow, *Sharing the Journey*, 297.

50. Tynes, February 7, 2004.

51. Wuthnow, *Sharing the Journey*, 299.

52. Stephen E. Fowl, *Philippians*, ed. Joel B. Green and Max Turner, The Two Horizons New Testament Commentary (Grand Rapids, MI: Eerdmans, 2005), 208.

53. Ibid., 220.

54. Ibid.

55. Ibid., 224.

56. Michael O. Emerson and Christian Smith, *Divided by Faith: Evangelical Religion and the Problem of Race in America* (New York: Oxford University Press, 2000), 130.

57. Ibid.

58. Ibid., 131.

59. Ibid., 132.

60. Ibid., 107.

61. Ibid., 131. Their conclusions seem both indebted to and to confirm the work of sociologists Jackman and Crane. Mary R. Jackman and Marie Crane, "'Some of My Best Friends Are Black': Interracial Friendship and Whites' Racial Attitudes," *Public Opinion Quarterly* (1986). Jackman and Crane challenged the long-held tenets of Gordon W. Allport's Contact Theory. Gordon W. Allport, *The Nature of Prejudice* (Reading, MA: Addison-Wesley, 1954). Allport, a psychologist whose work in 1954 addressed policy-making concerns around school desegregation, argued that prejudice resulted from whites' ignorance of blacks that fed and perpetuated misconceptions and stereotypes. Personal contact will correct and soften these misconceptions. Jackman and Crane, using data from a 1975 survey conducted by the Institute of Social Research at the University of Michigan, found that intimacy of relationships is less important than having a variety of contacts in changing beliefs and perceptions. Their results also cast doubt on Allport's basic assumption that prejudice was a form of ignorance that can be dispelled through cross-group contact. They found "that white's affective and social dispositions towards blacks change with greater ease than their beliefs about blacks, or...their racial policy views." Jackman and Crane, "Some of My Best Friends Are Black," 479. Further undermining Allport's support of individual friendship, Jackman and Crane showed that a relationship with an African American of higher socio-economic status had greater influence on a white's beliefs than a relationship of equality. In other words, the dynamic of inequality is more significant than friendship.

62. Emerson and Smith, *Divided by Faith*, 170. For a study of racial diversity in American churches, see Kevin D. Dougherty, "How Monochromatic Is Church Membership? Racial-Ethnic Diversity in Religious Community," *Sociology of Religion* 64 (2003): 65–85.

63. Emerson and Smith, *Divided by Faith*, 170.

64. Curtiss Paul DeYoung et al., *United by Faith: The Multiracial Congregation as an Answer to the Problem of Race* (New York: Oxford University Press, 2003).

65. Ibid., 168.

66. Christerson, Edwards, and Emerson, *Against All Odds*, 152. Returning to Allport's contact theory, they find that contact in a multiracial church or organization

is not sufficient to overcome what they call the *niche overlap effect* (members attracted to other organizations in which they are a better fit) and *niche edge effect* (members not part of the dominant group leave at a faster rate than those in the majority group), which work to destabilize these groups. Christerson, Edwards, and Emerson, *Against All Odds*, 156.

67. Their conclusions match the experience of Voice of Calvary in Jackson. Both John Perkins and Phil Reed of Voice of Calvary, attest to the almost inevitable instability of a multi-racial congregation, and the huge expenditure of energy such a congregation demands of its members to maintain diversity. While existing as a multiracial congregation for over thirty years, the high turnover of membership at Voice of Calvary, particularly among whites, means they remain a small congregation. John Perkins, interview by the author, October 12, 2004, Jackson, MS; Phil Reed, interview by the author, October 7, 2004, Jackson, MS.

68. Michael O. Emerson and Rodney M. Woo, *People of the Dream: Multiracial Congregations in the United States* (Princeton, N.J.: Princeton University Press, 2006), 193. See also George Yancey, *One Body One Spirit: Principles of Successful Multiracial Churches* (Downers Grove, IL: InterVarsity Press, 2003).

69. John Perkins criticizes Mission Mississippi's position that he characterizes as, "We ain't asking you to change your church." "What Mission Mississippi is trying to do," Perkins believes, "is try and change people outside the church," making Mission Mississippi, "a classic para-church organization." This strategy has two fundamental flaws for Perkins. First: "Organizations [to be successful] have got to be anchored within the local church" and the "support base" that provides. Second: Perkins asks, "is there such a thing as a white church and a black church, biblically? No!... You can defend it on the basis of culture, but you can't defend it on the basis of biblical truth." Perkins, 12 Oct. 2004.

70. In her interview, Lisa Maisel described the change in her perception resulting from involvement in Mission Mississippi that now enabled her to acknowledge the validity of African Americans' perception of systemic inequality:

> I just thought about the way my friend has made a comment... or I've heard women that I know say something. Like a person on the base say "Well that is because of my race." At first I'm going to go, "do you really believe that?" But then, what I do is I resist, I consciously suppress them. What does it matter? That is the perception so that is reality. It is something that pops up in me and I just consciously push it down and say that is perception and the perception is reality to those people or to anyone really. Maisel and Maisel, Oct. 5, 2004.

71. Not everyone who has participated in the prayer breakfasts has experienced the power for reconciliation that others described. One interviewee who attended prayer meetings annually when his church hosted the breakfast stated:

> I felt that they were a bit phony in the sense that you walked in there and they said a few words and you kind of prayed together and you left.... The negative part of it was you didn't know, in many instances, the people you

were praying with.... I think group prayer is better if you share some commonality with the people before you pray together. I think prayer can help create community but I always thought it was something lacking.

George Evans and Carol Evans, interview by the author, October 17, 2005, Jackson, MS. Another participant, committed to racial reconciliation initiatives found Mission Mississippi's prayer breakfasts frustrating:

Well, it's the same old same old. You have a devotional and then you divide up into groups and then you have some prayer for 15 minutes. The prayers are kind of surface in my opinion. I would like to see some permanent small groups building relationships.

Ben Beaird and Judy Beaird, interview by the author, October 6, 2004. Clinton, MS. Both of these interviews, rather than dismissing Mission Mississippi's efforts, express frustration at the unrealized potential in interracial intercessory prayer for reconciliation.

72. Maisel and Maisel, Oct. 5, 2004. Jackman and Crane note that whites attitudes change most significantly when their black friends are of a higher socioeconomic status. They hypothesize this change in attitude is a result of a reversed power dynamic. Jackman and Crane, "Some of My Best Friends Are Black": 480. In this example, the spiritual—not socioeconomic—power dynamic is reversed.

73. Maisel and Maisel, October 5, 2004.

74. Ibid.

75. James Baird, interview by the author, February 9, 2004, Flowood, MS.

76. Dietrich Bonhoeffer, *Life Together; Prayerbook of the Bible*, ed. Gerhard Ludwig Müller, Albrecht Schönherr, and Geffrey B. Kelly, Daniel W. Bloesch, and James H. Burtness trans., vol. 5, Dietrich Bonhoeffer Works (Minneapolis: Fortress Press, 1996), 90–91.

77. Ibid., 90.

78. See his description of the Pharisee as the disunited man in Dietrich Bonhoeffer, *Ethics*, ed. Ilse Tödt, et al., Reinhard Krauss, Charles C. West, and Douglas W. Stott trans., ed., vol. 6, Dietrich Bonhoeffer Works (Minneapolis: Fortress Press, 2005), 316.

79. Dietrich Bonhoeffer, *Act and Being*, ed. Hans-Richard Reuter and Wayne Whitson Floyd, H. Martin Rumscheidt trans., vol. 2, Dietrich Bonhoeffer Works (Minneapolis: Fortress Press, 1996), 128.

80. Ibid., 127. Being in Christ frees the individual even from the seemingly inescapable isolation of death. Charles Marsh, *Reclaiming Dietrich Bonhoeffer: The Promise of His Theology* (New York: Oxford University Press, 1994), 132. Geffrey B. Kelly and F. Burton Nelson, *The Cost of Moral Leadership: The Spirituality of Dietrich Bonhoeffer* (Grand Rapids, MI: W.B. Eerdmans Pub., 2003), 150.

81. Dietrich Bonhoeffer, *Life Together*, John W. Doberstein trans. (London: SCM Press, 1954), 77.

82. Tynes, Feb. 7, 2004.

83. Weathersby, October 12, 2004.

84. Pate, October 14, 2004.

85. Ibid.

86. Ibid.

87. Dietrich Bonhoeffer, *Sanctorum Communio: A Theological Study of the Sociology of the Church*, ed. Joachim von Soosten and Clifford J. Green, Reinhard Krauss and Nancy Lukens trans., vol. 1, Dietrich Bonhoeffer Works (Minneapolis: Fortress Press, 1998), 187.

88. Bonhoeffer, *Act and Being*, 123.

89. Although private confession had all but disappeared in the German Evangelical Church (EKD), at the time of the Reformation, Martin Luther had insisted on maintaining the practice of hearing private confession and absolution. In 1520, Luther wrote, "Of private confession, which is now observed, I am heartily in favor, even though it cannot be proved from the Scriptures; it is useful and necessary, nor would I have it abolished; nay, I rejoice that it exists in the Church of Christ, for it is a cure without equal for distressed consciences." From *Prelude on the Babylonian Captivity of the Church*, 4.13 in Martin Luther and Charles Michael Jacobs, *Three Treatises: [an Open Letter to the Christian Nobility of the German Nation Concerning the Reform of the Christian Estate. A Prelude to the Babylonian on Captivity of the Church. A Treatise on Christian Liberty. Introductions and Translations by C. M. Jacobs, A. T. W. Steinhaeuser and W. A. Lambert]* (Philadelphia: Muhlenberg Press, 1947).

90. Bonhoeffer, *Life Together* (1954), 108.

91. Bonhoeffer outlines the practice of confession. Ibid., 108–18. He roots this authority to forgive sins in Jesus' words, "If you forgive the sins of any, they are forgiven them; if you retain the sins of any, they are retained" (John 20:23).

92. Bonhoeffer, *Act and Being*, 123.

93. The confession does not necessarily remain secret. The details of sins forgiven form an essential part of the evangelical's testimony. However, the function of a testimony is not confession: rather it is to encourage other believers, bring glory to God, and to evangelize the unconverted. These, often lurid tales of sinful lives forever abandoned as a result of God's grace, can have the unfortunate result of confining sin, repentance and forgiveness firmly in the pre-conversion past. This creates what Bonhoeffer describes as a "pious community" in which "all have to conceal their sins from themselves and from the community." Bonhoeffer, *Life Together* (1954), 108.

94. Dietrich Bonhoeffer, "Thy Kingdom Come: The Prayer of the Church for God's Kingdom on Earth," 1932, in John D. Godsey and Dietrich Bonhoeffer, *Preface to Bonhoeffer; the Man and Two of His Shorter Writings* (Philadelphia: Fortress Press, 1965), 41.

95. De Gruchy, *Reconciliation: Restoring Justice*, 153.

96. In 1994, Edgar Ray Killen, an accomplice in the murder of three civil rights workers in 1964, threatened to make an appearance at a stall in the annual State Fair in Jackson. Dolphus Weary found himself torn between African American members of the board who wanted Mission Mississippi to call a boycott of the fair, and whites who believed such an action would simply give him the publicity he desired. Mission Mississippi took no public position on the issue. At the height of the controversy,

Dolphus Weary explained to a group of students, "I want Mission Mississippi to always be in the middle. To always be able to send out the same message...even if we disagree we love each other in the body of Jesus Christ." Dolphus Weary, "Get Set," Presentation at the Inter-Varsity Conference, "Jubilee VI: The Grace Race," Voice of Calvary Ministries, Jackson, MS, October 2, 2004. The whole story proved to be a hoax of white supremacist Richard Barrett. Jerry Mitchell, "Key Suspect in '64 Killings Planning Fair Appearance," *Clarion Ledger*, September 20, 2004; A.P., "Wife Says Edgar Ray Killen Not Attending Fair," *Jackson Free Press*, October 1, 2004.

97. Tynes, February 7, 2004.

98. Bonhoeffer, *Ethics*, 67.

99. Bonhoeffer demolishes the idea of separate spheres or realms—*regnum gratiae* and *regnum narurae*—in a section of his *Ethics*. Ibid., 55–68. Bonhoeffer is correcting Luther's doctrine of two spheres (throne and altar) when he writes, "Ethical thinking in terms of realms, is overcome by faith in the revelation of ultimate reality in Jesus Christ." Ibid., 61. One can comfortably extend his argument to include a critique of the Southern Presbyterian doctrine of the spirituality of the church and the "sphere sovereignty" of Dutch Calvinist Abraham Kuyper.

100. Dietrich Bonhoeffer, *The Cost of Discipleship*, Reginald H. Fuller trans. (London: SCM Press, 1986), 134.

101. Bonhoeffer, *Life Together* (1954), 79.

102. Moltmann, *The Church in the Power of the Spirit*, 119.

103. Bonhoeffer, *Sanctorum Communio*, 186.

104. Ibid.

105. Tynes, February 7, 2004.

106. This account is taken from two interviews. Chase, October 18. 2004; Paris, O October. 10, 2004.

107. Chase, October 18 2004.

108. Shelia Hardwell Byrd, "Barbour Signs Bills Increasing Penalties for Fleeing Lawbreakers," *Clarion Ledger*, May 3, 2004. The bill came after police pursuits led to the deaths of fifty people in Mississippi since 2000. Statistics from Victims of Police Pursuits in Jeremy Hudson and Jean Gordon, "Fatal Car Chase Leaves in Its Wake Shock, Questions," *Clarion-Ledger*, June 25, 2004.

109. Eric Stringfellow, "Breaking Speed Limit Should Not Merit Death," *Clarion-Ledger*, June 27, 2004.

110. Allen G. Holder, "Officer in Chase Only Doing His Job," *Clarion Ledger*, July 5, 2004.

111. Anonymous, "Negro Dies in Police Chase, Mammy & Friends Blame, Da Cops as Usual," June 26, 2004. Available: http://www.nnnforum.org/forums/index. php?showtopic=888 (accessed January 14, 2006).

112. Casey Parks, "City Buzz: Running While Scared?" *Jackson Free Press*, July 21, 2004.

113. Chase, October 18, 2004.

114. Ibid.

115. Ibid.

116. Brenda Donnell, interview by the author, October 5, 2004, Jackson, MS.

117. Chase, O October. 18, 2004.

118. Hudson and Gordon, "Fatal Car Chase Leaves in Its Wake Shock, Questions."

119. Paris, October 10, 2004.

120. Jean Gordon, "Man on a Mission," *Clarion-Ledger*, March 11, 2006.

CHAPTER 7

1. Michael O. Emerson and Christian Smith, *Divided by Faith: Evangelical Religion and the Problem of Race in America* (New York: Oxford University Press, 2000), 130–131.

2. Ibid., 109.

3. Office of the Press Secretary, The White House, "President Discusses Hurricane Relief in Address to the Nation," September 15, 2005. Available: http://www.whitehouse.gov/news/releases/2005/09/20050915–8.html (accessed September 16, 2005).

4. Nell Luter Floyd, "Churches Scramble to Meet Needs," *Clarion-Ledger*, September 5, 2005; Chris Joyner, "Faith-Based Volunteers Aid in Area's Recovery," *Clarion-Ledger*, November 16, 2005.

5. Mission Mississippi, "Mission Mississippi Responds to Hurricane Katrina" [Web Page] 2006. Available: http://www.missionmississippi.org/Home.dsp (accessed February 18, 2006); World Vision, "U.S. Gulf Coast: World Vision Donors Help Raise $12 Million to Rebuild Lives," Available: http://www.worldvision.org/donate.nsf/child/tawv_hurricane_katrina (accessed July 21, 2008).

6. Virginia Chase, interview by the author, February 17, 2006. Glenn Barth, the director of the Nehemiah Leadership Institute of Tentmakers Ministries (an evangelical leadership training organization whose aim is "to transform the world through Christ, one relationship at a time"), wrote an extensive on-line Blog covering the two months he worked with Mission Mississippi helping facilitate its work post-Katrina. Glenn Barth, "Glenn's Journal: Hurricane Relief" [Web log] 2005. Available: http://www.tentmakersym.org/other/blogearly.html (accessed December 27, 2005).

7. Charles L. Dunn, e-mail to author, March 2, 2006.

8. Federal Emergency Management Agency, "Volunteer Agencies Assist with Hurricane Katrina Recovery Efforts" [Web Page] September 21, 2005. Available: http://www.fema.gov/news/newsrelease.fema?id=19665 (accessed February 19, 2006).

9. John W. De Gruchy, *Reconciliation: Restoring Justice* (Minneapolis: Fortress Press, 2002), 75.

10. Elizabeth D. H. Carmichael, *Friendship: Interpreting Christian Love* (London: T & T Clark International, 2004), 199.

11. Neddie Winters, interview by the author, October 18, 2004, Jackson, MS.

Selected Bibliography

INTERVIEWS

All the interviews were recorded on tape cassette and are in the possession of the author.

James Baird, Flowood, Mississippi, October 9, 2004.
Ben and Judy Beaird, Clinton, Mississippi, October 6, 2004.
Owen Brooks, Jackson, Mississippi, October 8, 2004.
Will D. Campbell, Mt. Juliet, Tennessee, October 19, 2004.
Robert C. Cannada, Jackson, Mississippi, (telephone), June 21, 2005.
Virginia Chase, Jackson, Mississippi, October 18, 2004.
———, Jackson Mississippi (telephone), February 17, 2006.
Ronnie Crudup, Jackson, Mississippi, February 5, 2004.
Kane Ditto, Jackson, Mississippi, October 15, 2004.
Brenda Donnell, Jackson, Mississippi, October 5, 2004.
Jon Elder, Jackson, Mississippi, October 18, 2004.
George and Carol Evans, Jackson Mississippi, October 17, 2004.
Catherine Griffith, Charlottesville, Virginia, July 14, 2004.
Peggy Hammett, Jackson, Mississippi, October 5, 2004.
Thomas Jenkins, Jackson, Mississippi, October 18, 2004.
Ed King, Jackson, Mississippi, October 17, 2004.
Steve Lanier, Jackson, Mississippi, February 9, 2004.
Judith Layng, Charlottesville, Virginia, May 11, 2003.

Lisa and Ralph Maisel, Brandon, Mississippi, October 5, 2004.

Mabel Pittman Middleton, Jackson, Mississippi, October 8, 2004.

Jürgen Moltmann, Charlottesville, Virginia, April 29, 2005.

Ross Oliver, Jackson, Mississippi, October 14, 2004.

Lee Paris, Jackson, Mississippi, May 19, 2003.

————, October 10, 2004.

————, October 14, 2004.

Jackie Pate, Jackson, Mississippi, October 14, 2004.

John Perkins, Mississippi, October 12, 2004.

Frank Pollard, Jackson, Mississippi, (telephone), October 5, 2000.

Randy and Kathy Pope, Jackson, Mississippi, October 2, 2004.

Phil Reed, Jackson, Mississippi, October 7, 2004.

Jane Virden Ross, Mississippi, February 9, 2004.

Mike Ross, Jackson, Mississippi, February 9, 2004.

Kay Shurden, Jackson, Mississippi, February 7, 2004.

Miriam Smith and Dorothy Daniels, Jackson, Mississippi, October 16, 2004.

Victor Smith, Pearl, Mississippi, October 12, 2004.

Eric Stringfellow, Jackson, Mississippi, October 7, 2004.

James Turner, Jackson, Mississippi, October 7, 2004.

Sheree Tynes, Jackson, Mississippi, February 7, 2004.

John Urban, Brandon, Mississippi, February 8, 2004.

Jarvis Ward, Flowood, Mississippi, February 9, 2004.

James Washington, Jackson, Mississippi, October 13, 2004.

Dolphus Weary, Jackson, Mississippi, February 25, 2000.

————, Jackson, Mississippi, February 10, 2004.

Joel Weathersby, Jackson, Mississippi, October 12, 2004.

William Winter, Jackson, Mississippi, October 13, 2004.

Neddie Winters, Jackson, Mississippi, February 10, 2004.

————, Jackson, Mississippi, October 18, 2004.

SELECTED BIBLIOGRAPHY

All scriptural quotations, unless otherwise noted, are taken from the New Revised Standard Version Bible. Division of Christian Education of the National Council of Churches of Christ in the United States of America, 1989. Scriptural quotations marked NIV are taken from the Holy Bible, New International Version, International Bible Society, 1973, 1978, 1984.

The Constitution of the Presbyterian Church in the United States of America: Containing the Confession of Faith, the Catechisms, and the Directory for the Worship of God. Philadelphia: Presbyterian Board of Publication, 1841.

Jackson, the City Beautiful. Jackson, MS: Chamber of Commerce, 1927.

Minutes of the General Assembly of the Presbyterian Church in the United States of America. Philadelphia: Presbyterian Board of Publication, 1836.

Minutes of the General Assembly of the Presbyterian Church in the United States of America. Philadelphia: Presbyterian Board of Publication, 1837.

Allport, Gordon W. *The Nature of Prejudice.* Reading, MA: Addison-Wesley, 1954.

Alvis, Joel L. *Religion & Race: Southern Presbyterians, 1946–1983.* Tuscaloosa: University of Alabama Press, 1994.

Barnett, Victoria. *For the Soul of the People: Protestant Protest against Hitler.* New York: Oxford University Press, 1992.

Barrett, Russell H. *Integration at Ole Miss.* Chicago: Quadrangle Books, 1965.

Barth, Karl. *The Epistle to the Romans.* London, New York: Oxford University Press, 1968.

Bartley, Numan V. *The New South, 1945–1980: A History of the South; V. 11.* Baton Rouge: Louisiana State University Press, 1995.

Bauckham, Richard. *The Theology of Jürgen Moltmann.* Edinburgh: T & T Clark, 1995.

Bauckham, Richard. "Jürgen Moltmann." In *The Modern Theologians: An Introduction to Christian Theology in the Twentieth Century,* edited by David Ford, 209–24. Cambridge, MA: Blackwell Publishers, 1997.

Bentley, James. *Martin Niemöller.* London: Hodder and Stoughton, 1986.

Berryman, Phillip. *Liberation Theology: Essential Facts about the Revolutionary Movement in Latin America—and Beyond.* Philadelphia: Temple University Press, 1987.

Boman, Martha. "A Social History of Jackson, Mississippi: 1821–1861, State Capital in the Old South." MA thesis, University of Mississippi, 1952.

Bonhoeffer, Dietrich. *Act and Being.* Translated by H. Martin Rumscheidt. Edited by Hans-Richard Reuter and Wayne Whitson Floyd. Vol. 2, *Dietrich Bonhoeffer Works.* Minneapolis: Fortress Press, 1996.

———. *The Cost of Discipleship.* London: SCM Press, 1986.

———. *Discipleship.* Translated by Barbara Green and Reinhard Krauss. Edited by Kuske Kuske, Ilse Tödt, Geffrey B. Kelly and John D. Godsey, *Dietrich Bonhoeffer Works.* Minneapolis, MN: Fortress Press, 2001.

———. *Letters and Papers from Prison.* Translated by Reginald H. Fuller. Edited by Eberhard Bethge. London: SCM Press, 1953.

———. *Letters and Papers from Prison.* Translated by Reginald H. Fuller and John Bowden. Edited by Eberhard Bethge. Enlarged ed. London: SCM Press, 1971.

———. *Life Together.* Translated by John W. Doberstein. London: SCM Press, 1954.

———. *Life Together; Prayerbook of the Bible.* Translated by Daniel W. Bloesch and James H. Burtness. Edited by Gerhard Ludwig Müller, Albrecht Schönherr and Geffrey B. Kelly. Vol. 5, *Dietrich Bonhoeffer Works.* Minneapolis: Fortress Press, 1996.

————. *Sanctorum Communio: A Theological Study of the Sociology of the Church.* Translated by Reinhard Krauss and Nancy Lukens. Edited by Joachim von Soosten and Clifford J. Green. Minneapolis: Fortress Press, 1998.

————. *Ethics.* Translated by Neville Horton Smith. Edited by E. Bethge. London: SCM Press, 1960.

————. *Ethics.* Translated by Reinhard Krauss, Charles C. West and Douglas W. Stott. Edited by Ilse Tödt, Heinz Eduard Tödt, Ernst Feil, and Clifford J. Green. Vol. 6, *Dietrich Bonhoeffer Works.* Minneapolis: Fortress Press, 2005.

Bonilla-Silva, Eduardo. *Racism without Racists: Color-Blind Racism and the Persistence of Racial Inequality in the United States.* Lanham, MD: Rowman & Littlefield, 2003.

Braddock, Jomills Henry, Marvin P. Dawkins, and George Wilson. "Intercultural Contact and Race Relations among American Youth." In *Toward a Common Destiny: Improving Race and Ethnic Relations in America,* edited by Willis D. Hawley and Anthony Jackson. San Francisco: Jossey-Bass Publishers, 1995.

Brady, Tom P. *Black Monday.* Winona, MS: Association of Citizens' Councils, 1955.

Brown, Henry Billings. "Majority Opinion in Plessy V. Ferguson." In *Desegregation and the Supreme Court,* edited by Benjamin Munn Ziegler. Boston: D.C. Heath and Company, 1958.

Brown, Robert McAfee. *Kairos: Three Prophetic Challenges to the Church.* Grand Rapids, MI: Eerdmans, 1990.

Brundage, W. Fitzhugh. *The Southern Past: A Clash of Race and Memory.* Cambridge, MA: Belknap Press of Harvard University Press, 2005.

Campbell, Clarice T., and Oscar A. Rogers. *Mississippi, the View from Tougaloo.* Jackson: University Press of Mississippi, 1979.

Campbell, Will D. *And Also With You: Duncan Gray and the American Dilemma.* Franklin, TN: Providence House, 1997.

————. *Brother to a Dragonfly.* New York: Seabury Press, 1977.

————. *Race and the Renewal of the Church.* Philadelphia: Westminster Press, 1962.

Carmichael, Elizabeth D. H. *Friendship: Interpreting Christian Love.* London: T & T Clark International, 2004.

Carter, Hodding III. "Citadel of the Citizens' Council." *New York Times Magazine,* November 12 1961, 23, 125–26.

Chappell, David L. *A Stone of Hope: Prophetic Religion and the Death of Jim Crow.* Chapel Hill: University of North Carolina Press, 2004.

————. *A Stone of Hope: Prophetic Religion and the Death of Jim Crow.* Chapel Hill: University of North Carolina Press, 2004.

Christerson, Brad, Korie L. Edwards, and Michael O. Emerson. *Against All Odds: The Struggle for Racial Integration in Religious Organizations.* New York: New York University Press, 2005.

Church of England. *Common Worship: Services and Prayers for the Church of England.* London: Church House Publishing, 2000.

Classen, Steven D. *Watching Jim Crow: The Struggles over Mississippi TV, 1955–1969, Console-Ing Passions.* Durham, NC: Duke University Press, 2004.

Cobb, James C. *The Most Southern Place on Earth: The Mississippi Delta and the Roots of Regional Identity.* New York: Oxford University Press, 1992.

Cohodas, Nadine. *The Band Played Dixie: Race and the Liberal Conscience at Ole Miss.* New York: Free Press, 1997.

Colson, Charles W., and Ellen Santilli Vaughn. *The Body.* Dallas: Word Pub., 1992.

Crespino, Joseph Hardin. "The Christian Conscience of Jim Crow: White Protestant Ministers and the Mississippi Citizens' Councils, 1954–1964." *Mississippi Folklife* 31 (1998): 36–44.

———. *Strategic Accommodation: Civil Rights Opponents in Mississippi and Their Impact on American Racial Politics, 1953—1972:* PhD diss., Stanford University, 2003.

———. *In Search of Another Country: Mississippi and the Conservative Counterrevolution.* Princeton, NJ: Princeton University Press, 2007.

Cunningham, W. J. *Agony at Galloway: One Church's Struggle with Social Change.* Jackson: University Press of Mississippi, 1980.

Dansby, B. Baldwin. *A Brief History of Jackson College: A Typical Story of the Survival of Education among Negroes in the South.* Jackson, MS: Jackson College, 1953.

De Gruchy, John W. *Reconciliation: Restoring Justice.* Minneapolis: Fortress Press, 2002.

DeLaughter, Bobby. *Never Too Late: A Prosecutor's Story of Justice in the Medgar Evers Case.* New York: Scribner, 2001.

DeYoung, Curtiss Paul, Michael O. Emerson, George Yancey, and Karen Chai Kim. *United by Faith: The Multiracial Congregation as an Answer to the Problem of Race.* New York: Oxford University Press, 2003.

Dibelius, Otto. *In the Service of the Lord.* New York: Holt, 1964.

Dittmer, John. *Local People: The Struggle for Civil Rights in Mississippi, Blacks in the New World.* Urbana: University of Illinois Press, 1994.

Dockery, David S. *Southern Baptists & American Evangelicals: The Conversation Continues.* Nashville, TN: Broadman & Holman, 1993.

Dollard, John, and Yale University Institute of Human Relations. *Caste and Class in a Southern Town.* New Haven: Yale University Press, 1937.

Dougherty, Kevin D. "How Monochromatic Is Church Membership? Racial-Ethnic Diversity in Religious Community." *Sociology of Religion* 64 (2003): 65–85.

Dovidio, John F., Peter Samuel Glick, and Laurie A. Rudman. *On the Nature of Prejudice: Fifty Years after Allport.* Malden, MA: Blackwell, 2005.

Doyle, William. *An American Insurrection: The Battle of Oxford, Mississippi, 1962.* New York: Doubleday, 2001.

Emerson, Michael O., and Christian Smith. *Divided by Faith: Evangelical Religion and the Problem of Race in America.* New York: Oxford University Press, 2000.

Emerson, Michael O., and Rodney M. Woo. *People of the Dream: Multiracial Congregations in the United States.* Princeton, N.J.: Princeton University Press, 2006.

Fager, Charles. *Selma, 1965: The March That Changed the South.* 2nd ed. Boston: Beacon Press, 1985.

Farmer, James Oscar. *The Metaphysical Confederacy: James Henley Thornwell and the Synthesis of Southern Values*. Macon, GA: Mercer University Press, 1986.

Faulkner, William. "A Letter to the North." *Life* 40 (March 5, 1956): 51–52.

Ferris, William. "John Dollard: Caste and Class Revisited." *Southern Cultures* 10 (Summer 2004): 7–18.

Fowl, Stephen E. *Philippians*. Edited by Joel B. Green and Max Turner, *The Two Horizons New Testament Commentary*. Grand Rapids, MI: Eerdmans, 2005.

Fox-Genovese, Elizabeth, and Eugene D. Genovese. *The Mind of the Master Class: History and Faith in the Southern Slaveholders' Worldview*. Cambridge; New York: Cambridge University Press, 2005.

Garner, James Wilford. *Reconstruction in Mississippi*. New York, London: Macmillan, 1901.

Garrett, James Leo, E. Glenn Hinson, and James E. Tull. *Are Southern Baptists "Evangelicals"?* Macon, GA: Mercer University Press, 1983.

Garrow, David J. *Protest at Selma: Martin Luther King, Jr., and the Voting Rights Act of 1965*. New Haven, CT: Yale University Press, 1978.

Gillespie, G.T. "Defense of the Principle of Racial Segregation." *The Presbyterian Outlook* 137 (March 14, 1955): 5–9.

Gladwell, Malcolm. "The Cellular Church: How Rick Warren's Church Grew." *The New Yorker*, September 12, 2005, 60–67.

Godsey, John D., and Dietrich Bonhoeffer. *Preface to Bonhoeffer; the Man and Two of His Shorter Writings*. Philadelphia: Fortress Press, 1965.

Gorringe, Timothy. "Eschatology and Political Radicalism: The Example of Karl Barth and Jürgen Moltmann." In *God Will Be All in All: The Eschatology of Jürgen Moltmann*, edited by Richard Bauckham. Minneapolis: Fortress Press, 2001.

Hamilton, Alfred P. *Galloway Memorial Methodist Church, 1836–1956: A History Compiled from Very Scanty Records of Private Individuals, Archives from the Methodist Room, Millsaps College, General Minutes of the Church at Large and Mississippi Conference Journals, Minutes of the Woman's Society of Christian Service, and of the Official Board of Our Church*. Nashville, TN: Parthenon, 1956.

Hampton, Henry, Steve Fayer, and Sarah Flynn. *Voices of Freedom: An Oral History of the Civil Rights Movement from the 1950s through the 1980s*. London: Vintage 1995, 1990.

Hankins, Barry. *Uneasy in Babylon: Southern Baptist Conservatives and American Culture*. Tuscaloosa: University of Alabama Press, 2002.

Harris, Harriet A. *Fundamentalism and Evangelicals, Oxford Theological Monographs*. Oxford, New York: Clarendon Press; Oxford University Press, 1998.

Hart, D. G. *Deconstructing Evangelicalism: Conservative Protestantism in the Age of Billy Graham*. Grand Rapids, MI: Baker Academic, 2004.

Hart, Trevor. "Imagination for the Kingdom of God? Hope, Promise and the Transformative Power of an Imagined Future." In *God Will Be All in All: The Eschatology of Jürgen Moltmann*, edited by Richard Bauckham, 49–76. Minneapolis: Fortress Press, 2001.

Hartfield, Jimmie Ann Hampton, ed. *100th Anniversary of Cade Chapel Baptist Church. 1880–1980 Jackson, Mississippi*. Jackson, 1980.

Harvey, Paul. *Freedom's Coming: Religious Culture and the Shaping of the South from the Civil War through the Civil Rights Era.* Chapel Hill: University of North Carolina Press, 2005.

Haynes, Stephen R. *Noah's Curse: The Biblical Justification of American Slavery.* Oxford; New York: Oxford University Press, 2002.

Huffman, Alan. *Mississippi in Africa.* New York: Gotham Books, 2004.

Hunter, James Davison. *Culture Wars: The Struggle to Define America.* New York: Basic Books, 1991.

Jackman, Mary R., and Marie Crane. "'Some of My Best Friends Are Black': Interracial Friendship and Whites' Racial Attitudes." *Public Opinion Quarterly* 50 (1986): 459–86.

Johnson, Luke Timothy. *Brother of Jesus, Friend of God: Studies in the Letter of James.* Grand Rapids, MI: W.B. Eerdmans, 2004.

———. *The Letter of James: A New Translation with Introduction and Commentary.* New York: Doubleday, 1995.

Johnson, Thomas Carey. "The Presbyterian Church in the United States." *Journal of the Presbyterian Historical Society* 1 (1901).

Jones, L. Gregory. "Crafting Communities of Forgiveness." *Interpretation* 54 (April, 2000): 121–34.

———. *Embodying Forgiveness: A Theological Analysis.* Grand Rapids, MI: W.B. Eerdmans, 1995.

Katagiri, Yasuhiro. *The Mississippi State Sovereignty Commission: Civil Rights and States' Rights.* Jackson: University Press of Mississippi, 2001.

Kelly, Geffrey B., and F. Burton Nelson. *The Cost of Moral Leadership: The Spirituality of Dietrich Bonhoeffer.* Grand Rapids, MI: W.B. Eerdmans, 2003.

Kester, Howard. "Lynching by Blow Torch: A Report upon the Double Lynching at Duck Hill, Miss., April 13, 1937." In *Howard A. Kester Papers, 1923–1972,* edited by Edward M. Wayland. Glen Rock, N. J.: Microfilming Corporation of America, 1973.

Keyes, Kenneth S. n.d. A Brief History of the Developments in the Presbyterian Church in the United States (Southern) Which Led to the Formation of the Presbyterian Church in America. In Committee for Christian Education & Publications, http://www.fpcjackson.org/resources/apologetics/keyes.htm (accessed March 2, 2005).

Kimbrough, Julie L. *Jackson, Images of America.* Charleston, SC: Arcadia, 1998.

Kinder, Donald R., and Lynn M. Sanders. *Divided by Color: Racial Politics and Democratic Ideals, American Politics and Political Economy.* Chicago: University of Chicago Press, 1996.

King, Martin Luther, and James Melvin Washington. *A Testament of Hope: The Essential Writings of Martin Luther King, Jr.* San Francisco: Harper & Row, 1986.

Kosmin, Barry A., Egon Mayer, and Ariela Keysar. *American Religious Identification Survey 2001.* New York: The Graduate Center of the City University of New York, 2001.

Kull, Irving Stoddard. "Presbyterian Attitudes toward Slavery." *Church History* 7 (June 1938): 101–14.

Lewis, Morris. *Wholesaler-Retailer: The Story of the Lewis Grocer Company and Sunflower Food Stores, Newcomen Publication; No. 1021.* New York: The Newcomen Society in North America, 1975.

Longfellow, Henry Wadsworth. *Hiawatha: A Poem, by Henry Wadsworth Longfellow.* Chicago: Reilly and Britton, 1909.

Lopez, Steve. "Ghosts of the South." *Time,* 30 (April 2001), 64ff.

Luther, Martin, and Charles Michael Jacobs. *Three Treatises: An Open Letter to the Christian Nobility of the German Nation Concerning the Reform of the Christian Estate. A Prelude to the Babylonian on Captivity of the Church. A Treatise on Christian Liberty.* Philadelphia: Muhlenberg Press, 1947.

Machen, J. Gresham. *Christianity and Liberalism.* New York: Macmillan, 1923.

MacIntyre, Alasdair C. *After Virtue: A Study in Moral Theory.* Notre Dame: University of Notre Dame Press, 1981.

Maddex, Jack P. "Proslavery Millennialism: Social Eschatology in Antebellum Southern Calvinism." *American Quarterly* 31 (Spring 1979): 46–62.

Maddex, Jack P. "From Theocracy to Spirituality: The Southern Presbyterian Reversal on Church and State." *Journal of Presbyterian History* 54 (Winter 1976): 438–57.

Manis, Andrew Michael. *Southern Civil Religions in Conflict: Civil Rights and the Culture Wars.* Macon, GA: Mercer University Press, 2002.

Marsden, George M. *Fundamentalism and American Culture: The Shaping of Twentieth Century Evangelicalism, 1870–1925.* New York: Oxford University Press, 1980.

———. *Understanding Fundamentalism and Evangelicalism.* Grand Rapids, MI: W.B. Eerdmans, 1991.

Marsh, Charles. *The Beloved Community: How Faith Shapes Social Justice, from the Civil Rights Movement to Today.* New York: Basic Books, 2005.

———. *God's Long Summer: Stories of Faith and Civil Rights.* Princeton: Princeton University Press, 1997.

———. *The Last Days: A Son's Story of Sin and Segregation at the Dawn of a New South.* New York: Basic Books, 2001.

———. *Reclaiming Dietrich Bonhoeffer: The Promise of His Theology.* New York: Oxford University Press, 1994.

Martin, William. "Billy Graham." In *Varieties of Southern Evangelicalism,* edited by David Edwin Harrell, 71–88. Macon, GA: Mercer University Press, 1981.

Martin, William C. *A Prophet with Honor: The Billy Graham Story.* New York: W. Morrow and Co., 1991.

McCain, William David, ed. *The Story of Jackson: A History of the Capital of Mississippi, 1821–1951.* Vol. 1. Jackson, MS: J.F. Hyer, 1953.

McLemore, Richard Aubrey, ed. *A History of Mississippi.* 2 vols. Hattiesburg: University & College Press of Mississippi, 1973.

McMillen, Neil R. *The Citizens' Council: Organized Resistance to the Second Reconstruction, 1954–64.* Urbana: University of Illinois Press, 1971.

———. *Dark Journey: Black Mississippians in the Age of Jim Crow.* Urbana: University of Illinois Press, 1989.

Meredith, James. *Three Years in Mississippi*. Bloomington: Indiana University Press, 1966.

Middlebrook, Martin. *The Battle of Hamburg: Allied Bomber Forces against a German City in 1943*. London: Allen Lane, 1980.

Miller, Kevin D. "The Clumsy Embrace: Croatian Miroslav Volf Wanted to Love His Serbian Enemies; the Prodigal's Father Is Showing Him How." *Christianity Today*, October 26, 1998, 65 ff.

Mills, Gwen Ann. "A Social History of Jackson, Mississippi, 1920–1929." MA thesis, University of Mississippi, 1966.

Mintz, Steven. *Moralists and Modernizers: America's Pre-Civil War Reformers*, Baltimore: Johns Hopkins University Press, 1995.

Moltmann-Wendel, Elisabeth. *Autobiography*. London: SCM Press, 1997.

———. *Rediscovering Friendship: Awakening to the Power and Promise of Women's Friendships*. Minneapolis: Fortress Press, 2001.

Moltmann, Jürgen. *The Church in the Power of the Spirit: A Contribution of Messianic Ecclesiology*. London: SCM Press, 1977.

———. *The Crucified God: The Cross of Christ as the Foundation and Criticism of Christian Theology*. New York: Harper & Row, 1974.

———. *Experiences in Theology: Ways and Forms of Christian Theology*. Minneapolis: Fortress Press, 2000.

———. *Experiences of God*. Philadelphia: Fortress Press, 1980.

———. "Open Friendship: Aristotelian and Christian Concepts of Friendship." In *The Changing Face of Friendship*, edited by Leroy S. Rouner. Notre Dame: University of Notre Dame Press, 1994.

———. *The Source of Life: The Holy Spirit and the Theology of Life*. Minneapolis: Fortress Press, 1997.

———. *Theology of Hope: on the Ground and the Implications of a Christian Eschatology*. New York, Harper & Row, 1967.

———. *The Trinity and the Kingdom: The Doctrine of God*. San Francisco: Harper & Row, 1981.

———, *How I Have Changed: Reflections on Thirty Years of Theology*. London: SCM Press, 1997.

———, *A Broad Place: An Autobiography*. Minneapolis: Fortress Press, 2008.

Moltmann, Jürgen, and G. McLeod Bryan. *Communities of Faith and Radical Discipleship, Luce Program on Religion and the Social Crisis; 2*. Macon, GA: Mercer University Press, 1986.

Moltmann, Jürgen, and M. Douglas Meeks. *The Open Church: Invitation to a Messianic Lifestyle*. London: SCM Press, 1978.

———. *The Passion for Life: A Messianic Lifestyle*. Philadelphia: Fortress Press, 1978.

Moody, Anne. *Coming of Age in Mississippi*. New York: Dial Press, 1968.

Morley, Patrick M. *The Man in the Mirror: Solving the 24 Problems Men Face*. Brentwood, TN: Wolgemuth & Hyatt, 1989.

Newman, Mark. *Divine Agitators: The Delta Ministry and Civil Rights in Mississippi*. Athens: University of Georgia Press, 2004.

Noll, Mark A. *America's God: From Jonathan Edwards to Abraham Lincoln*. Oxford; New York: Oxford University Press, 2002.

Nutt, Rick. "The Tie That No Longer Binds: The Origins of the Presbyterian Church in America." In *The Confessional Mosaic: Presbyterians and Twentieth-Century Theology*, edited by Milton J. Coalter, John M. Mulder and Louis B. Weeks, 236–56. Louisville, KY: Westminster/John Knox Press, 1990.

Ownby, Ted. "Evangelical but Differentiated: Religion by the Numbers." In *Religion and Public Life in the South: In the Evangelical Mode*, edited by Charles Reagan Wilson and Mark Silk. Walnut Creek, CA: AltaMira Press, 2005.

Palmer, Benjamin Morgan. *The Life and Letters of James Henley Thornwell*. Richmond, VA: Whittet & Shepperson, 1875.

Perkins, John. *A Quiet Revolution: The Christian Response to Human Need, a Strategy for Today*. Waco, TX.: Word Books, 1976.

Perkins, Spencer, and Chris Rice. *More Than Equals: Racial Healing for the Sake of the Gospel*. Downers Grove, IL: InterVarsity Press, 1993.

———. *More Than Equals: Racial Healing for the Sake of the Gospel*. Revised & expanded. ed. Downers Grove, IL.: InterVarsity Press, 2000.

Polsgrove, Carol. *Divided Minds: Intellectuals and the Civil Rights Movement*. New York: Norton, 2001.

Powdermaker, Hortense. *After Freedom: A Cultural Study in the Deep South*. New York: Viking Press, 1939.

Putnam, Robert D. *Bowling Alone: The Collapse and Revival of American Community*. New York: Simon & Schuster, 2000.

Putnam, Robert D., Lewis M. Feldstein, and Don Cohen. *Better Together: Restoring the American Community*. New York: Simon & Schuster, 2003.

Reed, John Shelton. "The Banner That Won't Stay Furled." *Southern Cultures* 8 (Spring 2002): 76–100.

———. *Southerners, the Social Psychology of Sectionalism, Institute for Research in Social Science Monograph Series*. Chapel Hill: University of North Carolina Press, 1983.

Rhodes, J Stephen. "The Church as the Community of Open Friendship." *The Asbury Theological Journal* 55 (Spring 2000): 41–49.

———. "The Comfort and Challenge of Open Friendship." *The Asbury Theological Journal* 49 (Spring 1994): 63–69.

Rice, Chris. *Grace Matters: A True Story of Race, Friendship, and Faith in the Heart of the South*. San Francisco, CA: Jossey-Bass, 2002.

Richards, John Edwards. *The Historical Birth of the Presbyterian Church in America*. Liberty Hill, SC: Liberty Press, 1987.

Ritterhouse, Jennifer Lynn. *Growing up Jim Crow: How Black and White Southern Children Learned Race*. Chapel Hill: University of North Carolina, 2006.

Salter, John R. *Jackson, Mississippi: An American Chronicle of Struggle and Schism*. Malabar, FL: R.E. Krieger, 1987.

Sansing, David G. *Making Haste Slowly: The Troubled History of Higher Education in Mississippi*. Jackson: University Press of Mississippi, 1990.

———. *The University of Mississippi: A Sesquicentennial History*. Jackson: University Press of Mississippi, 1999.

———. "William Forrest Winter Fifty-Eighth Governor of Mississippi: 1980–1984." In *Mississippi History Now*. Mississippi Historical Society, January 2004.

Silver, James W. *Edmund Pendleton Gaines and Frontier Problems, 1801–1849*. PhD diss., Vanderbilt University, 1935.

———. *Mississippi: The Closed Society*. 1st ed. New York: Harcourt, 1964.

———. *Mississippi: The Closed Society*. New enl. ed. New York: Harcourt, 1966.

———. *Running Scared: Silver in Mississippi*. Jackson: University Press of Mississippi, 1984.

Smith, Christian. *Christian America? What Evangelicals Really Want*. Berkeley: University of California Press, 2000.

Smith, Frank Joseph. *The History of the Presbyterian Church in America*. Manassas, VA: Reformation Educational Foundation, 1985.

Smith, H. Shelton. *In His Image, But: Racism in Southern Religion, 1780–1910*. Durham, NC: Duke University Press, 1972.

Smith, H. Shelton. "The Church and the Social Order in the Old South as Interpreted by James H. Thornwell." *Church History* 7 (June 1938): 115–24.

Smith, Morton H. *How Is the Gold Become Dim! (Lamentations 4:1) the Decline of the Presbyterian Church in the United States as Reflected in Its Assembly Actions*. Jackson, MS: The Steering Committee for a Continuing Presbyterian Church, Faithful to the Scriptures and the Reformed Faith, 1973.

Smith, Oran P. *The Rise of Baptist Republicanism*. New York: New York University Press, 1997.

Sparks, Randy J. *Religion in Mississippi*. Jackson: University Press of Mississippi for the Mississippi Historical Society, 2001.

———. *On Jordan's Stormy Banks: Evangelicalism in Mississippi, 1773–1876*. Athens: University of Georgia Press, 1994.

Spofford, Tim. *Lynch Street: The May 1970 Slayings at Jackson State College*. Kent, OH: Kent State University Press, 1988.

Staiger, C. Bruce. "Abolitionism and the Presbyterian Schism of 1837–1838." *The Mississippi Historical Review* 36 (December 1949): 391–414.

Stanford, E.L. *The History of Calvary Baptist Church, Jackson, Mississippi*. Jackson, MS: Hederman Brothers, 1980.

Thomas, William. "The Meredith Event at the University of Mississippi: The Creaking of Modern America under Post-Modern Stress." MA thesis, University of Mississippi, 1998.

Thompson, Ernest Trice. *Presbyterians in the South*. 3 vols. Vol. 2: 1861–1890. Richmond, VA: John Knox Press, 1973.

———. *Presbyterians in the South*. 3 vols. Vol. 1: 1607–1861. Richmond, VA: John Knox Press, 1963.

———. *Presbyterians in the South*. Vol. 3: 1890–1972. Richmond, VA: John Knox Press, 1973.

————. *The Spirituality of the Church*. Richmond, VA: John Knox Press, 1961.

Thornwell, James Henley. *The Collected Writings of James Henley Thornwell*. Edited by John B. Adger. Vol. 4. Richmond: Whittet & Shepperson, 1871–73.

————. *Hear the South! The State of the Country. An Article Republished from the Southern Presbyterian Review*. New York: D. Appleton and Company, 1861.

————. *The Rights and Duties of Masters: A Sermon Preached at the Dedication of a Church Erected in Charleston Sc., for the Benefit and Instruction of the Coloured Population*. Charleston SC: Walker & James, 1850.

Thornwell, James Henley. "The Baptism of Servants." *Southern Presbyterian Review* 1 (June 1847): 63–102.

Tutu, Desmond. *No Future without Forgiveness*. New York: Doubleday, 1999.

Van Gelder, Craig E. "Growth Patterns of Mainline Denominations and Their Churches: A Case Study of Jackson, Mississippi 1900–1980." PhD diss., Southwestern Baptist Theological Seminary, 1982.

Van Til, Cornelius, and Karl Barth. *Christianity and Barthianism*. Philadelphia: Presbyterian and Reformed, 1962.

Volf, Miroslav. *After Our Likeness: The Church as the Image of the Trinity, Sacra Doctrina*. Grand Rapids, MI: William B. Eerdmans, 1998.

————. *Exclusion and Embrace: A Theological Exploration of Identity, Otherness, and Reconciliation*. Nashville, TN: Abingdon Press, 1996.

————. "Forgiveness, Reconciliation, & Justice: A Christian Contribution to a More Peaceful Social Environment." In *Forgiveness and Reconciliation: Religion, Public Policy & Conflict Transformation*, edited by Raymond G. Helmick and Rodney Lawrence Petersen, Philadelphia: Templeton Foundation Press, 2001.

————. *Free of Charge: Giving and Forgiving in a Culture Stripped of Grace*. Grand Rapids, MI: Zondervan, 2005.

————. *The End of Memory: Remembering Rightly in a Violent World*. Grand Rapids, MI: W.B. Eerdmans, 2006.

————. "The Social Meaning of Reconciliation." *Interpretation* 54 (April 2000): 158–72.

Warren, Richard. *The Purpose-Driven Life: What on Earth Am I Here For?* Grand Rapids, MI: Zondervan, 2002.

Washington, Raleigh, Glen Kehrein, and Claude V. King. *Break Down the Walls: Experiencing Biblical Reconciliation and Unity in the Body of Christ*. Chicago: Moody Press, 1997.

————. *Breaking Down Walls: A Model for Reconciliation in an Age of Racial Strife*. Chicago: Moody Press, 1993.

Weary, Dolphus, and William Hendricks. *I Ain't Comin' Back*. Wheaton, IL: Tyndale House Publishers, 1990.

Wells, W. Calvin. "Reconstruction and Its Destruction in Hinds County." In *Publications of the Mississippi Historical Society*, edited by Franklin L. Riley, 85–108. Oxford: The Mississippi Historical Society, 1906.

Wentzel, Fred D. *Day Is Dawning; the Story of Bishop Otto Dibelius, Based on His Proclamations and Authentic Documents.* Philadelphia: Christian Education Press, 1956.

Wigger, John H. *Taking Heaven by Storm: Methodism and the Rise of Popular Christianity in America.* New York: Oxford University Press, 1998.

Winant, Howard. *The New Politics of Race: Globalism, Difference, Justice.* Minneapolis: University of Minnesota Press, 2004.

Winter, R. Milton. "Division & Reunion in the Presbyterian Church, U.S.: A Mississippi Retrospective." *Journal of Presbyterian History* 78 (Spring 2000): 67–86.

Winter, William F., and Andrew P. Mullins. *The Measure of Our Days: Writings of William F. Winter.* Jackson: William Winter Institute for Racial Reconciliation: Distributed by University Press of Mississippi, 2006.

Wise, Sherwood Willing. *The Cathedral Church of St. Andrew: A Sesquicentennial History, 1839–1989.* Jackson, MS: Cathedral Church of St. Andrew, 1989.

Wittig, Michele Andrisin, and Sheila Grant-Thompson. "The Utility of Allport's Conditions of Intergroup Contact for Predicting Perceptions of Improved Racial Attitudes and Beliefs—Contact Hypothesis." *Journal of Social Issues* 54 (Winter, 1998): 795–812.

Wuthnow, Robert. *Sharing the Journey: Support Groups and America's New Quest for Community.* New York: Free Press, 1994.

Yancey, George. *One Body One Spirit: Principles of Successful Multiracial Churches.* Downers Grove, IL: InterVarsity Press, 2003.

Zangrando, Robert L. *The NAACP Crusade against Lynching, 1909–1950.* Philadelphia: Temple University Press, 1980.

Index